A Decade of Probation

PATTERSON SMITH REPRINT SERIES IN
CRIMINOLOGY, LAW ENFORCEMENT, AND SOCIAL PROBLEMS

A listing of publications in the SERIES *will be found at rear of volume*

PUBLICATION No. 66: PATTERSON SMITH REPRINT SERIES IN CRIMINOLOGY, LAW ENFORCEMENT, AND SOCIAL PROBLEMS

New York County, Probation Dept.

A DECADE OF PROBATION

(A Study and Report)

IRVING W. HALPERN

Chief Probation Officer
COURT OF GENERAL SESSIONS
County of New York

HV
9306
N6
A52
1969

With a New Introduction by
ELMER W. REEVES

Montclair, New Jersey
PATTERSON SMITH
1969

120979

Originally published 1939 by New York County,
Court of General Sessions
This edition copyright 1969 by
Patterson Smith Publishing Corporation
Montclair, New Jersey

SBN 87585-066-9

Library of Congress Catalog Card Number: 69-14930

INTRODUCTION TO THE REPRINT EDITION

This reprinting of Irving W. Halpern's *A Decade of Probation* offers a valuable exemplar of early exposition of methods of assessment and practical help in the probation process. Although the work suffers from some limitations unavoidable in a thirty-year-old text in an advancing profession, the basic concepts and procedures embodied in it retain their validity and general acceptance.

The timing of this reprinting is also of interest for the light it throws on a troubling issue underlying the entire field of social work. In the early years of the decade covered by Halpern's study (1927 to 1936), apprehension and concern in the field began to arise which were given historic utterance in Porter R. Lee's presidential address to the National Conference of Social Work in San Francisco, 1929. The title of this address, "Social Work, Cause and Function," refers to the problems that occur when the mission and zeal that inspire the social worker who is serving the "cause" of human betterment give way to preoccupation with the increasingly professionalized "function" that new techniques and institutionalized procedures enable him to bring to bear in the service of this cause.

Halpern saw the probation system as a social case-work method that balanced a cause, or mission, of reclaiming the offender with a function, or organized methodology, that derived from professional social work. In placing equal emphasis on the professionalization of the functional side of probation, Halpern was ahead of his time. During the late twenties and thirties the concept of probation as a second chance for convicted offenders was not yet fully accepted, and the appropriateness of adapting the methods and practices of social work to this end was often debated. In fact, the correctional social worker or probation officer was generally regarded as an illegitimate offspring of the broad field of social work.

At the present time, however, the trend has swept beyond Halpern to the point where the function of social work now often obscures its cause. An over-eagerness to apply a space-age technology to human problems, the increasing use of the computer, the striving to quantify elusive individual and societal variables, the disposition to discard that which cannot be computed, and recent proposals to move from a system in which the social worker is the vortex of treatment planning and implementation to a programmed bureaucratic system of rehabilitative practice — all are evidence of this trend.

In these frenetic days of increasing sophistication and thrust for change, the issue of "Social Work, Cause and Function" again confronts us as the community seeks to validate scientifically the social worker's function in our changing society without sacrificing the capacity of social service to inspire in him enthusiasm for the cause of human betterment. A reading of *A Decade of Probation* should prove of definite aid to beginning workers and students by returning to proper focus the probation officer's "cause," which is the true source of his professional identity and the only justification for his work.

The general reader of Halpern's work will recognize in it a simplistic approach to the psycho-dynamics of human behavior, and the sociologist will find much to criticize in the statistical design and evaluation of his post-probation study. Nevertheless the overview that Halpern gives of probation work in action is a good one, and the beginning worker in probation will find particularly useful the chapters on the philosophy of probation and the step-by-step process of investigation. The presentation of supervision methodology, although over-simplifying treatment practices, will be of great value to the worker who has had no graduate academic background in the behavioral sciences.

The late Irving W. Halpern was a pioneer in the field of probation who shared the pioneer's conception of probation as a helping process that was a substitute for traditional punishment. He saw correctional social work in probation as a cause for the amelioration of the plight of such offenders who might reasonably be expected to be reformed without imprisonment, and he had unlimited zeal for objective compassion. He firmly believed that the cause was reborn with each new client, and it was his genius to light and hand on the torch to others. This introduction would not be complete without an acknowledgment of my personal debt to Irving W. Halpern for his friendship and inspiration.

—ELMER W. REEVES
Chief Probation Officer

First Judicial Department
Supreme Court
State of New York
December, 1968

COURT OF GENERAL SESSIONS

PROBATION DEPARTMENT

NEW YORK

OFFICE OF THE
CHIEF PROBATION OFFICER

THE HONORABLE, THE JUDGES,
OF THE
COURT OF GENERAL SESSIONS,
COUNTY OF NEW YORK.

SIRS:

I herewith present a Study and Report of the work of the Probation Department, from January 1, 1927 to December 31, 1936.

Faithfully yours,

IRVING W. HALPERN,
Chief Probation Officer.

CONTENTS

PAGE

Foreword 7

Board of Judges 9

Probation Plan and Scope Committee 10

Chart of Organization 12

CHAPTER

I. PROBATION 13

Early beginnings in Massachusetts—Probation in the
Federal Courts—Throughout the United States—
Volunteer probation service in New York State—
Probation as State function—Increase in probation
service—Varying concepts of Probation—Successes
and Failures

II. PROBATION IN THE COURT OF GENERAL SESSIONS 23

Historical background—Present organization—Volunteer probation service—Contributions of Catholic
Charities of Archdiocese of New York—Establishment of Department—Institutes in Probation—Educational Activities—Psychiatric diagnosis and treatment—Slum survey—Judicial versus Administrative
Control

III. ORGANIZATION OF THE DEPARTMENT 35

Executive Division—Division of Investigation—Division of Supervision—Division of Accounts and
Finances—Division of Research—Clerical Division

4

IV. DIVISION OF INVESTIGATION 46

Volume of investigation—Sex of offenders—Ages of offenders—Offenses according to age groupings—Native and foreign born—Color of Offenders—Commitments—Offenders placed on probation—Factors contributing to crime—Alcoholism and drug addiction —Economic factors—Bad associates—Education of offenders—Broken homes—Personal deficiencies—Fraternity—Marital status—Religion—First offenders—Previous Juvenile Court, Institutional, Probation and Parole Records—Previous Adult Court, Institutional, Probation and Parole Records

V. DIVISION OF SUPERVISION 73

Philosophy—Function—Channels of Treatment—Volume of cases—Restitution and family support—Employment of probationers—Earnings of probationers—Success and failure—Discharge of probationers —Violations of probation—Issuance and dispositions of Bench Warrants—Incidence of violations

VI. THE PSYCHIATRIC CLINIC 92

Psychiatry in the courts—Need for psychiatric studies —General Sessions Clinic—Establishment—Aim—Mode of procedure—Volume of examinations—Classification of offenders — Intelligence — Mental Deficiency—Psychopathic personalities—Neuroses—Psychoses

VII. POST-PROBATION STUDY 102

Purpose—Method of study—Success and failure—Previous court records—Period of probation—Age—Sex —Color—Mental and physical status—Education—Family and Neighborhood—Vocational and employment situation—Recreation—Religion—Thrift—Attitudes—Future Prospects—Conclusions

VIII. MANUAL FOR PROBATION OFFICERS 117

Training of staff—Investigation methodology—Directions to officers—Channels of investigation—The pre-sentence report — Supervision methodology — Treatment—Departmental procedure—Channels of probation — Recording — Case studies — Forms and statistics

IX. THE COMMUNITY'S CONTRIBUTION TO CRIME 256

Purpose and nature of study—The slum and crime—Environment and delinquency—Housing and delinquency—Slum clearance and crime control—Abstract of findings

X. SUMMER CAMP WORK 270

Purpose—Procedure—Cooperating agencies—Volume—Period at comp—Evaluation

XI. STATISTICAL TABLES AND CHARTS 279

FOREWORD

This study was made, and the report was written, in the odd time which could be taken from the problems inherent in the administration of a large department. Such limitations as the study possesses, are the result of the conditions under which it was prepared. It does not pretend to present a complete evaluation of the source material contained in our files. Such an effort would be a time consuming and expensive project, for which we have neither the facilities, the funds, nor the staff.

We have endeavored to portray in these pages, in broad outline, the scope of our activities, the results achieved through socialized investigation and treatment programs, and the extent to which a Probation Department can assist in the socialization of the administration of justice.

Such constructive results as we have been able to obtain, are directly due to the zeal of the staff of this Department and their loyalty to the standards which govern our work. This report presents the end results of their efforts.

This medium affords the opportunity to express my own, as well as the grateful appreciation of the staff, to the Judges of the Court of General Sessions. Their broad vision and their deep interest have stimulated this Department to its greatest efforts.

It gives me pleasure to acknowledge the aid furnished me by Mr. Elmer W. Reeves of the Executive Staff in the preparation of this study, and I am particularly grateful to him for his collaboration in the Post-Probation Study and the Supervision Methodology.

The collaboration of Mr. William V. Chieco of the Executive Staff, in the preparation of the Chapter on the Division of Investigation, is also gratefully acknowledged.

I am also indebted to Miss Agnes Sullivan, Examiner of the New York State Probation Commission, who edited the Supervision Methodology, and to Dr. Walter Bromberg, for his aid in outlining the procedures used in the Psychiatric Clinic of the Court of General Sessions.

Irving W. Halpern

JUDGES OF THE COURT OF GENERAL SESSIONS

Hon. William Allen

Hon. Owen W. Bohan

Hon. Cornelius F. Collins

Hon. George L. Donnellan

Hon. John J. Freschi

Hon. Morris Koenig

Hon. Charles C. Nott, Jr.

Hon. Saul S. Streit

Hon. James Garrett Wallace

———

Edward R. Carroll
Clerk of the Court

9

PROBATION PLAN AND SCOPE COMMITTEE OF THE JUDGES OF THE COURT OF GENERAL SESSIONS

HON. CORNELIUS F. COLLINS,
Chairman

HON. MORRIS KOENIG

HON. CHARLES C. NOTT, JR.

———

IRVING W. HALPERN,
Secretary

"Every scrap of authentic information from those who have been waging war against crime and criminals, night and day, reveals that there is but one way to reduce crime. That is through a policy of prevention.

"If the criminal's past history gives good reason to believe that he is not of the naturally criminal type, that he is capable of real reform and of becoming a useful citizen, there is no doubt that probation, viewed from the selfish standpoint of protection of society alone, is the most effective method that we have. And yet it is the least understood, the least developed, the least appreciated of all our efforts to rid society of the criminal. . . By its intelligent extension, crime can be decreased, the over-crowded conditions in our penal institutions greatly ameliorated, and the necessity for building more and more prisons, for needlessly and ineffectively spending huge prison budgets, reduced. . .

FRANKLIN DELANO ROOSEVELT
"Looking Forward"

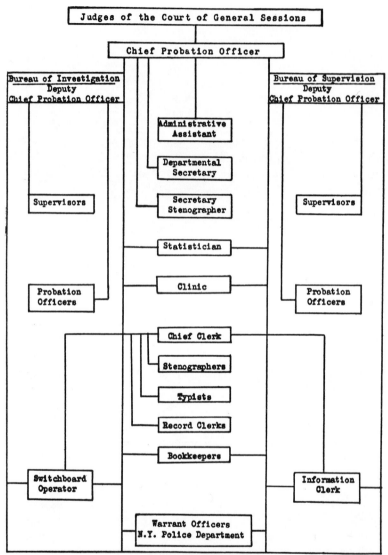

Court of General Sessions, Probation Department.

Chapter I

PROBATION

The penal system in this country was inherited from England and brought about the establishment of prisons, county jails and workhouses. Each state and the smaller communities within it, approached the problem in the light of their individual needs. As a result we have found that in some states enlightened views with reference to crime control and the adjustment of criminal offenders to normal life have to some extent prevailed. Other systems developed which depended upon the use of brutality, force and a revengeful attitude, in the belief that such methods terrorized the criminal and served to deter others from committing crime.

From the welter of confusion of thought and the diverse attitudes assumed toward crime and the criminal has come one contribution which is distinctly American—the probation system.

In criminal courts the probation system is utilized as a social control and discipline through suspension of sentence, sentence to a reformatory or prison, the execution of which is suspended, or through deferred sentence. Probation as the name of an official correctional service, commonly denotes the dual functions of the system, that of the investigation of offenders prior to sentence in order that the Court may have detailed information concerning the history of the offender, the etiology of the offense, and the control and treatment of offenders conditionally released on probation.

In probation agencies of recognized standing, investigations of offenders are developed in accordance with social case work principles, and supervision and treatment is administered in accordance with social case work techniques, which must be related to the authoritarian setting in which the probation system functions. Probation departments in addition to social investigation and the development of rehabilitative programs for those offenders released under probationary control, are also made directly responsible for the collection of varying amounts of money for restitution, reparation, and family support.

13

In probation agencies with acceptable standards, definite qualifications of education and experience are now being demanded prior to appointment of probation officers in contrast to the early methods of appointment through political preferment or for other undesirable reasons.

Probation has been criticized because of occasional conspicuous and spectacular failures, and because some probation departments have failed to develop a service which can stand comparison with the social services rendered by other agencies in the community. In the majority of instances, failure has been due to inadequate financial support, poorly qualified personnel, and failure to utilize standard methodologies of treatment. Another factor is the staggering case loads thrown upon probation officers, to which they are physically unable to give the individualized study and service which is inherent in the proper administration of the probation service.

The failure of probation departments to interpret to the community the social value of an adequately financed and properly staffed probation service, has been responsible for the lack of financial and public support, with the result that probation because of these handicaps is too often nothing but a routinized and mechanical form of haphazard surveillance.

Historical Background

From the early efforts to divert young offenders from criminal careers which were inaugurated by the cobbler, John Augustus, in the city of Boston, came the first recognition of the potentialities of this form of social discipline, and in 1878, Massachusetts passed the first probation law which required the city of Boston to appoint a probation officer.

In 1891 Massachusetts passed a general law requiring the criminal courts of the state to appoint probation officers. It was not until nine years later that probation legislation in general was passed. Only five states adopted probation legislation before 1900, and of these only three dealt with adult probation.

In the Federal Courts, prior to 1916 some Judges suspended sentence indefinitely by filing the case, or by deferring the sentence. This

14

method had been in use for over sixty years, when the Supreme Court of the United States held in the Killets case that a district Judge was without power to suspend or defer sentence indefinitely. As a result of this decision the Federal Probation Act was passed in 1925, but it was not generally used by the Federal Courts until 1930. Since that time the Federal probation system has been extended greatly both with reference to the increase in the number of probation officers appointed, and the number of persons placed on probation.

Although the probation system is of comparatively recent development, the concept of its effectiveness has been widespread, and at the present time adult probation is by law established in thirty-nine states, the District of Columbia, in most European countries, and in a number of the states of South America, Asia and Africa.

With such rapid development, probation for the most part has been governed by the same attitudes which brought about the development of penal institutions in this country, and because of these attitudes the effectiveness of the system has been seriously curtailed. Some of its faults have merited criticism and this criticism has had constructive value, because it brought about the determined effort to develop adequate standards, to recruit educated and trained personnel and to have probation workers classified in the competitive civil service, in order that the probation system might not become the football of politics.

The difference in the probation laws of various states are due to the contention that the conditions in these states warrant varying laws controlling probation. Thus we find that in some states probation is in a stage of development which approximates the earliest beginnings in those states which have since forged to the front by enacting enlightened social legislation concerning the probation system. Many of the states differ sharply in the types of offenses which may be subject to probation. In seven states there is no limitation on the offenses for which probation may be granted. Four exclude capital or life imprisonment offenses. Others exclude specific offenses, and the States of Alabama, Kentucky and North Carolina permit probation only for minor offenses.

15

Probation in New York

Probation was established in the State of New York in 1901 and it was first administered by volunteers. Those concerned with its extension and development recognized the need for a supervisory body which would make this form of correctional treatment more valuable and the New York State Probation Commission was established in 1907. During the years that it has served so effectively, this Commission has brought about the development of high standards and has continually exerted its efforts to make the application of these standards statewide.

The use of volunteers in the early stages of the development of probation in this state now can be said to have more or less hampered the proper development of the probation system, because those who were responsible for the finances of various communities were reluctant to support probation through public funds, when persons and organizations with generous inclinations were willing to supply personnel and finance this work. The State Probation Commission soon discovered that volunteer workers could not as effectively administer probation as could the publicly salaried probation officers chosen from competitive Civil Service lists, who were responsible to the courts and to the State Probation Commission.

However, praise must be given to volunteers, who in the early stages of probation history recognized its potentialities as a correctional treatment, but with the advent of the publicly salaried probation worker came a new concept of the prerequisites for such work, and the training and education which is essential to a proper and effective administration of the probation service.

Since 1908 the New York Courts have placed on probation 424,322 adults. In 1907 there was only 1,672 persons on probation as against 12,053 in penal institutions. In 1927 the number on probation had increased to 23,302 while the number in correctional institutions numbered 18,110. Since 1918 there have been more persons on probation each year than there were in correctional institutions, thus demonstrating the increasing confidence of the courts and the public in probation as a means of diverting offenders from criminal careers. The increase in the numbers of persons placed on probation, however, has not diminished

16

the number successfully treated, since an evaluation of the statistics shows that an excess of 70% continue to demonstrate that the probation system is an effective means of dealing with them.

Although the numbers on probation have shown a marked and steady increase through the years, the appointment of a sufficient number of probation officers to deal successfully with the manifold and complex problems presented by these persons has lagged far behind the general increase. Although probation has effectively demonstrated its capacities even in the face of the serious limitations imposed upon the system, financial support has been grudgingly given.

Varying Concepts

The varying concepts which have dominated probation and its application are significant. As in the field of social work, wherein sociological and psychological contributions to social case work changed the social workers' concept of the techniques and processes to be employed, so also did the views of the administrators of probation change through these contributions. In the early stages of probation there was little or no attempt to evaluate the problems presented in terms of subjective and objective factors, and the methods employed to cope with the problems were of the hit or miss type. Probation officers depended upon admonition and threats, and so-called friendly guidance. These methods were the result of the probation officer's subjective reactions to friendliness or antagonism on the part of the probationer, and the probation officer's planning, casual as it was, was limited to the knowledge which the probation officer had gained through his own experience. There was no controlling concept of probation treatment, and in many instances probation officers of the old school displayed marked antagonisms to the suggestions and aid offered by the better trained social worker who in some instances had contact with the probationer or his family. There was little or no attempt to evaluate causation and the problem of the offender was looked at only in a mass aspect. In most instances the legalistic concept was controlling. Offenders were judged in the light of their crimes and individualization of treatment was perceived by only a few probation administrators.

17

Although there was some interest in the problem of feeblemindedness and mental defect in its relation to delinquency and anti-social behavior, probation departments concerned themselves very little with intellectual factors until social workers became interested in the Binet-Simon scale of intelligence, which was first developed in 1905. During the intervening period between 1905-1911, this scale for measuring intelligence was used by social work agencies concerned with the problems of delinquency. Hailed as a significant forward step, this method of approach resulted in numerous studies by research groups connected with reformatory institutions. Although in the opinion of many it brought about for a time undue emphasis upon this factor as the most important underlying cause for delinquent conduct, nevertheless it served to emphasize the need for institutions to care for mental defectives with pronounced delinquent tendencies. Some of the probation systems began to avail themselves of the opportunities for conducting psychiatric and psychological examinations of offenders whose deficiency was outstanding, and in this manner were able to divert from probation consideration mental defectives who were potentially criminalistic and not amenable to the treatment which the probation system could afford.

The early studies of Dr. William Healy in the field of juvenile delinquency began to attract the attention of probation officers, and the publication of his INDIVIDUAL DELINQUENT in 1915, which contained case histories resulting from his five-year study of the behavior of the juvenile delinquent, was eagerly taken up by probation administrators because of its penetrating insight into motivating causes of anti-social behavior.

With the advent of the psychiatrist and psychologist into the field of delinquent behavior came a tendency on the part of probation officers to lean more and more upon their aid, with the result that probation administrators began to acquaint themselves with the results of research and its contributions. Although there was a rush to adopt every new psychological theory, which some were prone to accept as the basis on which all findings could be developed, nevertheless an attitude of receptiveness was fostered which inevitably brought about a broadening of vision and a widening of horizons. They listened to the educational psychologists who stressed the laws of association and behavior based upon the pleasurable results obtained and the avoidance of pain. They acquainted themselves with the teachings of the behavioristic school, which claims that behavior patterns can be traced to the conditioning brought about by stimuli in the early childhood of the subject.

They concerned themselves with the Freudian or psychoanalytical school with its searching inquiry into the subconscious and sex life, and probation officers began to evaluate personality in terms of sublimation, projection, transference, repressions, defense mechanisms and escape channels.

That confusion of thought developed concerning these various contributions and their application to probation techniques was inevitable. However, those concerned with the professional administration of probation were justified in their demands that probation officials and administrators should at least acquaint themselves with the various schools of thought in order that they might, without giving blind allegiance to any one group, develop and maintain a questioning attitude, accept the best workable programs which were offered, and apply them to the complex problems of personality with which probation officers have to deal.

It cannot be denied that in some instances extravagant claims were made as to the therapeutic value of some of the treatment offered. Some believed that these discoveries would result in the development of a cure-all for the problem of delinquency, but probation administrators of extended experience have accepted these findings with caution. They have wisely kept the middle of the road and have made use of the best which these schools had to offer as practical and workable tools which could be used in the social adjustment of criminal offenders. These contributions have led to emphasis on the individual, in addition to economic determinants and social and environmental stresses.

The probation officer began to see that nothing short of an individualized approach to the problem which each probationer presented could possibly help to eradicate the maladjustments responsible for the behavior patterns and the delinquencies. The probation officer became more understanding and less arbitrary in his demands, less dogmatic in his evaluations, and began to appreciate that it was in the mental attitudes of probationers that the most fertile field for his efforts could

19

be found. With this understanding and tolerance came also the realization that the probationer had to be educated to develop resources within himself, since some time or other the period of probation had to end and the probation officer no longer would be able to supply the crutch upon which the probationer could lean.

The potentiality of probation treatment as a means of bringing about permanent rehabilitation was envisaged, in contrast to the narrow view which once prevailed, that probation was merely a form of custodial care and that the probation system was relieved of responsibility with the discharge of the probationer from probationary oversight.

These changing attitudes have brought about a merging of the three avenues of approach; the sociological, the psychiatric, and the psychological. The great danger for probation officers in their reliance upon the interpretation given by the psychiatrist, however, is that they will adopt a hesitant attitude in placing confidence in their own interpretation of the material which their case histories contain, and permit the psychiatrist to do their thinking for them. No matter how well developed the methods used for character building, for the changing of mental attitudes, and for the transference of objectives, these techniques cannot be made workable unless the probation officer has the capacity, the vision, and the force to bend them to his will.

Successes and Failures

Through the years that the probation system has functioned, much information has been gathered with reference to first offenders and their potentialities for rehabilitation through this method of correctional treatment. We are now firmly convinced that probation treatment is not feasible for drug addicts, persistent alcoholics and mental defectives with well-developed criminal habits. We have learned also that because a person is for the first time convicted of a crime, such a circumstance in and of itself is no recommendation for his selection for probation. Investigation has repeatedly disclosed that some first offenders possess well defined anti-social habits, have had extended experience in criminal enterprise without having been apprehended, and have had continued contacts with underworld groups.

20

Probation has achieved a marked measure of success in dealing with criminal offenders who are young, whose personalities are pliant and whose offenses are casual. As yet, however, there have been no studies of value which have developed flexible criteria for the determination of continuing success or failure. In the main, throughout the United States, the reports of probation departments have merely classified persons discharged from probation as "Improved," "Committed" and "Absconded."

These classifications have little value since the critical standards by which these evaluations are made are the standards of the individual officer or the probation department. However, studies of the various reports which have been issued by probation departments and state divisions of probation reveal that an excess of 70% of those placed on probation have been discharged from probation as in some measure improved, and there have been investigations conducted at various times by independent commissions and research projects which have sustained these contentions. It would appear also that the failures could in a large measure be charged to ineffectual service due to a lack of staff and the granting of finances which were inadequate to bring about the development and proper administration of a probation service which could stand the test of decent standards.

It is exceedingly difficult to survey the successes achieved after release from probation because of the justifiable antagonism on the part of the discharged probationer to such investigations. Having conducted himself in such fashion as to merit his discharge from probation, and having established himself in many instances as the head of a family, as a respected employee, and sometimes as an employer, he is decidedly averse to being again approached after a lapse of years to submit himself to intensive questioning and investigation in order that he may assist in determining to what extent probation techniques and processes have been effective in bringing about his proper reestablishment in community life. However, such surveys have been made, and in Erie County in 1920, a review of the cases of two hundred discharged probationers showed that one hundred and eleven, or 72% of those discharged as improved, had continued to show improvement on the basis of better social and economic adjustments. A study in Wisconsin in 1926 showed that of sixty-five cases discharged from probation in 1922, of which number fifty-two could be found, only six had been subsequently arrested.

Despite the fact that probation has at times been regarded with suspicion and antagonism, and that it has been the subject in many instances of unjustified criticism, the system, despite the limitations imposed upon it by starvation support, has continued to grow. It has become through the years an accepted means of restoring to the community as productive and participating units, those who have violated the criminal law.

The future of probation will be written by the probation officers themselves. As they develop professional attitudes and give loyalty to the high standards which are being established, so will they profit from increased respect and confidence on the part of the public who must accept and support the probation system, if the service is to attain its maximum efficiency and usefulness as one of the social disciplines.

Chapter II

PROBATION IN THE COURT OF GENERAL SESSIONS

"The Court of General Sessions of the County of New York is the oldest criminal court in the United States. It dates from the early days of the colonial period when the Mayor's Court ('Generall Quarter Sessions') determined criminal matters.

"When Colonel Richard Nicholls captured New Amsterdam, September 6, 1664, and James II of England ceded it to the Duke of York, the so-called Mayor's Court was established. It was presided over by the Mayor, five Aldermen, sitting as Justices of the Peace, a Recorder, and a Sheriff, who combined the functions of prosecutor and constable.

"The old records reveal that whipping and branding were regular sentences of the Court. One of the cases records the following proceedings.

> 'J. Hatsell confessed of several thefts. Sentenced to the whipping post, to receive forty lashes and one, and to depart from the Citty and not to be found therein again upon penalty of severe punishment. To receive sayd punishment tomorrow morning by twelve of the clock.' "[1]

The Court of General Sessions has changed much since early colonial days. Today it consists of nine Parts in which trials are held daily, presided over by the nine Judges of the Court. The extent of its manifold activities can be judged by the volume of its criminal business. The Court between 1927 and 1936 disposed of 42,688 felony cases. Many felons and murderers, notorious in the annals of crime, have had their trials in the old dingy Criminal Courts Building, which houses this Court.

The Volunteer Service

Approximately thirty-five years ago, a volunteer probation system was established. After a short experimental period, this system was

---

[1] Judge John J. Freschi, Court of General Sessions, Address to New York County Criminal Courts Bar Association, June 13, 1933.

developed to include representation of the three principal religious denominations. Until 1927 all of the probation service of the Court of General Sessions, which included the investigation of the offenders arraigned for sentence, was carried on by the social workers assigned to these three religious divisions by the St. Vincent de Paul Society and Catholic Charities of the Archdiocese of New York, the Prison Association of New York, the Jewish Protectory and Aid Society, (now the Jewish Board of Guardians) and the Jewish Probation Society.

Although the social workers assigned to these Bureaus were actuated by a desire to properly develop the probation system into a well-rounded agency for the socialized treatment of first offenders, their efforts were limited by the meagre funds assigned for this work. This made it impossible for them to attain the objectives which they visioned as necessary to an efficient and constructive probation treatment of persons charged with criminal offenses.

Catholic Charities Contribution

In 1925, Cardinal Hayes of the Archdiocese of New York made the most outstanding contribution for the advancement of probation as a scientific form of correctional treatment that had ever been attempted in this country. Cardinal Hayes set up in the Court of General Sessions a Probation Bureau with a personnel well equipped by education and training to cope with the complex problems confronting the probation officer. This bureau also was equipped with an adequate clerical staff to compile case records and to aid in the preparation of thorough and detailed reports for the Court. A case record system which was a model of its kind was developed.

Cardinal Hayes, through his Secretary for Charities, Monsignor Robert F. Keegan, stated that this probation experiment would be conducted to ascertain the true value of an efficient and scientific probation system and would be carried on for two years, after which it was hoped that the City of New York would provide the funds for this work and maintain the high standards which had been established.

The Catholic Charities of the Archdiocese of New York recruited to this new venture in probation, young, alert men and women whose education and personality fitted them for this new type of endeavor. The staff were graduates of universities and every effort was made to meet and put into practice the Juvenile Court standard of minimum educational qualifications for Probation Officers.

The staff was divided into Investigation and Supervision Divisions, in order that each division might be given an opportunity to specialize in their respective fields. The work of this new venture in applying principles and practices which had heretofore only been discussed, attracted wide attention, received national publicity, and was commended in the highest terms by those qualified to appraise its work.

The experiment lasted for two years, at a cost of a quarter of a million dollars to Catholic Charities of the Archdiocese of New York. It demonstrated beyond doubt that if probation is administered by a well organized Department, adequately staffed with trained personnel, it can pay tremendous dividends in human salvage. It also demonstrated that this constructive work could be carried on through a public agency, if the standards which had been established by this privately established experiment were maintained.

Establishment of Department

The publicly maintained Probation Department began to function on January 1, 1927, after legislation had been enacted to provide for its establishment. From the very outset it has had the full cooperation and the splendid advice and guidance of the Judges of the Court, whose social vision and sincere interest have made possible its broad usefulness and accomplishments.

The Probation Department of the Court of General Sessions as it exists today, is a development of the Catholic Charities experiment. The standards and much of the methodology and techniques which were developed in the Catholic Charities Probation Bureau have been modified or broadened to meet changing conditions and the needs of a larger Department.

25

Commenting on the development of the probation service in this Court, Sanford Bates, then the Director of the United States Bureau of Prisons, stated:

> "By all odds the most efficient and progressive system of probation, that which has been the most intelligently devised and which has had the greatest measure of support, is that now officially adopted as part of the machinery of justice in the Court of General Sessions in New York City."[2]

The guiding principle of the new, publicly financed Department, was an individualized investigation into the personality and background of the delinquent and the development of an individualized program in each case, to meet the needs of those on probation. Without such an approach predicated upon a scientific and practical base, it was felt that the probation service could accomplish little of constructive and enduring value.

To attain these objectives, the calibre of personnel became one of the most important considerations. The new Department was fortunate in having a nucleus upon which to build its staff. Many of those who were qualified by education and training, who had been employed in the three social agencies which had theretofore carried on the probation work of the Court, entered the examinations conducted by the Civil Service Commission of the State of New York for the various posts in the new Probation Department. The executive heads of the three social agencies were classified in the civil service and were appointed to the positions of Chief Probation Officer and Deputy Probation Officers. The twenty-seven positions of Probation Officer which had been established were filled from the lists established by the State Civil Service Commission after open competitive examinations. A clerical staff was appointed from Civil Service lists.

Rules and regulations governing the new Department were adopted by the Judges of the Court of General Sessions, and a standard methodology of investigation and case work treatment programs were developed for the guidance of the staff, which was divided into two

---

[2]Bates, Sanford, National Conference of Catholic Charities, New York City, October 3, 1933.

groups under the direction of the Deputy Chief Probation Officers. Those qualified to conduct investigations to determine the personality and social maladjustments which lead to anti-social conduct, were assigned to the Division of Investigation. Those whose temperaments and specialized equipment qualified them to give the intricate and detailed services which are a basic part of probation treatment were assigned to the Division of Supervision.

In the ten years of its existence, the staff has been increased from 54 to 89 employees, its present strength. With the enlargement of the staff, the refinement of techniques, and the intensification of social investigation and probation treatment, there arose the necessity for more executive controls and the positions of Case Supervisors (Assistants to the Deputies) were created. The present set-up approximates that which can be found in any large social service agency of recognized standing.

Institutes in Probation

The administrators of the Department realized that previous educational training in Universities and Schools of Social Work were not sufficient, in and of themselves, to fully qualify the new staff for the grave responsibilities which it had to assume. It therefore became necessary to develop means to stimulate the staff to an awareness of these problems and to keep them abreast of the latest developments in the social sciences and in the field of case work practice. Staff conferences and case discussion sessions are a regular procedure in the Department, and in addition every opportunity has been afforded the field workers to individually confer with the executives. In the early years of the Department, speakers who were experts in various fields of social work, at intervals were invited to address the staff.

In 1932, the Probation Department established the "Institutes in Probation." The guest lecturers are outstanding authorities in the fields of sociology, law and psychiatry, and members of our staff have actively participated in the Institute programs as lecturers and discussants.

The purpose and value of these Institutes received the approval of the New York Academy of Medicine, which offered its cooperative aid in the enlistment of lecturers in the fields of psychiatry and medicine.

27

In commenting on the constructive educational value of these institutes, the Journal of the American Institute of Criminal Law and Criminology stated:

> "This is the most comprehensive course of instruction so far developed within a Probation Department. . . It is hoped that many other courts will follow the example of the Court of General Sessions and will include definite training courses and institutes for their workers as part of the day's work."

Regular sessions of the Institutes are held for six months in each year.

The members of other probation and parole departments and social workers in the employ of private and public agencies are invited to participate. This intensive training with its constant stimulation for the staff to adhere to the standards which this Department has established, has had marked results in developing a greater degree of efficiency and morale.

Educational Activities

The Department in a further effort to broaden the social vision and equipment of the probation officers, established a library for the use of the staff, which today numbers approximately three hundred volumes. Each year the best books published in the fields of the social sciences are added, as well as social work magazines, pamphlets and reports of other agencies. The staff, in addition, has been encouraged and aided to take further training in schools of social work, and some of the members of the staff since their appointment, have attended classes at the New York School of Social Work and the Fordham University School of Social Service. Others have taken lecture courses on special subjects.

State and National Conferences on Probation and Social work have been attended by members of the staff. The executives have contributed papers on the subject of probation at these conferences.

Much remains to be done through educational efforts to inform the community as to the objectives of probation and what it can and cannot

28

accomplish. Too often the public fails to distinguish between parole and probation and the faults and failures of one are too often charged to the other. Probation has been the subject of attack whenever some conspicuous failure is broadcast in the public press. Its successes are accepted as a matter of course, and without comment.

In accordance with the fundamentals upon which the probation system is founded, probation in the Court of General Sessions countenances no coddling of the criminal. We disclaim that the service is a cure-all for crime and know that many criminal offenders are unfit for this form of correctional treatment. The probation system has no desire to provide the means by which criminals can be released to commit more crimes, nor to assume responsibility for those whose attitudes and past records reveal that they will be probation failures.

Every effort is being made to disseminate wideley the knowledge that probation is not a form of mercy, nor is it just "another chance." It is a legally established branch of the correctional system of the State and a proper administration of probation means the weeding out through comprehensive and far-flung investigations of all those unfit for probation treatment. For every probationer, it means the application of programs of rehabilitation based on practical and workable procedures, which will result in eradicating malformations of character and which will change the mental attitude which produce anti-social behavior.

Professor Sheldon Glueck of Harvard University has pointed out that "One of the great tasks to be performed by workers in delinquency is to evaluate existing practices in this field, and present them in their true light to judges and leaders of public opinion. It is necessary that more tribunals like that of the New York Court of General Sessions, for example, consciously enter upon a scientific program of probation practice. Probation needs to be far more than another 'lenient disposition' of cases."[3]

Probation can perform no miracles. Since the human equation is the most important factor in this form of correctional treatment, failure must always be considered as a possibility. The Probation Department of the Court of General Sessions, while proud of its successes, is trying

---

[3]Glueck, Sheldon, and Eleanor T., *500 Criminal Careers*, pages 331-332.

to carefully appraise its failures in order to learn from them why the system does not work in some cases. While there are many reasons to which failures can be traced, the Judges have adopted the best possible means of limiting them; a most careful selection of those chosen for probation supervision and rehabilitation.

This Department has long been engaged on a program of public education in order that an informed public opinion might be developed to bring about a true evaluation of the probation system as a form of correctional treatment. Social and psychiatric studies have been made of the source material contained in the case histories compiled by the Department, and special articles have been written for the press and for magazines. Lectures have been given in universities and public forums. Crime commissions and research bodies have studied our cases and techniques. Students from schools of social work have been accepted for training, and the speakers bureau of the Department has rendered valuable service in helping to crystallize public thought.

The Department is a member of the Delinquency Section of the Welfare Council of New York City. The Chief Probation Officer is a member of the Board of Governors of the National Probation Association, has served as a member of the Advisory Committee of the National (Wickersham) Crime Commission, was a member of Governor Lehman's Crime Commission, and he and other members of the staff are members of national and state social service organizations and neighborhood councils. The Chief Probation Officer is a member of the faculty of the Law School of New York University where he lectures on criminology to classes of lawyers admitted to practice.

These extra activities are undertaken in order that the Department may have close personal knowledge of the work which other social service agencies are doing, and in order that our work may be interpreted to the public and integrated into the general program of social work and crime treatment which is being carried on by the community.

Psychiatric Diagnosis and Treatment

The Probation Department has always recognized that many persons charged with anti-social conduct present problems which require the aid of psychiatric diagnosis and treatment. Through the cooperative relationship established with the clinics of the various hospitals of the city of New York, such examinations and treatment were procured, but it soon became apparent that the clinics were unable to meet the flow of cases which were being referred to them.

In December, 1931, the Probation Department, through the aid of the Judges of the Court of General Sessions, and a committee of public officials, psychiatrists and social workers procured the establishment of the Psychiatric Clinic of the Court of General Sessions. This clinic, which is maintained by the Psychiatric Division of the Department of Hospitals of the City of New York, conducts the mental and physical examinations of all offenders investigated by the Probation Department of the Court of General Sessions.

Every person who is convicted of an offense in this Court is referred to the Clinic for examination by the Probation Department. Approximately 2800 examinations are made each year. Where psychiatric treatment is indicated by these examinations and the offender is released on probation, the cases are referred back to the clinic for treatment.

The method of dealing with the criminal offender through the sentencing power of the Court has had its defenders and its critics. It has been argued that the disposition of the offender by Judges is generally on the basis of legalistic concepts with little heed being given to changing social conditions and individualization of the needs of the offender and the community. Much has been said about mass treatment of offenders and some proponents of another approach have demanded that the sentencing power be turned over to sentencing boards to be composed of experts in the field of law, criminology and psychiatry.

The Judges of the Court of General Sessions, in imposing sentence, predicate the disposition which they make upon a wide and searching social investigation and a comprehensive psychiatric and physical examination. In each case the Judges have before them the report of the Probation Department and a report from the Psychiatric Clinic, which, in effect, combines in the pronouncement of judgment, the legal, the social, and the psychiatric approach, to a proper disposition of the offender.

31

Survey of the Slums

The Probation Department feels that in order to make constructive contributions to crime control and crime prevention, it must concern itself with the entire problem of crime, its causation, and its treatment.

In order to bring to the general public a consciousness of the factors which are responsible for the development of criminal attitudes and conduct, this Department, in 1935, at the request of the New York Housing Authority, undertook an exhaustive survey of the slums of this City.

The findings which resulted from this survey were published in the book entitled "The Slum and Crime," compiled by this Department. One thousand copies of this book were published through a grant of Federal funds, and have been distributed to libraries, universities and interested agencies here and abroad.

Judicial vs. Administrative Control

Suggestions have been made that all probation departments of the City of New York should be consolidated into one Department to render probation service to every criminal court in the city. However attractive it may appear in theory, such a plan is not practicable in the City of New York. It will lead to bureaucracy with its resultant ills and mechanized functioning. Such a department can easily became a political pawn, standards can be leveled down and the efficiency and social usefulness of the Probation Department of the Court of General Sessions seriously curtailed if the service is taken out of the Courts and deprived of the protection and oversight of the Judiciary.

Those concerned with the administration of probation and those interested in its development are constantly stressing that its techniques and processes must be individualized to the needs of each probationer. This is true also of probation departments, which must not be permitted to grow cumbersome and routinized. The service in each court must be highly specialized to meet the problems inherent in the cases arraigned in the various courts. Probation units should be comparatively small and mobile so that the probation administrator may know the capacities of each individual in his Department and the specialized service which each can render.

32

It has been amply demonstrated that the probation service of this city has never received the financial support necessary for its greatest development. In sharp contrast, the Probation Department of the Court of General Sessions, through the mandatory powers vested in the Judges by the legislature, has been organized and developed in such a manner as to bring to the public a far-reaching and constructive social service. Such mandatory powers will never be conferred upon a Director of Probation of the City of New York, who will be forced to plan his work in accordance with such funds as the fiscal authorities see fit to grant, which destroys any hope of a probation service which will measure to the standards which should govern such an undertaking.

An analysis of the funds allotted for probation work in this city reveals that the cost approximates $762,000. An estimate of the amount necessary to maintain a consolidated probation department in accordance with the standards which govern the work of the Probation Department of the Court of General Sessions is $2,787,000, an increased cost of more than two million dollars. If we are to judge from past experience, it is futile to assume that even an approximate amount of this sum will be furnished for such a purpose.

This leads logically to a discussion of whether or not probation is an administrative or a judicial function. While it can be argued that it is administrative insofar as the probation officers administer the service, nevertheless it remains a judicial function because the Court always is in control of the probationer, and acts through the probation officer, who is the agent of the court. In contrast to parole, which is purely administrative, the probation administrator possesses none of the powers of the parole commission or board, which has the sole right to release and to determine whether parole shall be continued or revoked. The probation officer must submit to the Judge on the question of acceptance of probationers and with reference to the revocation of probation, or of any modification of the Order of the Court in placing a person on probation. If the probation departments should be consolidated, the judiciary will be relieved of all responsibility for the administration and functioning of the system. Such a change would be extremely detrimental to the future development of probation.

Good probation work costs money, but it pays high dividends. Every court in this city can secure a good probation service, if an informed public opinion demands that the fiscal authorities shall properly support this sound and constructive method of changing social liabilities into social assets.

The Citizens Budget Commission has reported that, "The Probation Department of the Court of General Sessions in New York County has been cited many times as a model."[4] The Department has made contributions to a better understanding of the human motivations and the vitiating influences which produce anti-social behavior. It has developed and carried through rehabilitation programs which have resulted in changing a large number of social liabilities into social assets. We believe that its standards, its effectiveness and its further usefulness can best be maintained in its present setting.

---

[4]Citizens Budget Commission—A Report on the Administration of the Judicial System of the City of New York, 1935, page 21.

Chapter III

ORGANIZATION OF THE DEPARTMENT

The Department is divided into an Executive Division, a Division of Investigation, a Division of Supervision, a Division of Accounts and Finances, a Division of Research, and a clerical staff.

The Executive Division consists of the Chief Probation Officer, the Deputies and their Assistants, the Assistant to the Chief, a Chief Clerk, and a small clerical staff.

The Chief Probation Officer, subject to the direction of the Judges of the Court of General Sessions, is the administrative head of the Probation Department. The standards which govern the work of the members of the staff are developed and maintained by the executive officers of the Department, and conferences for this purpose are held daily. The executive officers also act as the case consultants, and direct the field activities of the staff. This Division is the liaison group between the Court, the Department, and the social agencies of the community.

All programs designed to further develop the capacities of the staff, to increase their knowledge of the social sciences, and the techniques and processes in use for the investigation and treatment of social, physical, and mental maladjustments, are initiated in this Division.

The Probation Department now has eighty-nine employees. The professional staff, who are university trained men and women, number fifty-one. The other employees are bookkeepers, clerks, stenographers, typists, etc. Two detectives are permanently assigned by the Police Department to act as warrant officers.

The Judges of the Court of General Sessions and the Chief Probation Officer in recruiting the professional staff, have had in mind the development of a career service. Merit has been recognized through promotion examinations. Every member of the Department is in the classified civil service. All of the executives have attained their present rank as a result of their service as Probation Officers of the Court of

35

General Sessions. The high standards which govern the work, and the qualifications of education and training which are demanded of these appointed to the staff, have governed the establishment of the salary of Three Thousand Dollars annually, which is paid to probation officers. The depression period and the program of retrenchment which resulted from it, has prevented the establishment of a schedule of regular salary increments for probation officers. An effective probation service demands a highly individualized effort on the part of the probation officer, and a definite salary increase to which he can look forward, is an urgent necessity if he is to be stimulated through the continuing years of his service to the best endeavors and contributions which he can make.

The entrance salary of this Department guarantees a choice of the best type of probation worker, but without some material reward for continued effort, his enthusiasm cannot be expected to remain at top-pitch. A minimum and maximum salary schedule with regular pay increases is of paramount importance to the continued effectiveness of this Department.

The work of the probation officers is under constant direction and supervision, and semi-annual ratings of their efficiency, which includes further educational development, are compiled by the Personnel Board of the Department, which consists of all of the executives. The findings are submitted to the Chief Probation Officer, and the ratings are filed with the State Civil Service Commission.

Former members of our professional staff who received their training in this Department, are now executives in other agencies, and two hold professorships in leading universities.

In commenting upon the development of the probation service in New York City, the Prison Association of New York has expressed the hope "that there will be in the other departments of the City a level of personnel and work equal to that now in the Court of General Sessions."[6]

So far as can be ascertained, this Department was the first to commit itself to the policy of a divided staff in order that there might

[6]90th Annual Report of the Prison Assn. of New York, 1934.

be specialization in social investigations and in the supervision of probationers, and the major Bureaus of this Department are the Division of Investigation and the Division of Supervision.

The Division of Investigation conducts the investigations of defenedants preliminary to sentence, and its inquiries, findings and interpretation of the legal, social, mental and physical factors are contained in reports which the Judges have before them when imposing sentence. Probation Officers who possess marked investigative ability and the capacity to evaluate human conduct and motivations are assigned to this unit.

The Division of Supervision is responsible for the supervision, direction and probation treatment of all persons paroled in the custody of this Department, and the probation officers assigned to this Division are chosen because of special aptitudes, sympathetic understanding, and ability to carry into effect workable plans for the rehabilitation of offenders.

Probation Officers are not required to spend any of their time in the Court room during the imposition of sentence, except in those rare instances when a Judge directs that they be present. The Department communicates the results of its pre-sentence investigations, the analyses of its treatment programs, reports of probation violations, and all other communications to the Court, in writing on forms which have been developed for these purposes. Verbal communications and reports are not permitted. The greatest value of such a system is that it permits the use of the full time of the probation officers for field activities.

The Division of Finances and Accounts is concerned with the collection and disbursement of restitution, reparation and family support, and also is responsible for maintaining accurate accounts of the expenditure of funds appropriated by the fiscal authorities of the city for the maintenance of the Department. The financial transactions of the Department are audited annually by the Department of Finance of the City of New York.

The Division of Research, if adequately staffed with trained research workers, could be developed into one of the most important branches of the Department. The studies which could be undertaken by this Division, in which the great amount of source material which has been gathered by this Department could be utilized, would be extremely valuable to public and private agencies engaged in coping with the problem of crime and its causes.

The Clerical force is composed of stenographers, typists and clerks. This Division prepares the reports for presentation to the sentencing Judge, and the detailed stenographic work necessary to conduct the inquiries of the Department. The case records, every one of which is typed, are kept in accordance with the best practices in use in recognized social service agencies.

Division of Investigation

This Division is in charge of a Deputy Chief Probation Officer who is assisted in the direction of this Division by two assistants who act as the Case Supervisors. Nineteen probation officers are assigned to this unit.

At National and State Probation and Social Work Conferences, it has been authoritatively stated that in order to adequately investigate, evaluate and interpret all the factors in the life of an individual which converged to make him an offender, a case load of twelve investigations monthly is all that a probation officer can efficiently carry. This Department has attempted to adhere to this standard but the volume of work has steadily increased, and with this increased volume, more and more cases have been thrust upon the officers assigned to this Division.

To envisage the factors in the life of an individual, to conduct investigations which will comprehensively evaluate these factors, and to present them in such a manner that they will serve to portray the individual as a distinct personality, requires time, special training, initiative and painstaking effort. If the standards which have been established for investigations of this character are to be adhered to, the staff assigned to this Division will have to be increased.

The Judges of the Court of General Sessions have established a system of investigations which is unique in that every offender arraigned in this Court who either pleads guilty or is convicted of a crime, is referred to the Probation Department for investigation. The investigation is initiated by a Court Order directing the Department to conduct such an investigation and to submit its report to the Court.

In the conduct of this investigation, the following methods are used. Triplicate fingerprints of the offender are taken by the Police fingerprint expert assigned to the Court. The probation officer who is assigned to the Investigation Division for the purpose of checking criminal records, compares the fingerprints with the records at Police Headquarters, the New York City Department of Correction, which controls the city institutions, the Parole Commission of the City of New York, the Division of Parole of the State of New York, and the Magistrates Courts. In each case an original fingerprint record is forwarded to the Identification Division of the United States Department of Justice, Washington, D. C.

In addition to this search of the criminal records, the record officer also visits nine other agencies to ascertain whether the offender, as a juvenile, appeared in the Children's Court or was committed through the Department of Public Welfare to institutions caring for children, or by the Board of Education as a truant.

Every case is cleared through the Social Service Exchange, and if the offender came to New York from another town or city, the case is cleared through the social exchange in that vicinity, to ascertain whether he or his family are known to the social agencies there.

During the interview with the offender, the probation officer exerts every effort to induce the offender to give a detailed and truthful statement of his life and the conditions under which his life developed. He is urged to discuss freely his childhood, his family, his employment and his reactions to it, his leisure, his religious observances, his ethical concepts, and the mental attitudes which prompted him to engage in criminal activity.

The next step for the probation officer after he has initiated his investigation is to prepare an Outline of History. This outline was formerly submitted to one of the cooperating hospital clinics or to the City Prison Physician in order that a Psychiatric and Physical examination of the offender might be conducted. All persons confined in the

City Prison were examined in that Institution, and those at liberty on bail were referred to the various clinics in the city.

Since the establishment of the Court of General Sessions Psychiatric Clinic in 1931, psychiatric, psychological and physical examinations of every offender convicted in the Court of General Sessions are made there. This Clinic is located in the Criminal Courts Building, in close proximity to the offices of this Department.

The field of investigation comprises an analysis of the offense, and an evaluation of the life of the offender and of the factors which converged to create the offender. This includes interviews with teachers and school nurses, a visit to the defendant's home, interviews with the family, his landlord, neighbors, friends, etc., communication with all social agencies which have had contact with him or his family and an analysis of the Court, Institution, Probation or Parole records, if he has previously been arrested or convicted of an offense. His employers are interviewed and their records of the defendant are studied and checked to establish the legitimacy of his employment and to evaluate his reaction to the type of work in which he was engaged. His fellow employees are interrogated to determine his relations with them and his reactions during employment hours.

The leisure-time activities of offenders, when they are more or less free to come and go as they please and choose the recreation they desire, are carefully investigated because they reveal fundamental characteristics. The associates they choose and their emotional reaction to the influences which surround them during their leisure, are essential to complete analyses of the personalities of offenders.

The report of the psychiatrist is studied in order that a diagnosis of his personality may aid to explain the defendant's conduct in terms of causation and motivation.

All this information is recorded upon the field sheet of the case and from the very valuable information gleaned through a comprehensive and painstaking investigation, the report of the Court is evolved.

This Department furnishes copies of these reports to the institutions to which offenders are committed in order that our findings may be utilized in their plans of treatment. A copy in each case is also furnished to the State Division of Parole and to the City Parole Commission.

Division of Supervision

The Division of Supervision has the responsibility for the supervision and rehabilitation of persons placed on probation by the Judges of the Court of General Sessions, and is in charge of a Deputy Chief Probation Officer who is assisted by two case supervisors. Twenty-one Probation Officers are assigned to this Division.

To properly study the subjective and objective factors in the lives of the persons placed on probation, and as a result of such studies to develop practical and workable programs of rehabilitation, requires painstaking effort, patience, keen insight and the ability to stimulate the development of attitudes which will make constructive plans acceptable to the probationers. Fifty cases, it has been stated authoritatively time and again, is the maximum that a Probation Officer can carry if he is to influence constructively the behavior of those entrusted to his care. This Division has attempted to adhere to this standard, but as the numbers placed on probation have increased, Probation Officers have been forced to assume the burden of more and more cases. Summer vacations, unexpected illnesses of Probation Officers, and other reasons, have at times compelled Probation Officers assigned to this Bureau to assume burdens far beyond their capacities to carry, and render effective service. In addition, despite the desire of the Judges to maintain a staff adequate to cope satisfactorily with the responsibilities of this Division, the retrenchment programs of the fiscal authorities have decreased the personnel assigned to this Division. More Probation Officers are needed for assignment to this Division, if it is to attain its maximum efficiency.

The minimum standard for the work of this Division is social case work in accordance with the best practices in use in recognized social service agencies.

The city is mapped into districts in accordance with population areas, and to these districts are assigned probation officers specially qualified to deal with the inhabitants and the conditions which prevail there. Probation Officers assigned to this Division are chosen with regard to the religious and racial origin of the groups they will supervise, and insofar as possible and wherever practicable, all probationers are assigned to probation officers of the same sex and religious faith.

Probationers at the inception of the probation period, are required to report weekly. The rules of the Department require that Probation Officers shall visit the homes of probationers twice monthly, and shall verify their employment once each month.

Extreme care is taken to avoid intermingling of probationers, and privacy when reporting is obtained through the use of the private offices in the Probation Department.

Reports are made by probationers between the hours of 5 P. M. and 8 P. M., in order that conflict with their employment may be avoided, and every probation officer assigned to this Bureau is on duty until 8 P. M. two nights each week. The offices of the Department are open until 8 P. M. every working day of the week, except Saturday, when they are closed at 12 Noon.

When a probationer fails to report, the rules of the Department require that a visit be made within twenty-four hours to ascertain the reasons for his absence, and if within forty-eight hours no satisfactory reason for his failure to report is forthcoming, the probation officer is required to clear the probationer's fingerprints through Police Headquarters to ascertain whether he has lapsed into delinquent conduct and is under arrest.

The maximum probation period for felonies is the maximum term of imprisonment which can be imposed under the law for the offense committed. For a misdemeanor the maximum probation period is three years. Generally, the judges of this Court place individuals on probation for the maximum period. In instances where a shorter probation period is deemed advisable at the time of sentence, the probationer must by his development of behavior patterns which conform to the accepted norms, prove that he is eligible for discharge at the expiration of his probation period. Should it appear that he is in need of further rehabilitative measures, the Chief Probation Officer submits a request for an extension of the probation period to the sentencing Judge, which invariably is granted.

When the Court places a person on probation, he or she is escorted to the Probation Department by a Court Attendant. The probationer is then interviewed by the Deputy Chief Probation Officer in charge of this Bureau, and the rules of probation and the general requirements are explained in detail to the probationer. The probationer is then introduced to the probation officer in whose district he resides, and under whose care he will remain during the probation period.

This initial interview, which marks the beginning of the long contact which the probationer will have with this Department, is carefully and tactfully carried on by the probation officer who attempts to establish a common meeting ground as a basis for mutual understanding. Plans for the probationer's future are discussed in broad outline, and thereafter the probation officer maps his program of treatment.

In every case the plan of treatment is developed about one month after the probationer has been entrusted to the care of this Department. This case analysis, in writing, presents the problems with which this Department must concern itself, the causal factors and the plan of treatment which has been evolved after careful observation and an analysis and evaluation of all the factors which influenced him toward anti-social conduct.

This case plan is revised and modified every three to five months, and is consulted constantly by the supervising officer in order that he may keep in step with the changes in the personality and life of the probationer, and his progress or retrogression.

The Probation Department which attempts to carry on its function as an isolated unit, is doomed to routinized effort, stagnation and failure. In determining a course of treatment for the probationer, the probation officer must outline a plan based upon an exhaustive inquiry into the school history, home, family life, industrial history, mental and physical health, and the recreational outlets of the probationer. His evaluation of these factors and his desire to change conditions and attitudes within the family group will necessarily lead to a utilization of all the community resources which can aid him to bring about the necessary changes for a better social adjustment of the probationer and his family. This Department has received the whole-hearted cooperation

43

of all the social agencies of the community, without whose aid it would have been impossible to have carried on effectively its program for social betterment, through the restoration of offenders to good citizenship and as participating social units.

Complete and detailed histories are prepared in each case. The present form of these case histories are the result of continuous experimentation. The earliest form of case recording used in this Department was the "chronological" or "diary type." These types of case histories are in use in a large number of public and private social agencies. However, it was readily seen that this type of recording in a probation department, where repetitive data was obligatory and case loads are heavy, presented the danger of creating mechanical, routinized and inadequate case histories.

Therefore in the Fall of 1934 a committee of seven members of the staff of this Department was organized to study the problem of case recording.

The result was the formulation of two outlines which were to be used as a guide by the probation officer in organizing his material before and as he recorded it. The first was for an initial entry which marks the transition of the record from the work of the Division of Investigation to the Division of Supervision. The second was for a periodic monthly summary which is narrative record providing for flexibility and for the presentation of a coherent integrated picture of fact or event in logical sequence with an opportunity for interpretation and diagnosis. In addition, we have also developed various other forms incidental to the procedure and the methodology of this Department.

The forms now in use have served as models for other Probation Departments throughout the country. The detailed case history is a running story of the supervisory process and endeavors to portray the progress made through the rehabilitative measures utilized and the reactions of the probationer to the forms of treatment which his particular needs make necessary. It serves a two-fold purpose in that it aids the probation officer to improve the quality of his service to the probationer whose performance or non-performance of obligations created by law it records, and provides efficient rapid and useful means to the executives to direct and evaluate the work of the probation officer. It is from these case histories that we secure necessary statistical and descriptive data which have been and are being used for research purposes not only by this Departmnt but by other public and private agencies.

When the probation period is about to terminate, a detailed report concerning the probationer's conduct during the probation period, and a recommendation for his discharge is submitted to the Judge who placed him on probation. Discharged probationers are urged to keep in touch with the Department and in many instances aid and guidance has been furnished them years after their official relations with the Department have terminated.

Chapter IV

DIVISION OF INVESTIGATION

Every person who either pleads guilty or is convicted of a crime in the Court of General Sessions is referred to the Probation Department for investigation. Sentences are adjourned from ten days to two weeks, in order that the Division of Investigation may make a searching inquiry into the social, mental and physical factors which moulded the defendant's personality and which conditioned him toward anti-social conduct.

The mere gathering of objective information such as employment records, school histories, family backgrounds, etc., cannot sufficiently reveal the offender as a personality. An individualized approach to a proper disposition of the offender requires a detailed investigation to determine in what way, from his earliest years, he has been conditioned by the influences with which he came into contact.

The investigations conducted by this Division are aimed toward that end and the inquiries made are as broad and as searching as the limitations of time and the volume of work will permit.[1]

This Division serves to "filter" those offenders who are deemed fit for probationary treatment and supervision and the reports compiled by this Division also form the basis for correctional treatment plans developed by the custodial institutions to which approximately four-fifths of the offenders who pass through this Court are committed.

During the decade beginning January 1, 1927 and ending December 31, 1936, the Probation Department conducted preliminary sentence investigations into the careers of 25,872 convicted offenders who had been indicted for felonies and arraigned in the Court of General Sessions. Of this number 14 were discovered after investigation to be under the age minimum of sixteen, and referred to the Juvenile Court. These cases were deducted from the total of 25,872, and the statistics which appear in the following pages are based on the resulting total of 25,858. These investigations, in form, content and techniques utilized,

---

[1] *The Investigation Methodology* (Chapter 8) details the investigation procedures.

followed the standard investigation methodology which is detailed elsewhere in this report.

The yearly average of cases referred by the Court to the Probation Department for investigation was 2,587, but this figure is in no sense constant. The annual total ranged from 2,218 in 1928, to 2,927 in the peak year of 1930. The following year, 1931, was close behind in volume, when 2,917 criminal histories were added to the records of the Department.

The volume for the three-year period subsequent to 1929 rose to 8,707, and for the ten-year period, except for 1934, they are the peak years. On the other hand, for the three-year period up to and including 1929, a total of 6,890 referrals were made by the Court, or a number 1,817 less than the second three-year period.

Sex of Offenders

The number of women investigated by the Probation Department for the ten-year period aggregated 960, or 3.71% of the total intake, as against 24,912 men, or 96.29% of the total.

Ages of Offenders

For purposes of classification, offenders investigated by the Probation Department were fitted into five-year age groups. These statistics reveal that the first two groups, those from 16 to 20, and those from 21 to 25, virtually dominated numerically.

For the ten-year span, the first group represented 25.78% of the total departmental intake, while the second group accounted for 24.57% of the total. Combined they represented 50.35% or more than half of the number of offenders who passed through the Probation Department.

The age of 19 appears as the most susceptible from the standpoint of incidence, followed by the 18-year-old group, after which follow in order those in the 20, 21, 22, and 23-year-old classification.

Why should the crime scene be numerically dominated by our younger criminals? To this ever-perplexing question numerous hypotheses have been evolved from time to time which temporarily appeal to

47

popular fancy but which fail to stand the test of scientific investigation. Can it be that the stage of transition into early manhood is of itself a pre-disposition to criminality? Is this stage most susceptible because there has not yet been a full ethical and moral development with the consequent impatient disregard of the consequences of criminal conduct?

Is it possible that the combination of conditions which we have found contribute to criminality reach their maximum strength during this period in the offender's life? What causes a break at this time in the moral make-up of young men who have long been subjected to deleterious influences? Is the desire for easy money stronger? Is the fascination and pull of commercialized recreation greater? How strong or weak was the home environment and the influence of parents? Would the steadying influence of a good home or of gainful employment have outweighed many of these factors at that time? Just what weight should be assigned to conflicts arising from faulty emotional adjustments to society's conventional codes of conduct?

These conditions and other variables were present in many cases studied, but their relationship to each other and their relative weight in contributing to criminal conduct remain as challenging questions.

Whatever group of causes combined to produce criminality, the fact is that the majority of our felons are young men. A comparison of these figures with comparable age groups in the general population is illuminating. For the year 1930 the statistics compiled by the U. S. Census Bureau reveal that for New York City the age group between 15 to 19 numbered 599,286, or 8.65% of the total population. For the first five-year period, despite the fact that 16 years is the minimum age for arraignment in this Court, the offenders in this group investigated by this Department approximated 22.15% of the total, or more than two and one-half times their representation in the general population.

For the group between the ages of 20-24, the same federal agency reported a total of 687,417 or 9.92% of the total general population in the City of New York. For the same five-year period, offenders in this age group passing through this Department totaled 27.41%.

A comparison over the ten-year period reveals that the percentage of total investigations in this Court for the group 16-19 aggregated

48

20.31%. Compare this figure with that for the general population, which, even including 15-year-olds, is but 8.65% of the total.

The 20-24-year-old group represented 25.89% of the entire number of investigations over the ten-year period. Comparison of percentage with the federal census figures indicates that in 1930 this group in New York City represented but 9.92% of the general population.

While it is in all likelihood true that these groups should be assigned a higher ratio in the law abiding population in 1936 as against 1930, the gravity of this problem is apparent when it is noted that the preponderance of younger offenders is attained by comparing only General Sessions convictions against the non-criminal population, with no consideration of arrests or convictions in other county courts in the City of New York, and excluding convictions in our inferior courts.

Individual behavior, whether law abiding or anti-social is dependent upon numerous pre-disposing conditions and psychological processes dating back to the early developmental years. The community, if for no other reason than the selfish one of protecting its investment in these young men, and diminishing the ever mounting cost of incarcerating the criminal, must act to ameliorate those conditions in its society which have appeared so frequently in our case histories as the pre-determinants of criminality.

Offenses According to Age Groupings

An analysis of the types of offenses committed according to age groups reveals that younger offenders not only contributed most heavily numerically but that they perpetrated the most serious crimes and frequently used weapons in perpetrating them.

Over the ten-year period the age group 16-20 perpetrated 38.34% of the total number of robberies for which convictions were had in this court. This offense, which involves theft from the person by the use of violence or threat of injury, is one which necessitates daring and some degree of premeditation in planning. It is also, under average circumstances, one of the most hazardous to perpetrate successfully in the County of New York. Conviction brings the infliction of heavy penalties. There is the ever-present menace of death or serious injury to the criminal, and the possibility that the death of an assaulted victim will lead the offender to the electric chair. Although these circumstances are known to the average criminal, and despite the fact that the rewards frequently are negligible in proportion to the risks, the reckless, young and optimistic criminal seems to be strongly attracted to this type of crime.

As a rule the law-breaker who feels that a gun or other lethal weapon will contribute to his success encounters little difficulty in arming himself. Speedy automobiles are left unlocked and unattended in our city streets. The desire for spectacular recognition, the fleeting sensation of temporary dominance over his victims, the appeal of "easy money" and the lure of dangerous adventure combine to form a powerful attraction.

For the age group 21-25, the percentage for this offense represented 35.54% of the total number of robberies.

Those from 16 to 25 years old were responsible for 73.88% of the total number convicted of robbery. The 26 to 30-year group perpetrated 18.81% of the total robberies. Thereafter, the distribution curve undergoes a steep drop.

Burglary

For this crime the highest incidence was in the group 21 to 25, which accounted for 28.10% of the total number of burglaries, as against 21.50% for the younger classification. However, it is not to be assumed that this type of crime was without appeal to the 16-20-year-old defendants, for an analysis of the statistics relating to the convictions for Unlawful Entry, which is an offense identical with burglary but perpetrated under conditions and in a manner not warranting a burglary classification with its more severe punishment, indicates that 44.97% of the total convictions for unlawful entry fell into the younger grouping. This figure is nearly double that for the 21-25 group. Together, the defendants ranging in age from 16 to 25 were responsible for 68.65% of the total number of convictions for unlawful entry.

50

Petit Larceny

For this offense the youngest group was once again responsible for the largest number of convictions, although the representative percentage receded from 35.10% for the first five-year period, to 29.40% for the latter, thus providing a ten-year average of 32.25% of the total convictions for this crime. For the older group there is an even and steady recession in the distribution curve.

Grand Larceny

For Grand Larceny offenses, the 21-25-year group led with 21.29% of the total convictions, as compared with 16.9% for the younger group. The 16-20 group was also exceeded numerically in this classification by the defendants in the 26-30-year-old group, which accounted for 19.73% of the total convictions for Grand Larceny.

Forgery

As one would expect, the older groups predominated in the forgery classification. This crime, which demands for successful consummation the exercise of well-developed skills and techniques, and often an extensive knowledge of business practices, proved to be least attractive to the younger group. The group from 26-30, with 22.24% of the total forgery convictions, led the others, followed by the 31-35, and by the 36-40 groups. Those in the 21-25 classification ranked fourth numerically, after which came the 41-45 classification. The 16-20 group accounted for only 6.72% of the total convictions of forgery.

Assault

Under this classification are listed Felonious Assaults, involving Pugnacity, and Sex Offenses. Here the age group 21-25 predominated numerically, being responsible for 24.85% of the entire number of criminal assaults. Thereafter, followed the 26-30 year group, with a percentage of 20.46%. The youngest age group accounted for 17.30% of the total convictions in this category.

Pugnacity

Felonious Assaults involving pugnacity averaged 12.95% of the total number of investigations.

Sex Offenses

Crimes involving sex dereliction of any kind, including Abduction, Bigamy, Prostitution and Impairing Morals, comprised 6.12% of the total number of criminal investigations conducted by this Department. Under this classification, convictions of Assault in the Third Degree, involving sex, were numerically predominant.

Acquisitiveness

By far the majority of offenses investigated by the Probation Department involved acquisitiveness. A grouping of all offenses involving theft, such as larceny, forgery, burglary, unlawful entry and robbery, indicates that they aggregated 69.56% of the total number of criminal investigations over the ten-year period. This percentage would be a larger one if other offenses which involved acquisitiveness but not listed in these major classifications were included.

Native and Foreign-Born

An exhaustive report relating to this phase of criminality was made by the National Commission on Law Observance and Enforcement (Wickersham Commission) and was published in 1931 as the "Report on Crime and Foreign Born." This volume, number ten, of the reports published by this Commission, surveys the available statistical data, and attempts, as far as possible, to draw some conclusions, in spite of the general *inadequacy* of available statistics. The following is included in this report:

> "It (the report) does not cover the prevalence or the tendency to crime among American-born descendants of parents one or both of whom are foreign born. Crime statistics can hardly be said to have attempted to segregate and compile the data necessary for any inquiry as to the latter group. Whether or not the current impression of excessive criminal propensities among so-called "foreigners" generally can partially be justified by the existence of criminal propensities among children of foreign-born parentage, it is impossible either to affirm or deny. Within

52

the limits of the problem which it has been possible to study, we are now in a position definitely to say that any such impression as to the foreign-born is at variance with the facts. The conclusions ... from ... statistical studies are in proportion to their respective numbers the foreign-born commit considerably fewer crimes than the native born; that the foreign-born approach the record of the native-born most closely in the commission of crimes involving personal violence, and that in crimes for gain the native-born greatly exceed the foreigners."

For the ten-year period, 19,213, or 74.30% of the offenders investigated by this Department were found to be native-born, while 1,013, or 3.92% were born in dependencies, protectorates or possessions of the United States.

The foreign-born accounted for 5,620, or 21.73% of the total number of investigations by this Department.

The native-born colored offenders, totalling 6,366, represented 86.45% of the total colored criminals investigated, as against 12,818 native-born whites, or 69.75% of the total white criminals investigated by this Department.

Nativity of Offenders

The native-born offenders have steadily increased in number over the ten-year span. In 1927, they were charged with 68.77% of the total number of criminal investigations, while those defendants born in United States dependencies represented 3.09% of the total.

By the end of 1936, the native-born were responsible for 79.59% of the total, while those defendants born in dependencies had increased to 5.25%.

On the other hand the criminal investigations relating to the foreign-born offenders has shown a consistent decline from the peak-year in 1927, when they accounted for 28.01% of the total investigated. By the end of 1936, they had reached the lowest point of 15.16%.

Native-born of Native Parents

For the white group, 4,250 offenders or 33.16% of the total native-born were found to have been born of native-born parents. For the negro group of similar classification, 5,903 or 92.73% of the total colored American-born were the offspring of native-born parents.

Native-born of Foreign-Born Parents

The white American-born defendants of foreign-born parents totalled 7,132, or 55.64% of the American-born white offenders. There were 189 or 2.97% of the native-born negro defendants of foreign-born parents.

Summary

It is seen that for the whites, the American-born of foreign-born parents heavily outscored the native-born defendants whose parents were born in America, exceeding the latter group by 2,882, or 22.48%. The reverse was true for the negro group of native-born, where it was found that 92.73% of the negro native-born had native-born parents, while only 2.97% of the native-born negroes were the offspring of foreign-born parents.

These findings coincide, generally speaking, with other studies on the subject. Glueck's study revealed that the native-born sons of foreign-born parents contributed more than their share to the criminal ranks, and that there were two and a half times as many persons native-born of foreign or mixed parentage in the Reformatory group studied as were found in the general population.[2]

According to the investigations carried on by this Department, the average immigrant was found to be hard-working but of limited industrial training and as a result placed in the lowest income group. He was attracted to low-cost tenements partly because he could mingle with his own racial group, but mainly because of economic necessity.

As a rule he received small returns for his labor and worked long hours. The family income was augmented by small earnings contributed

---

[2]Glueck, S., and E. I., *500 Criminal Careers*, 1933, p. 119.

by the wife who worked either in the home or away from it. The children of the immigrant, however, were less constrained to resign themselves to long daily labor for small income and resented parental insistence that any work is better than none.

The homes of immigrants were frequently marked by ill-concealed hostility between the father and older sons, especially where extended unemployment had reduced the group to marginal existence. Work-weary parents knew little of their children's activity outside of the home and less of their friends and associates. There was little social intercourse carried on by them in the home, which usually was regarded only as a place to eat and sleep.

Often the street-wise youth held his well-meaning but industrially unsuccessful parent in contempt, and the parent's recognition of the widening breach caused him to resort to direct disciplinary measures which bred further resentment and usually led to an open break.

In those cases where probationary treatment was applied, it was only by a slow process of education that the parent and offspring were brought to a recognition and appreciation of mutual rights and enabled to make the mental and emotional adjustments necessary for a balanced family life.

Offenders by Color

The white defendants convicted and arraigned in the Court of General Sessions aggregated 17,801 men and 575 women, or a total number of 18,376. This figure represents 71.07% of the total intake.

Offenders classified as belonging to the negro race numbered 6,980 men and 384 women, or an aggregate total of 7,364, or 28.48% of the total number of offenders investigated by the Department.

Orientals accounted for 104, or .40% of the total, while defendants classified as being of the red race totalled 14, or .05% of the total.

While the rate of criminality among whites, insofar as convictions in the Court of General Sessions is concerned, shows a wide fluctuation during the decade under consideration, the rate among negroes has steadily climbed.

In 1927, for example, a total of 530 men and 30 women of the negro race were convicted in this Court and investigated by this Department. This represented a number which was 23.41% of the total investigations for 1927. In that year the white offenders totalled 1,824, or 76.25% of the total number investigated.

By 1936, after some degree of fluctuation, the white offenders had dwindled to 1,443 for a representative percentage of 61.09% of the total, while the number of negro offenders had mounted to 899, or 38.06% of the total investigated.

Commitments

Of the total number of 25,858 defendants investigated by the Probation Department for the ten-year period, 18,595 men and 588 women were sentenced to penal and correctional institutions. These commitments represented 74.15% of the total number of convicted offenders.

The proportion of male defendants committed to penal and correctional institutions to the number investigated was 74.64%, while 61.25% of the total number of female defendants were similarly committed.

Male offenders who were committed to institutions for defective delinquents and to institutions for the insane, totalled 336, or 1.35% of the total number of men investigated. Only 8 women, or .83% of the total women investigated were committed to these institutions.

At no time were there more than 53 commitments in one year to institutions of this type. In 1932 only 9 were so classified and disposed of accordingly.

A combination of the totals for men and women indicates that 344, or 1.33% of the total number of investigations were listed in this category.

Placed on Probation

A total number of 5,693 offenders were released to this Department under probationary oversight. This number represents 22% of the total number investigated for the ten years.

A total of 5,374, or 21.57% of the men investigated were placed on probation, while 319, or 33.23% of the women were released under probationary supervision.

A more detailed analysis of this section will be found elsewhere in this report.

Factors Contributing to Crime

In presenting the following material relating to crime causation, it cannot be emphasized too strongly that this data can be interpreted only for the bare facts enumerated. The individual offender has been considered as a living, changing being in a constantly changing environment. As far as possible, the outstanding factors present in the histories of the offenders studied have been gathered and objectively tabulated. No attempt will be made to utilize this factual data to draw conclusions regarding the specific *causes* of crime, or the importance of one set of conditions over another set in being responsible for crime.

If our study has made no other contribution, it has revealed that crime is attributable to deep-rooted psychological processes, and is the product of many variables. It has indicated the impossibility of separating the individual from the physical and social forces which condition his development.

It is scientifically unwise to attempt even a separation of terms like "heredity and environment" much less to ascribe variables to each and weigh them against each other in an effort to form a basis for the understanding of human motivation. In anti-social behavior, the intent which motivated the activity is frequently of greater significance than the overt act itself. This principle is recognized in law, as criminal intent must be established to label an act a crime.

The tendency to select an unusual or spectacular event in the life of the criminal and ascribe his unlawful behavior solely to it should be avoided. He may have suffered a head injury as a child; he perhaps was maltreated by a brutal father or spoiled by an over-indulgent mother; or he may have suffered a shocking experience in childhood. Of course these factors would be important in any consideration of crime causation, but they are insufficient in themselves as an explanation

57

for criminal conduct. Neither is it adequate to ascribe criminality solely to the pressure or effect of unfavorable environmental or social influences as unemployment and poverty, the prevalence of slums, inadequate recreational facilities, etc.

In an increasing degree the individualization of treatment and the individualization of punishment are being emphasized in recognition of the fact that criminality is being traced to individual differences in the offender.

Crime is the resultant of many variables which do not affect human beings in the same manner. Neither is the effect of these variables on a given group constant.

Dr. Sheldon Glueck states:

"One of the most necessary and crucial lines of research, not only in the causation of delinquency but in education and many other problems of life in a complex society, is a careful inquiry into the introjective processes of various types of human beings; into the why and wherefore of the conscious and unconscious acceptance or rejection by different persons of certain bits of the environment. This process of weaving of environmental elements into the fabric of personality is the key to many a problem of behavior."[3]

Criminals are alike only in that they have been apprehended and convicted and labelled law-breakers. But they may differ in every other respect. Situations which encourage crime in some do not in others. As Cyril Burt observed, "It is the personal reaction to a given situation that makes a man a criminal, not the situation itself."[4]

Let us not forget that studies of crime causes have in the main been limited to *apprehended* and *convicted* criminals. While the data from this group is illuminating and instructive it is quite probable that many criminals are never brought to justice. It is likely too that many individuals have perpetrated a single crime, or several criminal offenses un-

---

[3]Glueck, Sheldon, *Crime and Justice*, 1936, p. 179.
[4]Burt, Cyril, *The Young Delinquent*, 1925, p. 179.

letected, and have thereafter led law-abiding careers. This fact should
emind us that at best we are treating conditions in a situation which
an never be studied as a whole.

Alcoholism and Drug Addiction

Alcoholism and drug addiction as contributory factors to criminality
are linked in this discussion, although the former is by far more commonly associated with crime. The effects of chronic intoxication and
drug addiction have frequently been prominent in consideration of
causes of crime. It has been contended by some that either the excessive
use of alcohol or the continued use of drugs was the direct cause of
criminal behavior, but the validity of such a conclusion is open to
question. There are many responsible law-abiding individuals who use
alcohol in varying degrees of moderation, or excess, just as there are
drug users who never come to the attention of correctional agencies.

Intoxicating liquor is comparatively easy to obtain. In a general way
its use tends to weaken the coordinating centers and lessens control over
muscular activity. In attempting a discussion of this kind we are once
more faced with the problem of individualization, for not alone does
the use of intoxicating liquor affect different individuals in various ways,
but its effect is unpredictable even upon the same person, depending
upon the state of his mental and physical condition at various times.

Because alcohol destroys the finer adjustments it would seem that
drunkenness would encourage the perpetration of crimes where these
finer adjustments are not essential. Sullivan[5] contended, and was supported by others, that the drunkard was inclined to commit minor
offenses, and that sex offenses constituted the serious crimes.

Goring[6] reported that in his study of the subject he found the
relationship between alcoholism and crime was insignificant when intelligence was made a constant, but that this relationship was significant
in crimes involving personal violence.

[5]Sullivan, W. C., *The Criminology of Alcoholism* in T. N. Kelynock's Symposium on
The Drink Problem.
[6]Goring, C., *The English Convict,* 1913, pp. 277-286.

Over the ten-year span alcoholism was considered to be a contributing factor in 5,755 cases investigated, a figure representing 22.26% of the total.

Drug addiction was found to be an important contributing factor in only 525 investigations, or 2.03% of the total. This relatively small figure is perhaps due to the fact that crimes involving the illegal use of drugs are disposed of in the Court of Special Sessions. This Court also passes on crimes involving petty thefts, usually perpetrated by the drug addict for funds to purchase drugs.

Once again the importance of individualized study is demonstrated, if the question of a significant relationship between drug addiction and crime is to be examined. There are numerous kinds of narcotics which produce varying effects in individual behavior, depending on the quantity used, and the physical and nervous condition of the addict at the time.

The power of drugs in displacing or subordinating normal objectives to the procurement of an adequate supply of narcotics is a strong one. Because of this, the economic status of the addict is most important in any consideration of drug addiction and its relation to crime causation.

The excessive or extensive use of alcohol and narcotics aside from their more specialized effect on individual conduct, have the general properties of affecting normal inhibitions and creating a state which is likely to express itself in anti-social behavior as the more convenient method of release.

Alcoholism and drug addiction, like criminal conduct itself, are frequently symptoms of basic mental or physical inadequacy or disorder. In that sense they may be regarded more as effects of existing predisposing conditions than causal agents.

Regardless of the original causes for the establishment of these habits, when the victims fall into criminal behavior, it is recognized that they represent the most trying and difficult problems from the standpoint of rehabilitation under probationary oversight. Institutionalization invariably is needed and as a result this type of offender rarely is referred for probationary treatment.

Economic Factors

Economic security and regular employment are among the foremost safeguards to normal and orderly life. The stabilizing influence of steady work frequently has been found to have counteracted and neutralized unfavorable social conditions commonly found to have contributed heavily to criminal conduct.

A steady job is valuable not only because its regular income encourages independence and responsibility, but because it imposes a disciplinary regimentation on the worker that makes for the development of patterns of orderly behavior. Unaccustomed idleness, on the other hand, speedily undermines good personal habits. Slovenliness frequently results, personal discipline is relaxed, family and social activities are subordinated and curtailed, and an increased leisure is made available to individuals rarely trained to use it constructively. Should the period of idleness be prolonged and the pressure of poverty added to an attitude of hopelessness, the temptation to criminal conduct is increased.

From 1927, when 41.79% of the total number of defendants investigated were found to be unemployed at the time of arrest, the rate increased steadily until in 1931 the jobless at time of arrest represented 66.76% of the total offenders. From 1931 the rate decreased until in 1936, 51.86% of the defendants were idle at the time of their arrest. For the ten-year period the average for this classification was 56.76%.

Poverty and economic incompetence were found to have contributed significantly as crime causes in 19.38% of the total over the ten years.

Obviously, it is difficult here to attempt an isolation of factors. Unemployment, economic incompetence, poverty, employment of mothers out of the home, etc., are all so closely related to each other and to other conditions such as poor housing, limited educational opportunity, unfavorable recreation, etc., that it is perhaps advisable, except for statistical classification, to consider these factors collectively rather than singly.

Low income families are under numerous handicaps. They can formulate no long-range plans for general improvement but must solve the day-to-day problems incident to providing the bare necessities of life. They are restricted to the low-cost deteriorated sections of the city which as a rule afford the least advantages. Their children are shunted into haphazard and often unhealthful employment early in life at the expense of formal or vocational education, and it is this group that regularly contributes its crop of industrial misfits to the steadily increasing army of unemployed.

While it is undoubtedly true that the influence of poverty is present in many homes of delinquents and criminals, it is present in many families which are law-aiding. One must be wary in pointing to the influence of poverty alone as a primary contributory factor to criminality.

Bad Associates

The influence and effects of undesirable companions have long been recognized as important factors in causing crime. Especially weighty has been this influence as a causal factor in juvenile delinquency, but it is by no means limited to that group.

Those highly sensitive to these influences are usually those from families where discipline is either too severe or has broken down; where the family relationships are strained, or where conditions exist that make street life more desirable than the home.

The immature, poorly supervised adolescent is attracted to older more street-wise companions whose comradeship he values, and whose precepts and habits of thinking become his own.

Glueck found that 95% of the Reformatory inmates studied had bad associates prior to their commitment.[7]

In 3000 cases Healy and Bronner concluded that in 62% of them bad associates could fairly be regarded as a causative factor in the delinquency.[8]

Because of the train of other deteriorating factors which usually accompany the influence of bad associates, it is difficult to attempt an isolation of this factor from other harmful conditions which have

---

[7]Glueck, S. and E. I., *500 Criminal Careers*, 1933, p. 128.
[8]Healy, Wm. and Bronner, Augusta, *Delinquents and Criminals*, 1926, p. 179.

affected the offender. The law-breaker who is affected by the suggestions and urging of vicious companions and commits crime, might have engaged in anti-social activities in any event. It is recognized, however, that an inclination to wrong-doing is greatly stimulated and reinforced by companions whose approbation is desired, and that a crime perpetrated by a group tends to lessen individual guilt and responsibility in the minds of the culprits.

"Bad associates" was found to have been present as a significant causal agent in 15,136 cases, or 58.54% of the total investigated, and was the factor most frequently encountered.

Education of Offenders

One of the most striking facts that commands attention in studies of delinquency and criminality is the meagre formal schooling of the subjects under consideration. One of the most frequently met conditions is that the criminal has failed to complete the grammar grades. This finding has been variously interpreted and has been responsible for some interesting conclusions. For example, the Hon. Rodney H. Brandon, Director of Public Welfare in Springfield, Mass., was so impressed by his findings when he discovered less than one hundred and seventy-five high school graduates among more than ten thousand men in the prisons of Illinois, that he formed the conclusion "that a high school diploma is practically immunity from prison."[9]

Dr. Sheldon Glueck found a similar limitation in a study of 454 reformatory inmates studied. Only 4.4% of them had spent one or more years in high school, while only .2% had completed high school studies. 4.6% had reached the 9th grade in elementary school; 45.8% had attained the sixth to the eighth grade, while 42.6% had reached the fifth grade or less.

Dr. Glueck was able to compare his findings with comparable nondelinquents, and found that the "schooling of the reformatory group is far less than that of the general population as represented by Boston school children."[10]

---

[9]Brandon, Hon. Rodney H. in Clifford R. Shaw's *The Natural History of a Delinquent Career*, 1931.
[10]Glueck, Dr. Sheldon and Eleanor T., *500 Criminal Careers*, 1933, pp. 132-134.

Healy observed that statistics on education are only of negative value, and concluded that "illiteracy arising through lack of opportunity plays no important part in the production of delinquency as we have seen it in our city population."[11]

The experience of the Probation Department is studying 25,858 offenders over the ten-year period reveals that the preponderant majority had but limited schooling. There were 19,955, or 77.17% who had terminated their school careers in some grade of elementary school, and of this number, but 3,286, or 12.71% were elementary school graduates.

Of the number who had attended high school, 3,688, or 14.26%, only 558 or 2.16% had completed such studies.

Those who had attended college numbered 530, or 2.05% of the total, while 193, or .75% were college graduates.

The defendants who had had training in continuation schools, vocational or business schools totalled 543, or 2.10% of the total, while those defendants who had had no schooling whatsoever totalled 1,018, which represented 3.94%.

These statistics indicate that the criminal group, insofar as the County of New York is concerned, were subjected to a limited formal schooling, and in some measure parallel the observations of other studies of similar groups. However, care should be exercised in seizing upon this factor as a causal agent.

As Sutherland points out, many attempts have been made to prove that criminal behavior is the result of limited formal schooling, and that even if there were a significant and definite correlation between illiteracy and crime, it might indicate only that both were caused by the same unfortunate conditions. He found no good grounds for the conclusion that an increase in illiteracy produces crime, and no evidence that formal scholastic education is a significant factor in increasing or decreasing crime.[12]

In any evaluation of formal school training, it is obvious that the effect of school attendance upon the individual must be considered. This effect will vary, being dependent for the most part on the pupil's reac-

[11]Heally, William, *The Individual Delinquent*, 1929, p. 152.
[12]Sutherland, Edwin H., *Criminology*, 1924, p. 172.

tion to school discipline, what feature of school life he responds to, and the training he carries over with him when not at school. Education, as we know it, is virtually a continual process which is not limited to school attendance, and of which the school is only one phase, though an important one. However, also important is the environmental setting, the home, parents, recreation, and other similar conditions which exert a powerful influence in the shaping of behavior.

In view of these circumstances, it is perhaps unfair to expect the school to bear the major responsibility for the development of good character, especially when it is clear that the average delinquent spends so small a part of his career at school. In many instances, however, the school represents the first contact with extra-familial discipline, and because of its importance in the community, the school is in a position to initiate broad and constructive programs for mental, emotional and physical improvement, in cooperation with other agencies who can furnish more specialized service. In this way the influence of the school can be extended and developed into a potent force for good in the lives of those who give early indication of maladjustments which form the basis for subsequent delinquent conduct.

The limitations imposed by meagre schooling are apparent. Lacking an educational background, deprived of constructive mental stimulation and vocationally untrained, these individuals represent that group who are rarely gainfully employed. They are the last to be hired and the first to be discharged, and the attitudes of mental shiftlessness and irresponsibility which result, contribute to the formation of an anti-social viewpoint.

While it cannot be shown that limited schooling per se is a "cause" of crime, it becomes increasingly evident from the cases studied in this Department that this lack provides a fertile field which nurtures and stimulates the growth of more positive conditions which contribute to criminal behavior.

Broken Homes

While it is not known just how many homes are broken or disrupted in the non-criminal population by reason of death, divorce, desertion or separation, the effects of the "broken home" appear as significant contributing causes in the development of anti-social attitudes. This condition is important because it gives rise to other conditions which make for poor development, such as bad home conditions, lack of religious or moral training, and frequently, institutionalization during formative years.

In a group of over 1,600 delinquent boys in New York State studied by Slawson, 45.2% came from homes disrupted by the death of one or both parents, or where the parents were separated or divorced. This figure was compared with a large control group which showed 19.3% were similarly affected. He concluded that there appeared to be two or three times as many broken homes for the delinquents as for non-delinquents.[13]

It has been estimated from census reports that probably 25% of children in the United States live in broken homes.[14] Crime studies in relation to this caption reveal that the figure for delinquent groups is approximately twice as great. A study of delinquent girls in Chicago by Miss Hodgkiss showed that 66.8% of the delinquent girls were from broken homes.[15]

While conclusive evidence is lacking, some investigators are of the opinion that homes broken by divorce or separation of parents have a more harmful effect on children than homes disrupted because of the death of a parent.

There can be little doubt that a normal family life with both parents is invaluable for the development of good character. Of greater importance appears to be the type of parents in the home. Children whose parents are shiftless, immoral, feebleminded or drunkards, are exposed to vicious influences which severely handicap them.

It is apparent that a home broken during the child's developmental years would be expected to have a greater effect than a home broken in later life.

---

[13]Slawson, J. D., *The Delinquent Boy*, 1926, p. 8.
[14]Shideler, E. H., *Family Disintegration and the Delinquent Boy in the United States*, Journal Crim. Law and Criminology 9; 715, January, 1918.
[15]Hodgkiss, M., *The Influences of Broken Homes and Working Mothers*, Smith College, Stud. in Social Work 3:259-274, January, 1918.

In this department for the ten years it was found that 12,245, or 47.35% of the defendants investigated were the products of broken homes when they were sixteen years of age or under.

From 1927 to 1931, for the first five-year period covered in this survey, "broken homes" were included in the classification "bad home conditions." For the last five-year period, however, broken homes were separately classified. Combining bad home conditions and broken homes where the effect of home disruption was considered a significant causal factor, these captions appeared 11,372 times, or 43.98% of the total.

Personal Deficiencies

Under this caption is included certain personal weaknesses and defective attitudes which were developed in the individual usually because of the interplay of other damaging factors.

A weak will, for example, which rendered an individual readily susceptible or easily influenced by situations or associates toward criminal behavior was found in 7,174 cases or 27.74% of the total.

Irresponsibility and carelessness appeared as significant factors in 4,654 cases, or 17.80% of the total.

Laziness and a general attitude of shiftlessness was present in 2,795 cases studied, which represented 10.8% of the whole.

Attitudes developed by a feeling of inferiority which operated sufficiently to be considered an important factor, appeared 1,064 times, or 7.98% of the whole number.

There were 2,878, or 11.13% whose lack of wholesome interests contributed to criminal conduct, while those with an anti-social attitude numbered 2,330, or 9.01% of the total number investigated.

An excessive love of pleasure and luxury was found to have been important in 3,334 cases, or 12.89% of the whole. Love of adventure, greed, excessive ambition and gambling combined were found to have operated significantly in 11.92% of the cases studied.

Fraternity

Studies conducted into the families of delinquents with the view of ascertaining the relationship of the size of the family to the development of anti-social attitudes are as a rule of little significance because of absence of comparable statistics for the general population. However, this information becomes valuable when considered in conjunction with poor housing, low family income, and limited opportunity. Glueck found that reformatory inmates studied came from families appreciably larger than the average Massachusetts family, and concluded that this fact, when considered with the associated evils of crowding, bad sanitation and poor neighborhood conditions, was of true significance. It was impossible, however, to ascribe precise weight to this factor.[16]

The study conducted by the Probation Department revealed but slight differences in the incidence of criminality in families which had from one to five children. There were 3,313, or 12.81% who were the only child in the family; 3,480 or 13.46% came from families where there were two children; 3,774, or 14.59% from families with three children. Defendants from families with four children totalled 3,750, or 14.50%; while 3,152 or 12.19% of the total were from families of five children.

There was, however, a sharp increase in the number of defendants who came from families of six or more children. There were 8,191 so classified, which represented 31.68% of the total investigations.

Marital Status

By far the greater majority of the defendants arraigned in this Court were unmarried. The unmarried male offenders totalled 15,437, or 62% of the total males investigated, while the unmarried female offenders numbered 304, or 31.69% of the total women investigated. A combination of this caption shows that 15,741 or 60.87% of the total male and female investigations were not married.

Men who had been married at the time of their investigation numbered 6,308, or 25.33% of the total males investigated, while 329 or

---

[16]Glueck, S. and E. T., *500 Criminal Careers*, 1933, p. 120.

34.31% of the women were so classified, for a combined total of 6,637 or 25.67% of the total investigations.

2,143 men (8.61%) and 200 women (20.86%) were separated at the time they came to the attention of this Department, for a total of 2,343, or 9.06% for this classification.

There were 505 (2.03%) widowers, and 77 (8.03%) widows, while 258 (1.04%) men and 32 (3.34%) women for a total of 290 (1.12%) had been divorced.

234 men (.94%) of the men, and 17 women (1.77%) for a combined total of 251 or (.97%) of the total were living in common-law relationships.

Religion of Offenders

The offenders investigated were mainly in the three numerically predominant religious denominations. There were 13,103 Catholics, who represented 50.67% of the total; 8,911 were of the Protestant groups, representing 34.46% of the total, while the defendants of the Jewish faith numbered 3,261, or 12.61% of the total investigated. The defendants of these three major religious denominations represented 97.74% of the grand total.

The remaining 2.26% were scattered through numerous religious faiths, which included Greek Catholic, Greek Orthodox, Christian Science, Mohammedan, Confucian, Buddhist, Shintoist, Seventh Day Adventist, Mormon, Spiritualist, and Freethinkers. There were 39 Atheists, representing .15% of the total, while 16 could not be ascertained.

First Offenders

The number and percentage of first offenders investigated by this Department shows a wide variation over the ten-year period. The greatest number of first offenders were investigated in 1930, when 1,233 or 42.20% of the total number passed through the Probation Department. In 1931 the first offenders totalled 1,142, or 39.22% of the total investigated, while in 1927, although the number investigated was 1,044, the percentage of 43.65% was the highest for the ten-year period. The average percentage of first offenders investigated by the Probation Department over this period was 35.59%.

The caption "first offender" is meant to apply to those defendants whose records revealed that they had never previously come to the attention of any court, police or correctional agency. Frequently investigation brought to light the fact that first offenders had perpetrated previous crimes for which they had not been apprehended, but this group was small. It is mainly from the group of first offenders that material for probationary treatment was obtained.

Previous Juvenile Court Records

The following statistics relating to previous Court arraignments apply only to the five-year period from 1932 to 1936.

Of the defendants investigated, 2,611, or 19.81% had been previously arraigned in Juvenile Courts, and 2,310 or 17.59% had been convicted of delinquency in those courts.

Those who had been committed to Juvenile Institutions prior to their arraignment in this Court numbered 1,661, or 12.65% of the total, while 1,397 or 10.64% had been at one time on probation to Juvenile Courts. Of those who had been on probation to Juvenile Courts and who were subsequently brought to General Sessions Court, 298 or 21.33% had violated their probation as juveniles, and 189, or 13.53% had been committed for such violation of probation.

There were 1,020 or 7.77% who had been on parole to institutions for juveniles, and 354 or 34.71% of such parolees had violated the conditions of their parole, as a consequence of which 292, or 28.63% had been committed for such violation.

Previous Adult Court Records

The defendants investigated during the five-year period ending 1936 who had appeared in Courts as adults previous to their arraignment in General Sessions numbered 8,403, or 64.02% of the total, while 6,944, or 52.52% had prior convictions in courts of adult jurisdiction.

5,088 or 38.76% of these investigated had been convicted in lower courts, while 3,915 or 29.83% had been convicted in higher courts for more serious crimes. Individuals who had been convicted of crimes in courts of Federal jurisdiction, including court martials, totalled 442, or 3.37% of the total.

There were 2,277 or 17.35% who had been convicted in both lower and higher courts, while those defendants who had been convicted in both juvenile and courts of adult jurisdiction numbered 1,480, or 11.28% of the total.

2,912 or 22.18% of the total investigated had appeared in the Court of General Sessions previously, while 2,464, or 18.77% of the total had been convicted previously in this Court. 1,954, or 14.89% had previously come to the attention of the Probation Department.

Previous Adult Institutional Records

During the five-year period ending 1936, 5,444 or 41.47% of the total defendants investigated were found to have been committed previously to institutions of adult jurisdiction on one or more occasions. 1,132, or 8.62% of the total had been inmates of State Prisons, while those who had spent time in various institutions for mental ills and for the insane totalled 132, or 32% of the total investigated.

There were 971 or 7.40% who had served terms in both juvenile institutions and in institutions for adults.

Previous Adult Probation Records

For the five-year period ending in 1936, the number of defendants investigated by this Department who had been at one time on probation totalled 1,707, or 13% of the total. 815, or 6.21% had had previous contact with probation in lower courts, while 929, or 7.08% of the total had been on probation to higher courts prior to their arraignment in General Sessions.

Defendants who had been on probation both to juvenile courts and to courts of adult jurisdiction numbered 258, or 1.97% of the total, while 532, or 4.05% of the total had formerly been on probation to the Probation Department in the Court of General Sessions.

Those who had violated the terms of probation, including the situations where the present offense constituted the violation, totalled 708, or 5.39% of the total investigated.

Previous Adult Parole Records

Among the defendants investigated during the latter five-year period, 2,896, or 22.07% were found to have been on parole at one time or another, prior to their arraignment in General Sessions. 1,993, or 15.18% of the total were classified as parole violators, including those instances wherein the present offense had resulted in placing them in this category.

* * *

The objective factors presented here, outline some of the predisposing causes of crime, but criminal activity must be regarded as the reaction of an individual to a specific situation. Each situation is the sum total of innumerable complex factors, some of which are apparent, and some of which may be so subtle as to defy isolation, without a long and continuous period of study. Isolation of objective factors is important only insofar as they illuminate the inter-actions of the personality and social situation of the individual offender, and provide us with source material to aid in understanding crime causation and developing constructive plans for crime prevention.

Within the limitations of these pages, however, it is impossible to tabulate those intangibles which enter into the moulding of personality. In each case investigated by this Division, we have endeavored to make such an evaluation in the Pre-Sentence Report. This presents to the Court, in addition to the objective factors in the offender's history, an analysis of the offender's behavior patterns in the light of the inter-related influences which have played upon him.

For the decade covered by this study, 25,858 reports of this type are contained in our files. It is our hope that this Department will be provided with research facilities, so that we will be able to utilize this large and valuable amount of source material, to further clarify the personality and social maladjustments which produce criminality.

Chapter V

DIVISION OF SUPERVISION

The individual who has committed a criminal act and who is arraigned in a criminal court to answer for it, has indicated in a very definite way that for any number of reasons, he has failed to make a proper social adjustment. The mechanics of placing him on probation do not bring about any magical changes in his personality, his behavior patterns or his sense of social responsibility. His arrest, incarceration, and his reaction to the formalisms of the law, may create in him a sense of temporary fear, but such an element, unless transmuted into a conscious and ungrudging respect for authority, is a very poor influence through which any permanent change of character can be effected. We have learned that changes in personality and in social attitudes must be predicated upon more constructive and lasting influences.

The criminal offender has been conditioned from the beginning of his formative years by a variety of favorable and adverse influences. His behavior patterns have in many instances become fixed. His weakened sense of social responsibility, or the lack of it, is the result of pressures and influences exerted upon him by weak parental controls, the conditions of the home, the environment in which he has lived, his economic inefficiency, his associates, and a great number of other influences which have converged to affect his growth as an individual.

It is conceded that all who commit criminal acts are not inherently vicious. It is recognized that criminal behavior is symptomatic. Probation has been developed as a branch of our jurisprudence because it is recognized that in each offender, as in every human being, there are potentialities for evil and for good. A constructive administration of probation envisages a period of social treatment designed to develop the best potentialities of the probationer. It is predicated upon an individualized study which will sharply bring into relief the conditioning influences responsible for his anti-social behavior and it requires the development of practical plans which will change him from a social liability into a social asset.

The probation system, when properly administered, performs a dual function. It rehabilitates the individual and by reclaiming him from the criminal class in which he has placed himself by his criminal act, protects society.

The Division of Supervision of this Department assumes this responsibility through two approaches. The first is legalistic and entails strict oversight of the probationer's activities insofar as they relate to the community's safety through his avoidance of further delinquent behavior. This involves reporting, checking home conditions, verification of employment, investigations into habits and associates, and returning to the Court those who by their conduct and refusal to participate in plans for their rehabilitation, indicate that they are potentially criminalistic.

The second approach is through the application of social case work principles and techniques for the adjustment of the individual within himself, his relation to those groups which are primary, and to society as a whole. This approach is evolved through individualized treatment processes aimed at adjustment and rehabilitation. The objective which is the underlying principle in all treatment plans developed in this Division, is the development of resources within the individual which will stand him in good stead in time of stress and temptation, and which will help him to effect a permanent rehabilitation.

Mere custodial care during the period of probation has no place in our philosophy of treatment. Our program of supervision involves two patterns which interlock. The first deals with the probationer as an individual and involves the growth within him of a sense of social consciousness which will provide him with the realization that he can live in an orderly, law-abiding manner, and in this way derive a maximum amount of satisfaction and security. It involves assisting him to adopt desirable ideals, transferring his objectives and loyalties, and insofar as the human equation permits, the development of desirable characteristics and attitudes. The second phase is control and guidance, which involves the utilization of the social pressures and community resources to meet the probationer's needs, thus developing in him a perception of them, and the ability to satisfy them through personal effort.

74

In the development of administrative checks and controls in this Division, and in the utilization of the treatment programs, we have adopted from the field of social work those principles and techniques which have stood the test of time and which are of practical value.

Generically, social case work deals with effecting an adjustment between the individual and his social environment. The social case work movement during the past fifty years has been marked by change, flux and shifting emphasis. In its development one may discern separate phases which however are so merged that there is apparent continuity and progress.[1]

The first phase was corrective and was the direct result of the recognition of the existence of social problems such as poverty, dependency, old age and disease. Emerging out of this area was the field of human problems upon which definite treatment measures could be directed. This stage concerned itself with the recognition and attempted treatment of individuals and groups such as widows, parentless or neglected children, under-privileged families, etc.

From these two approaches there evolved the third stage described by Social Diagnosis[2] which analyzed the problem and provided the concept of the individual as a social problem. However, during this phase, treatment was still aimed toward a rearrangement of the environment so as to remove the detrimental aspects of it and to create a pattern which would fit the plan made by the worker. The logical outcome of this approach was not only a thorough study of environmental factors, but also a desire to know more intimately, the individual who presented the problem.

Thus we see the gradual shift in emphasis from an approach wherein causes of maladjustment were located in the environment to one wherein the problem becomes more subjective and the causes are sought in the individual and the meaning that his experiences have for him.

In this way, case work slowly progressed from an environmental to a psychological level. The transition was slow and fraught with major difficulties. When case workers first dealt with the psychological area

[1] Robinson, Virginia P., *Changing Psychology in Social Case Work.*
[2] Richmond, Mary E., *Social Diagnosis; What is Social Case Work.*

there was a tendency to avoid treatment per se and to place emphasis upon the individual's past history so that a social plan could be evolved. However, with increased knowledge, social workers were gradually able to undertake the responsibility for that type of treatment which is inherent in the relationship which exists between the worker and the individual who presents a problem. This approach though utilizing the techniques of its predecessors recognizes that "rehabilitation" cannot be foisted upon a person. In essence, through relationship, we now attempt to change the individual so that he can live a satisfying and productive life in his immediate surroundings. The problem case cannot become adjusted unless he himself reaches the conviction that it is imperative for his personal satisfaction and welfare that he live a mode of life which meets with social approval.

This evolution in trends of treatment processes has resulted in the recognition of the utilization of the general case work field to supplement the individualized or specialized type of case work. The difference between case work as practiced by this Department and as practiced by any social work agency is administrative.

Inherent in such administration is the proper and intelligent use of the authoritarian factors which are present in the initially forced relationship between the probationer and probation officer and the legalistic and authoritative background of probationary supervision. Experience in this Department has revealed that this authoritarian setting need not hinder but can be developed into an asset in carrying into effect constructive treatment programs.

The probation officers of this Department have endeavored to influence the thinking and emotions of the individual probationer so as to cause him to improve his situation and insofar as possible, to modify and change his viewpoint in relation to the average norms of conduct and individual responsibility.

Thus, in treatment, we have laid stress upon the analysis and proper evaluation of certain psychological factors which are believed to determine personality formation. These include constitutional or hereditary factors, acquired reactive tendencies, family influences, influences of the social environment, and the general ideological trends which are evident in the cultural patterns of any given individual.

76

After a sound and practical diagnosis has been made, the probation officer utilizes certain definite mechanics of therapy. These are based upon the psychological mechanisms of motivation, transference, identification, mental catharsis, conditioning, and mutual planning.

Although the probation officers in this Division mobilize and make available community resources, every effort is made to make the probationer cognizant of his personal responsibilities, which he may be consciously or unconsciously trying to evade. The probation officer's primary function is to interpret the probationer's needs to him and to the community, to stimulate him to use the available resources, and to develop in him receptiveness to plans aimed at further economic and social growth, through direct and indirect guidance. This, of course, involves recognition of the probationer's limitations and the extent to which his capacities for growth can best be developed. The action and interaction of the personalities of the probationer and the probation officer constitute the dynamics of treatment.

In treating the probationer and his problems, the Division of Supervision lays stress upon

1. The individual.
2. His situation.
3. The relation between the probation officer and the probationer.
4. Recognition by the probation officer of the skills which are to be used.
5. Recognition by the probation officer of the probationer's needs, both psychological and material.
6. Adaptation of resources available to assist the individual in his adjustment.

Treatment is carried on through interviews with the probationer, his family, and others whose influences affect him; and through home visits and contacts with case work and other assisting agencies. Emphasis is placed upon a formulated plan of adjustment which utilizes the basic approaches of discipline, the family, mental and physical health, recreation, education, employment, thrift, and spiritual development.

Probationary supervision, like case work treatment, is planned guidance which, to be effective, must be administered by probation officers who are mentally, emotionally and professionally equipped to formulate and carry through constructive programs. The probation officers assigned to this Division are selected because of special aptitudes and training, but the executives of the Department have recognized that practice does not necessarily bring with it increased proficiency.

In order that the probation officers may recognize and understand emotional and intellectual drives, and develop disciplined thinking, systematic analysis and objective appraisals of attitudes and reactions, there has been developed a departmental in-service training program. This involves individual conferences each week with the case supervisor, which entails discussions of specific cases presenting unique problems, analyses of case records and application of departmental procedures; weekly staff conferences; lectures at the office by specialists in allied fields (Institutes in Probation); suggested and prescribed readings; circulation of available literature, such as books, magazines, pamphlets and bulletins; encouraging the staff to take additional courses at universities and schools of social work; urging members of the staff to attend lectures given under professional auspices; allowing the staff time to attend and participate in state, regional and national conferences in probation, social work and allied fields; integrating staff activities with community social welfare programs; semi-annual ratings of each staff member based upon capacity, performance and professional growth; and transfers from one Division to the other.

THE CHANNELS OF TREATMENT:

Discipline

We recognize that in an authoritarian agency such as this, it is our primary duty to subject probationers to the normal regimentations which make for orderly life. Our approach through this channel has as its objective the development of a program of discipline which will inculcate habits of industry, restraint, consideration for the rights of others and the development of an attitude of obedience to and acceptance of normal codes of conduct. These objectives we have learned, however, cannot be attained through any mechanized approach to the problem of those on probation or by any routinized methods of dealing with them. To properly understand and meet the needs of the probationer, it is necessary that the probation officer study him as an individual, learn to what influences he reacts, know how to meet his needs, and substitute understanding for force and scientific knowledge for aimless meddling.

The Family

Through the family we trace the roots of the individual. His family usually represents his place in the social scale and the influences which are thrown about him in his family life are as far reaching as any other contacts which he makes. His social codes find their basis in this fabric and to a large extent he gives expression in his daily life to the influences which play upon him in these relationships. The attitudes of parents, friction and discord, lack of sympathy and understanding, neglect and antagonism, both subtle and apparent, all have their places in the making of the offender.

Family disorganization, congestion, economic incompetency, poverty, lax behavior or a broken home, are problems to which every probation officer must actively apply himself if he is to have any hope of changing the mental attitudes which result in behavior patterns conflicting with the law.

Each probationer is a part of a unit, and that unit is the family. To meet the needs of the family, to bring about an adjustment of its problems, is to bring about the solution of some of the probationer's problems. To build up the family economically and socially means the rendering of a similar service to the probationer, for with this building-up process which must be educational and practical, the entire family is aided to develop a higher sense of group responsibility. To bring this about, the Probation Department utilizes all the social resources of the City of New York and has enlisted the cooperation of social workers trained in family case work.

Mental and Physical Diagnosis

The diagnosis and proper evaluation of the subjective factors to which can be traced the behavior patterns of offenders require extended and searching inquiry and the psychiatric approach to this problem, therefore, has been welcomed by this Department. In order to have understanding, in order to develop plans of treatment which will be practical and which will have as their goals constructive results, every person on probation should be examined either in a clinic or by an independent psychiatrist. The process of mental and behavioristic growth are confusing to those without specialized training. Since behavioristic processes are clouded and cannot be positively determined as consecutive steps even by the psychiatrist, the probation officer must utilize the scientific aid which the psychiatrist brings, to determine the factors which motivated these processes.

We have recognized the advantage of such a diagnosis in each case, furnishing as it does a scientific basis for the plan of treatment which must follow, and each probationer has been subjected to a mental examination.

Physical examinations have also been conducted for the determination of physical capacities and the knowledge of physical limitations and ills. To attempt to bring about adjustments without such knowledge is to make futile gestures. In physical conditions may lie, to some extent, the answer to behavior patterns. From a sense of inferiority induced by physical handicaps and disease, may lie the germ of an offender's gangster growth.

The psychiatric and medical fields are greatly interested in the problem of abnormal behavior and are constantly probing and analyzing to determine from what soil abnormal conduct springs. In our early years we successfully interested the clinics, hospitals, and the physicians of this city in our problems of personality diagnosis and obtained from them invaluable scientific aid. To aid us to understand the emotional patterns, personality drives and mental conditions of criminal offenders and probationers, we brought about the establishment of the Psychiatric Clinic of the Court of General Sessions.

Recreation

The quest for new experiences and for adventure to offset the humdrum and often depressing influences of home environment, appears as one of the impelling influences which drive boys and young men to associate with disorderly companions in groups or gangs. Their desire for association with those who are congenial and whose codes of conduct are more or less similar to their own, also impels them to participate in the recreation which they find desirable and urges them toward the commercialized form of amusement, such as the "shady" poolroom, dance hall and undesirable type of candy and cigar store which are so often the congregating points for groups from which delinquents are recruited.

Centers of commercialized amusement, where low standards of conduct are tolerated, have in a large measure influenced and weakened the offender before he becomes a ward of the probation officer. To wean the probationer from these influences is no small task and it cannot be accomplished overnight. A program of spare time activities which has value in building character and which serves to enlarge the social consciousness of the probationer must be substituted but it cannot be an acceptable program unless it is an effective and interesting substitute for the glamour and lure of the unwholesome recreational activities from which the probationer must be diverted.

It has been the objective of the Probation Department to drive home to the community through constant repetition, the thought that as the youth of the community is conserved through supervised and properly directed leisure, so will this city profit by removing the influences which serve to develop delinquency.

Education

It is well known that education materially affects the personality of an individual, broadens his outlook and gives him understanding. The education of those with whom the probation officer deals is at best fragmentary, and in many instances the probationer has not even completed the grammar school grades. To deal adequately with his needs, it is necessary to point out and stimulate his interest in a world outside of his limited vision. To establish him as a productive social unit requires training and at times re-education.

It has been shown that those who are placed on probation are not so much anti-social as they are non-social, and this attitude has been due to their lack of appreciation of their obligation to their fellows. The awakening of this obligation and sense of responsibility is an educational process for which many approaches are available.

In conformance with this idea, this Department has enlisted the cooperation of the Public Library of New York City and through the splendid interest manifested by Miss Jennie M. Flexner, Reader's Adviser of the Public Library System, selected courses of reading suited to the mentality and interests of the probationers have been developed.

Those desirous of engaging in specialized reading have been referred to Miss Flexner, who, after an interview and evaluation of the probationer's mental equipment, has prepared outlines of reading which are especially suited to the probationer's interests and needs. Other probationers have been referred to the branch libraries of the city with a card of introduction from Fiss Flexner to the librarian in charge. We have found that this educational process has brought about a broader vision which has been productive of good results.

Through our membership in the New York Adult Education Council, we are kept informed of the educational opportunities available for probationers. The probation officers, in accordance with the standards established by this Department, have applied themselves to the stimulation of interest in furthering the education of the probationers in their charge. Some have been induced to participate in specialized educational projects and others to enroll in the evening classes of the public school system.

Employment

We have found that many of those entrusted to the care of the probation officers are mechanically apt and require only the guidance and stimulation of interest to accept the training which will fit them for the economic struggle.

Vocational testing, vocational guidance and placement and economic maladjustment represent fundamental needs on the part of the probationer that must not be overlooked. During the period of depression which now exists and when the probation system has the grave problem of unemployment to cope with, this Department has exerted every effort to place in trade schools those who can profit by special training in order not only to aid probationers toward economic adjustment, but also to prevent them from loitering about the streets in idleness.

Studies were conducted of the vocational aptitudes of probationers through the cooperation of Dr. Joseph V. Hanna, Vocational Director of the Young Men's Christian Association, and the analyses made by Dr. Hanna aided us materially in developing programs for the vocational adjustment and placement of these probationers.

As another aid in the field of vocational adjustment, we established a cooperative relationship with the Junior Consultation Service which during 1934 and 1935 was conducted by the Junior Division of the New York State Employment Service and the Vocational Service for Juniors. Trained vocational counsellors interviewed the probationers referred to the bureau and discussed with them their school backgrounds and work histories in relation to possible training or employment. They were tested so that special aptitudes and skill could be discovered and efforts were made to place them in schools or industry.

We intend that every probationer shall be studied in order that programs for economic stability through educational processes, trade training and vocational placement can be developed. This plan, however, could not be carried through because the fiscal authorities failed to appropriate the money for the position of vocational director. It is hoped that this position, so essential to constructive probation service, will be established when the depression has passed.

Thrift

Crimes of acquisitiveness are an invasion of the property rights of the community and, in the majority of instances, those who commit this type of crime have no consideration for the property rights of others because th y possess so little of material value themselves. To teach them to conserve their earnings so that their sense of security can be developed, is to give them a feeling of confidence and responsibility, and the knowledge that possessions honestly acquired with difficulty are entitled to those safeguards which the state through its laws throws about every person.

However, before they can be taught to conserve their earnings, those on probation must be taught to make a wise distribution of them. The family budget is nothing new. It has been utilized with good effect by every social agency dealing with family problems. A proper disbursement of income has far reaching effects upon the stability of family life and upon the mental attitude of those who constitute the family. The unwise dissipation of income and the mortgaging of future earnings mean that the period of stress will eventually appear, making doubly burdensome the problem of the probation administrator.

The development of security means the building of resources and this Department insists that such resources be created in each case through savings accounts and life insurance. We have aided the development of habits of industry and habits of saving—two factors which exert a wholesome influence which is far-reaching.

Spiritual Development

Our surveys reveal that the age of offenders has been slowly descending through the years, and that in recent years the graver crimes have been perpetrated by youthful offenders. The majority of these offenders have drifted away from the influence of the church for a variety of reasons. To bring them back to this constructive influence has been the every day problem of the probation officers. To enlist the aid of the church is to bring to the probationer a more far reaching influence than casual church attendance. In addition to religious influences, probationers derive benefit from participation in the recreational activities which the churches today are providing, and through contact with fine people willing to aid in making effective the program developed by the probation officer.[3]

A haphazard mechanized utilization of these channels can achieve no constructive results. These basic approaches are individualized to the needs and capacities of each probationer, since no matter how broad the analysis made, nor how skillfully the channels are used, they can have little value unless the probationer's cooperation is secured and there is instilled in him a willingness to accept plans made for his adjustment.

[3]The detailed application of these channels is presented in the Supervision Methodology.

84

Shortly after the probationer is received by this Division, a plan of treatment must be evolved by the probation officer to whom he is assigned. This will present the etiological factors responsible for the behavior patterns of the probationer and an evaluation of his potentialities in terms of social liabilities and assets. The plan must present the practical and workable means which are to be employed to influence the probationer to a higher level of responsibility and social consciousness. The plan must be submitted to the Case Supervisor for approval and from time to time as the retrogression or progress of the probationer is noted, the plan must be changed to meet the changed conditions.

When the Department was established on January 1, 1927, the social agencies which had previously supervised probationers in the Court of General Sessions, transferred to the new Department 677 cases. In the ten years covered by this study, 5,394 males and 334 females were placed on probation to this Department, making a total of 6,605 cases supervised. Of this number, 70 males and 4 females were received on transfer from other Courts.

The yearly percentage of those placed on probation in relation to the total number investigated by the Department, has fluctuated between a high of 26.66% and a low of 19%.

Those who were placed on probation for the first time, represented 91.38% of the total received on probation. 11.81% were on probation for less than a year; 23.52% remained on probation for two years; 48.53% were on probation for 3 years; 14.72% were on probation for 5 years or longer.

Those between the ages of 16 and 20 years totalled 32.18%. Those between the ages of 21 to 25 totalled 21.47%, and those between the ages of 26 to 30 totalled 14.06%. There was a steady decline in the percentage of the older persons placed on probation, those between the age limits of 31 and 35 numbering 9.82% and those between the ages of 46 to 50 numbering 2.75%.

The Division of Supervision, among its other duties, is responsible for the collection of restitution, reparation and family support. In the period covered by this study, the probationers through this Department paid the following amounts:

Restitution $594,811.11
Family Support 100,602.00

Total $695,413.11

These monies were paid from the earnings of the probationers, and in many instances they entailed not only privation for them but hardship for their families.

The depression created problems in the lives of the probationers and their families which had to be met with counter-balances in order to prevent new delinquencies as a means of obtaining funds for immediate needs. Through the efforts of this Division and the cooperative aid of social agencies and employment bureaus, there has been a steady effort to keep probationers employed and in many instances to aid in securing employment for members of the families of probationers. Since the depression began, regular employment has hovered in the vicinity of 50% with an additional 25% of part time employment. In 1936, 49.36% were employed regularly and the total percentage of those employed, which included part time work, was 78.39%.

In 1934, the statistics of this Department were enlarged to include a yearly total of the earnings of probationers. For the three years that these statistics have been compiled, the earnings amounted to $2,107,564.35.

Year	Employment Full Time	Employment Part Time	Employment Relief Projects	Total
1934	$559,007.11	$73,033.07	$65,812.00	$697,852.18
1935	514,883.07	59,821.43	97,391.45	672,095.95
1936	543,352.79	51,597.31	142,666.12	737,616.22
Totals	$1,617,242.97	$184,451.81	$305,869.57	$2,107,564.35

These earnings in abnormal times such as these, should give pause to those who question the value of probation as a form of correctional treatment.

In order to teach probationers the value of security which comes from savings, we have insisted that wherever possible, each probationer shall lay aside some of his earnings for this purpose or for the payment of protective insurance premiums. These savings of probationers from 1934 to 1936, when we began to keep yearly records for this purpose, amounted to $102,639.61.

Year	Savings	Insurance Premiums Paid In	Total
1934	$13,567.00	$11,707.20	$25,274.20
1935	25,780.88	12,397.83	38,178.71
1936	28,287.32	10,899.38	39,186.70
Total	$67,635.20	$35,004.41	$102,639.61

Success and Failure

Our studies reveal that the average probationer placed in the custody of this Department by the Court for control and social treatment, is a young man whose background is poor and who is a member of a family which lives either on a marginal income, or one in which poverty is a prominent factor. His social vision in general is limited to the codes of conduct which govern the attitudes of his associates and which prevail in the immediate neighborhood in which he lives. His education is scanty. His equipment for a place in the economic struggle leaves much to be desired. He seldom has developed in himself resources which make for that element which we call character and he rarely, if ever, has any objective which makes for the immediate development of a socialized viewpoint. His leisure is spent on the streets, in poolrooms, and in cheap dance halls. He is not easily diverted from the deteriorating influences which play upon him in these environments.

In measuring the extent to which probation has succeeded or has failed in reconstructing the lives of probationers, we have applied the same exacting standards which we use in judging our techniques and procedures. In each case, the probationer, whether discharged as improved or as a failure, is the subject of a detailed report to the Court in which the methods employed to divert him from further criminal activities are portrayed and his reactions are presented. This makes for a more detailed analysis and evaluation than the usual methods of discharging probationers as "improved" or "unimproved," but as yet no studies have been published in the field of probation which would serve to bring about the establishment of flexible criteria for a more exacting evaluation of success or failure.

In our evaluation of successes, we have given due consideration to the potentialities of probationers after discharge, in relation to the irremedial limitations which confronted us during the probation period. We have in these cases discharged probationers as successful, but with a "guarded prognosis." This classification is used because consideration must be given to the many deteriorating factors we have been unable to neutralize, which have developed in the lives of these offenders, both before they committed criminal offenses and after they became subjects for probation treatment. Under these classifications have been placed those persons discharged from probation at the close of the maximum period, whose futures are problematical because they are of borderline intelligence, emotionally unstable, economic misfits or inefficients, or are the subjects of devitalizing influences in the family and environmental spheres which could not be changed during the period of probation treatment and which present little prospect of change in the future.

These probationers, however, were the subjects of individualized study and treatment and were in contact with the personality of probation officers equipped to understand their needs and meet them insofar as conditions and the personality difficulties of these individuals permitted programs of treatment to be evolved and utilized. We do not claim a full measure of success for this group, but we feel that their vision has been enlarged, constructive influences have affected them and they have learned a measure of self-discipline. Were we concerned only with the care of this group during the probation period, we could claim complete success, since they remained law-abiding and did not become involved in any form of anti-social activity during the probation period. However, because of their limitations, they are classified as "prognosis guarded." This group has approximated about 8% of our successes.

There has been a steady upward growth in the ratio of probationers successfully treated during the years embraced by this study. For the years 1927 to 1931 the failures amounted to 18.06%. In 1932, the failures, because of the intensified efforts of the Division of Supervision, had dropped to 10.55%. In 1933, the failures were at their lowest, 8.98%. In 1936 the failures amounted to 9.94%.

Violation of the terms of probation can be traced to many causes, the primary cause being the refusal of the probationer to accept the plans developed for his adjustment. His resentment and rebelliousness may find expression in the commission of new crimes, or he may give concrete expression to his refusal to conform, by continuing his old mode of life, in overt defiance of the efforts made to divert him to better standards of living. In cases of this type, every effort of the probation officer which is intended to improve the condition of the probationer, is repelled, because he has found greater satisfaction in his old codes of conduct and mode of life. This conflict may exist over a long period, but in the majority of instances a period of six months sees its culmination, and the probationer, in an effort to rid himself of a situation which he cannot control, seeks escape by absconding.

Probationers disappear for other reasons. Their immature attitudes and the same inability to cope with their immediate problems which led them into criminal enterprises, prompts them to run away from responsibility. In other instances, family bickerings, which they cannot adjust or overcome, are responsible. The inability to bring about an economic adjustment as quickly as they desire, sometimes prompts others to escape from reality by absconding. This type of probationer, when again taken into custody, is generally found after investigation to have refrained from further criminal activity, and is restored to probation. The time that he remained hidden from oversight is added to his probation period. The violators whose attitudes and behavior patterns indicate that they may again become involved in crime are committed to reformatories and prisons.

The probation system, if it is to continue to be a constructive force in controlling and rehabilitating those entrusted to its care and if it is to develop Society's approval of its use as a correctional device, must speedily apprehend and return to the Court those who violate the mandates of the Court. With this policy in mind, those who have violated probation, are carried as active cases until we can return them to custody. The fingerprints of these violators are cleared at regular intervals both in this city and with the Department of Justice at Washington and through these media and others which we employ, we have been able to return to the Court from all parts of the United States, sometimes through bitterly fought extradition proceedings, violators of probation who had disappeared from oversight for a large number of years. Only 247 (13.09%) of the warrants issued in the last ten years have not as yet been executed.

During the years embraced by this study, 1,887 Bench Warrants were issued. From 1927 to 1931, 38.82% of these Warrants were issued because probationers were arrested for new offenses. In 1936 this percentage had declined to 24.75%. The remaining Bench Warrants were issued at our request because of a lack of responsiveness on the part of the probationers involved, or because we felt that to permit them longer at liberty was a responsibility which we could no longer assume and properly safeguard the community's interest.

Of the total number of Bench Warrants issued, 846 (44.83%) were committed to institutions; 519 (27.50%) were continued on probation after a thorough investigation into the motivating causes responsible for the violation and 204 (10.81%) were closed through commitment on new charges, etc. The remainder either died, were deported, or were in penal or insane institutions. 247 (13.09%) are as yet unapprehended.

The maximum number of Violations of probation occurred in the first six months of the probation period. Of the number who violated, 264 (13.99%) committed their violations during the first three months; 321 (17.01%) violated the terms of probation within the three to six month period. The next largest number of violators occurred within the period embracing a year to a year and a half after they had been placed on probation. During this time 310 (16.34%) became violators. As the probation period advances, there is a sharp decrease in the percentage of violators running from 11.61% in the period of one and a half to two years to 3.49% for the period embraced by three to five years.

The foregoing pages, within the necessary limitations of space, have endeavored to present the function and mode of procedure of the Division of Supervision. It is relatively simple to specify function and objective. However, the problem of portraying methodology and evaluating results in a field of treatment based essentially upon relationship, is difficult. The definite attainments of this Division must be measured

n terms of the community safety and in the improvement of the social
nd economic situation of the individual probationer.

A further effort has been made to depict those intangible results
f supervision manifested in the attitudes of probationers. These re-
lect an increased social consciousness and the ability to lead not only a
roductive but a self-satisfying life in a community with which they
vere formerly in conflict.

We believe that the efforts of this Division have done much to
ring to the public a consciousness of the social benefits which can be
lerived from an intelligent and understanding approach to the treatment of the criminal. It is hoped that this will find expression in a
more generous general support and extension of the system of proba-
ion, in accordance with the standards which have been fostered by the
Judges of the Court of General Sessions.

Chapter VI

THE PSYCHIATRIC CLINIC

The establishment of psychiatric clinics in courts is a comparatively recent concept. In the main, the emphasis to establish such clinics originally was placed on the need for such services in juvenile courts, in order to afford proper correctional and rehabilitative treatment for the juvenile delinquent.

The use of the service of psychiatrists in courts of criminal jurisdiction first envisaged only the determination of insanity and mental defects, but as knowledge of mental abnormalities and personality drives have increased, the psychiatrist has more and more given aid in determining responsibility, or that degree of conscious or unconscious irresponsibility which should be considered by the Probation Departments and to which the Courts should give consideration in the determination of a proper disposition of the convicted offender.

Dr. Selling points out that "it is the opinion of most psychiatrists, who are familiar with the subject, that most criminal impulses are more likely to have been uncontrolled than uncontrollable . . ."[1]

Criminal conduct is the most direct exemplification of nonconformist behavior. Abnormal behavior is symptomatic. Psychiatric research in its probing for the causes of such behavior inevitably had to concern itself with the problem of crime. Inevitably, too, a sharp conflict was bound to arise between the legalistic concept bolstered by tradition, legal precedent, and a certain rigidity of treatment, and the medical concept concerned mainly with the offender as a mental and physical problem resulting from tangible and intangible pressures and influences.

Unfortunately, and this will not be denied by the psychiatrists themselves, too often in criminal trials the question of mental responsibility has become a pitched battle between psychiatrists who have expressed divergent views predicated upon the same symptoms and conduct, with the result that the public has been confused and encouraged in its sceptical attitudes towards psychiatric opinion in criminal cases.

---

[1]Selling, Lowell S., *Diagnostic Criminology*.

Those concerned with the problem of crime and its treatment have long known that crime in general is a social phenomenon, like the phenomena of disease, poverty and other devitalizing influences, and that in order to understand the symptomatic behavior which is criminalistic, a searching inquiry had to be made into the hidden, complex motivations for such conduct. It was felt that the psychiatrist, if he held no brief for one side or the other, but conducted his inquiry and rendered his findings impartially, could render an aid to the social investigation, which would be of great value in the determination of what disposition should best be made of criminal offenders. Such an approach has resulted in bringing the psychiatrist into the Court, either on a part time or a full time basis, with the result that to-day the psychiatric influence in the determination of the proper treatment of the convicted offender is being noticed more and more.

"A survey made chiefly by Dr. Winfried Oberholser under the joint auspices of the National Committee for Mental Hygiene and the National Crime Commission, revealed that 110 courts in the United States (9.4%) report themselves to be served regularly by a psychiatrist, either employed by the court on a full time or part time basis, or furnished by some other public agency. These courts are distributed through thirty-one states and the District of Columbia. Moreover, of 259 public penal and correctional institutions, 93 (39.9%) employ psychiatrists on either a full time or part time basis. Eighty-five (32.8%) so employ psychologists."[2]

The psychiatrist has given invaluable aid in helping criminologists to formulate public opinion with reference to the need of a departure from old penological methods. Every experienced Judge and probation officer knows that each day offenders appear in the courts whose personality maladjustments cannot be treated in the average prison or reformatory, the influences of which only serve to intensify their emotional instabilities.

Specialized institutions with adequate psychiatric service are an urgent need if offenders are to be diverted from careers of crime and

[2]Menninger, Carl A., *The Human Mind.*

restored to the community upon their release, equipped mentally, physically, and economically to be law-abiding and self-supporting.

General Sessions Clinic

An awareness of these conditions caused the Probation Department upon its establishment in 1927 to enter into a cooperative arrangement with the clinics of the various hospitals of the City of New York to conduct mental and physical examinations of offenders referred to them by the Department. Those who were awaiting sentence and were at liberty on bail were referred to these clinics. The offenders who were held in custody in the City Prison while awaiting sentence were referred to the physician of that institution, who was a qualified psychiatrist. It was soon demonstrated that this method of procuring mental and physical examinations left much to be desired. The large volume of cases precluded any possibility of an examination in each case. Some offenders who were on bail failed to keep the clinic appointments. Limitations of staff, both in the Probation Department and in the clinics prevented the preparation of adequate social histories and psychiatric reports.

The Judges of the Court welcomed and aided the procurement of psychiatric and psychological diagnoses of the personality maladjustments responsible for the criminality of the offender, and the Probation Department in accordance with the recommendations of the American Bar Association and the American Psychiatric Association "that there be available to every criminal and juvenile court a psychiatric service to assist the court in the disposition of offenders,"[3] began to develop plans to bring about the establishment of a clinic as an official branch of the Probation Department of the Court. The Judges and the Chief Probation Officer enlisted the advice and support of a distinguished group of public officials, psychiatrists and social workers who aided in framing legislation for this purpose. Although the act was passed by both houses of the legislature, objections were voiced from various quarters with reference to the expense which such a venture would entail and the Department was unable to attain its objective.

---

[3]Meeting of the American Bar Association, Memphis, 1929.

In the meantime this Department in collaboration with interested public officials and social agencies had aided in amending the law in relation to probation to include the following: "Whenever desirable and facilities exist therefor they (probation officers) shall also obtain a physical, mental and psychiatric examination of such defendant or such child and report thereon in like manner to the Court prior to sentence or adjudication."[4]

In December 1931, the need for a separate clinic having become increasingly urgent, the Judges and Chief Probation Officer, aided by a group of outstanding authorities in the field of law, sociology and psychiatry,[5] brought about the establishment of the Psychiatric Clinic of the Court of General Sessions as a branch of the Psychiatric Division of the Department of Hospitals of the City of New York. The personnel, assigned from the Bellevue Psychiatric Hospital, consists of two senior psychiatrists, one junior psychiatrist, one psychologist, three stenographers, two clerks, and one clerical employee.

Dr. Walter Bromberg is the Senior Psychiatrist in charge of the Clinic. The other members of the professional staff now assigned are Dr. Charles B. Thompson, Dr. Frank Hale, and Solomon Machover, psychologist.

All persons convicted of crimes in the Court of General Sessions are referred by the Probation Department to the Clinic for examination. In each case an outline of the social history and the offense committed by the defendant is furnished to the Clinic. Whenever cases present mental and personality patterns which require extended study by the psychiatrists, sentences are further adjourned for this purpose. Reports

---

[4]Section 931 of the Code of Criminal Procedure.

[5]The group consisted of Judge Cornelius F. Collins, Chairman and Judge Morris Koenig and Judge Charles C. Nott, Jr., of the Probation Plan and Scope Committee of the Court of General Sessions; Edwin J. Cooley, the former Chief Probation Officer; Irving W. Halpern, the present Chief Probation Officer; Mayor James J. Walker; Dr. William Schroeder, Jr., the Commissioner of Hospitals, who was succeeded by Dr. J. G. William Greef; Dr. Menas S. Gregory, then Director of the Psychiatric Division; Dr. Vernon C. Branham, Deputy Commissioner of the Department of Correction; Mr. Edward R. Cass, President of the American Prison Association; The Prison Association of New York; Commissioner W. L. Butcher and Miss Jane M. Hoey of the State Crime Commission, Sub-Committee on Causes; The New York State Committee for Mental Hygiene; Dr. C. Floyd Haviland, Dr. Frankwood E. Williams, Dr. George H. Kirby, Dr. Sylvester R. Leahy, Dr. Mortimer W. Raynor, Dr. Lawson G. Lowrey, Dr. Sanger Brown 2nd, Dr. William L. Russell; the National Probation Association, the American Psychiatric Association and the Academy of Medicine. Further endorsements were made by Senator Hon. Caleb H. Baumes, Chairman of the State Crime Commission, Hon. Newton D. Baker, Chairman of the National Crime Commission, Hon. George H. Wickersham, President of the National Probation Association, and Professor Raymond Moley of the Department of Public Law and Jurisprudence, Columbia University.

in each case are submitted to the Judge before whom the offender appears and to the Probation Department.

Examination of the prisoner includes a study of the mental condition, the intelligence, the personality and the physical condition of the prisoner.

The study of the intelligence is aimed at finding the mental endowments of the individual as measured by comprehension, reasoning power, judgment, discrimination, memory, general information and ability. These functions are measured by the well-known psychological tests (Stanford-Binet, Porteus Maze, Pintner-Patterson Performancy, Healy P. C. II, Army Alpha and Beta, Otis, Stenquist Mechanical Ability test, Gray's Oral Reading, etc.) as given by the staff psychologist. The aim of the psychologist is to give a complete battery of tests, and hence the examination may utilize anywhere from one to fifteen types of tests. Since the psychological examination takes at least an hour, and as there is but one psychologist for three psychiatrists in the Clinic, obviously all cases are not given a psychometric test. All cases in the lower mental levels are referred to the psychologist. About one-fifth of all cases are given psychometric tests.

Those of obviously average intelligence or above are given mental level estimates by the psychiatrists whose examinations include some of the standard psychometric problems. In estimating psychological levels in the Clinic, due consideration is given to educational opportunity, social milieu, practical ability and familiarity and contact with intellectual material. The decisions in questionable cases like those in the Borderline Defective or High Moron Group (I. Q. 65-75) are therefore made not so much on the basis of I. Q. as these other factors. Thus, it is easily seen that individuals may have an I. Q. below 70 and not be defective. For these reasons, every defective or case of questionable mentality is seen in conference by all the psychiatrists and psychologist to rule out emotional, organic or medical factors which may influence a low mental rating.

The mental condition is studied to determine the condition of the defendant's mental functioning and to ascertain whether he exhibits abnormal, emotional, intellectual or behavior traits such as are clearly recognized among psychiatrists as denoting a psychosis. In this instance, an elaborate examination is given according to the more or less standardized technique of psychiatric examination. The official classification of the American Psychiatric Association, used throughout the country in state hospitals, psychopathic institutions and by practising psychiatrists, is employed.

A personality study aims to illuminate the individual regarding his capacities, interests, drives, background, psychosexual and social tendencies and attitudes. The commonly accepted classification of psychopathic personalities, including chronic alcoholism, unstable types with organic mental disease and psychoneuroses, are utilized.

In addition, offenders who are not abnormal, psychopathic or insane, are studied from the standpoint of the balance of their personality factors. The purpose of this study is to assist the Judges and the probation officers in their further handling of the case, in the illumination of any outstanding (although normal) personality traits which may appear. In this section of the examination, psychiatric observations, and knowledge of the family life, parents, activities, cultural background, schooling, social interests are considered.

A physical and neurological examination is made. This includes a thorough physical examination of the offender. The examiner looks for obvious physical defects in the various internal organs; evidence of contagious diseases, venereal disease, structural abnormalities and endocrine (glandular) defects. It also includes special examination of those with disease of the nervous system, such as locomotor ataxia, various types of paralysis, sleeping sickness, etc. When necessary, patients are referred to the Bellevue Psychiatric Hospital for laboratory checkup, x-rays, encephalograms, spinal tests, etc.

The report is arranged to cover the four "panels"—mental state, intelligence, personality and physical or neurological disease. Each of these is dealt with and discussed in detail if important. In all cases where problems of personality abnormality, insanity or any particular neurological condition arise, a conference of all the psychiatrists is held in order to arrive at a more balanced opinion.

Besides the routine examinations, the Clinic and the Probation Department have instituted a follow-up system in which probationers are re-examined, observed and treated. The selected offenders are seen at regular intervals, varying from weekly to yearly. This service was started in 1935, when 23 follow-up cases were seen. It was extended in 1936 to 65 cases. It is hoped that this type of psychiatric aid to probationers will be developed in the follow-up clinic.

A psychotherapeutic clinic, which meets in the evening, was established in 1937 as part of the follow-up system with the purpose of doing intensive psychotherapy with a limited group of probationers.

The material in the Clinic and special studies are utilized for lectures at the Probation Institutes conducted by the Probation Department for the Medical Psychology Club of New York University, and as preparation for papers for recognized medical and psychiatric associations.

Monthly and annual reports, covering the year's activities, with analysis of results, particularly psychological data, are prepared and forwarded to the Director of the Bellevue Psychiatric Hospital, the Commissioner of Hospitals, the Judges of the Court of General Sessions, the Chief Probation Officer, and other interested agencies.

In the first five years (1927-1931) of the Probation Department's existence, 4,332 cases were examined in hospitals, clinics, or by the Tombs physician. This represents 33.99% of the total number of investigations which were conducted by the Department for those years.

A five-year study of the work of the Probation Department[6] published in 1932, revealed that of the number examined, 80 were found to be of superior intelligence. This group represented 1.85% of the total number examined. The mentally defective and retarded represented 381 or 8.80% of the total number examined. Those with psychopathic personalities represented 7.55% of this group. Psychopathic personality was found among those of superior and normal intelligence, in addition to the mental defective.

---

[6]Halpern, Irving W., *Probation and the Criminal Offender.*

MENTAL CONDITIONS
1927-1931
(Inclusive)

EXAMINED

Superior	80	1.85%
Average	2,219	51.22%
Dull	1,072	24.75%
Mental Defectives	381	8.80%
Psychopathic	327	7.55%
Neurotic	240	5.54%
Psychotic	13	.30%
Total	4,332	(33.99% of total investigations)

From 1932 to 1936 inclusive, the Psychiatric Clinic conducted 12,703 examinations. One hundred and seventy-nine were found to be of superior intelligence, representing 1.41% of the total examinations and 4,321 representing 34.01% of the total examined were of average intelligence. Those who were of borderline intelligence represented 5.63%. The defective represented only 2.09% of the entire group and the psychotic (insane) numbered 53 or .42% of the group.

MENTAL STATUS OF OFFENDERS

1932-1936

Year	Total Exam.	Su-per-ior	% of Total Exam.	Aver-age	% of Total Exam.	Dull Nor-mal	% of Total Exam.	Bor-der-line	% of Total Exam.	Mental-ly De-fective	% of Total Exam.	Psy-cho-tic	% of Total Ex-am.
1932	2,216	92	4.15	631	28.47	380	17.15	126	5.69	47	2.12		
1933	2,477	16	.65	145	5.85	157	6.34	134	5.41	59	2.38		
1934	2,982	1	.03	170	5.70	180	6.04	126	4.23	63	2.11		
1935	2,590	36	1.39	1,756	67.80	529	20.42	189	7.30	57	2.2	21	.81
1936	2,438	34	1.39	1,619	66.41	570	23.38	140	5.74	40	1.64	32	1.31
Total	12,703	179	1.41	4,321	34.01	1,816	14.30	715	5.63	266	2.09	53	.42

NOTE: During 1932, 1933 and 1934 a total of 5,348 cases or 42.10% of the total number examined by the psychiatric clinic were noted as "Not Defective but not definitely classified." This notation is intended to apply to those cases which were subjected to examination to determine only whether or not they were mentally defective. Because of the pressure of work, these subjects were not given psychometric tests.

The following table reveals a sharp decrease in those classified by the clinic as "psychopathic personalities." In 1932, the first year the Clinic operated, offenders classified as psychopathic personalities repre-

99

sented 18.6% of the total examined that year. In 1936, this percentage had dropped to 5.53%.

Year	Psychotics		Psychopathic Personalities		Neuroses		Total Exam.	Total Abnormal
	No.	%	No.	%	No.	%	No.	%
1932	16	.72	413	18.6	50	2.2	2,216	21.5
1933	13	.52	792	32	54	2.1	2,477	34.62
1934	15	.53	697	23.3	105	3.3	2,982	27.43
1935	21	.81	97	3.74	138	5.29	2,590	9.84
1936	32	1.3	135	5.53	162	6.65	2,438	13.48

The Clinic accounts for the marked decrease in this number after 1934 by two important reorientations. One amendment in the criteria of psychopathic personality diagnosis was made by eliminating the immature emotional group from the category of psychopaths. This was based on the experience of seeing individuals diagnosed as psychopathic in 1932, 1933, and 1934, return in 1935 and 1936, with altered personalities; thus, within two or three years, these youths had lost many of their traits of aggressivity, callousness, sexual maladjustment, egocentricity, etc., etc. As a result of this experience, which the psychiatrists believe furnishes a valid justification for their action, these subjects are now regarded as maladjusted adolescents.

A second reorientation was in the direction of discounting as much as it was possible, anti-sociality as a criteria of personality, on the assumption that the commission of a crime does not in itself justify a diagnosis of psychopathic personality. Dr. Bromberg points out: "A proper viewpoint is required; the psychiatrists must know more of society and how it influences our emotional life. We should know how our notions about common things like sex, money, clothes, work, our bodies, government, social justice develop, in order to appreciate how the nervous patient reacts with his distorted ideas about life. In other words we are brought face to face with a social, rather than an individual orientation in the field of mental aberrations."[7]

As the Probation Department and the Clinic function, and a vast amount of source material accumulates, it becomes apparent that we cannot to any appreciable degree ascribe criminality to mental defect

---

[7]Bromberg, Walter, *The Mind of Man.*

or mental derangement. The findings of the clinic show but a small number of mentally defective and psychotic offenders. Although the dull normal and the borderline classifications combined represent slightly more than 12% of those who were examined, we are confronted with the question of whether or not this is a greater ratio than that which will be found among the law abiding population. There are, at the present time, no statistics by which such comparisons can be made.

It would also appear, as our sum of knowledge increases, based on more intensified investigations and studies, that the personality of the offender must loom largest in our consideration of why he chooses to become criminalistic. To understand that personality, all the environmental and hereditary influences which affected him from his earliest years must be studied. Where necessary, new approaches and new techniques must be developed to meet the needs of those who in the future may become anti-social, in order that they may be diverted from criminal careers. Psychiatric clinics in Courts can make an outstanding contribution toward the attainment of such objectives.

101

Chapter VII

POST-PROBATION STUDY

For an evaluation of society's approach to the problem of crime, its treatment and its prevention, it is imperative that reliable descriptive and statistical data be secured. This can only be done through well rounded research programs. However, research in problems of social maladjustment presents serious obstacles not the least of which are the difficulties involved in the very nature of the information to be secured, its variability and the lack of adequate source material.

Misconceptions concerning the probation system and much misinformation with reference to it are the result of the lack of adequate, detailed, reliable information with reference to the human material with which it concerns itself, its treatment programs and the effectiveness of its therapy. Too often probation is subjected to criticism and attack because of some outstanding failure which because of its publicity value, is sensationally portrayed. Those who rally to the defense of the probation system are generally forced to indulge in defensive apologetics, due to the fact that, in addition to the absence of reliable information, much which masquerades under the guise of probation is, in reality, an empty gesture which neither rehabilitates the offender nor affords the community that protection which the probation system should provide.

However, statistical and descriptive data cannot be accurately compiled because in so many probation departments probation officers are so badly overburdened with cases that it is a physical impossibility for them to keep the necessary records. Case histories, to adequately reveal the information which is basically necessary for a study of probation success and failure, require careful analysis and careful recording. The lack of clerical aid in probation units throughout the country is also a contributory factor to the existence of faulty and inadequate records.

Although the past seven years have shown some improvement in the compilation of records, nevertheless, the criticism of The National (Wickersham) Commission on Law Observance and Enforcement is

102

still for the most part applicable. In 1931 that body pointed out that:

"Statistics concerning probation, like statistics concerning nearly every other aspect of work with offenders, are distressingly inadequate in the United States."[1]

Recognizing that approximate methods of evaluation have little real value and that agencies and institutions which deal with crime and delinquency have lagged behind other fact-finding groups in the field of social science in the use of devices for measuring their work, this Department upon its establishment in 1927, developed and throughout its existence has furthered methods for the gathering of information of social value. These have had value in advancing our own methodology and gauging our successes and failures.

Although this material gathered in the cases of 25,872 criminal offenders is contained in our files, the community has as yet failed to make full use of this extremely valuable source material, because of a lack of funds necessary for such purposes. It is our hope that studies of our records and others, similar in scope and quality to them, will eventually be utilized by trained research workers in the determination of the underlying physical, personality and social maladjustments which create criminality, and in the development of generally accepted methods of treatment.

The success or failure of probation does not rest primarily upon the conduct and attitudes of probationers while under supervision. It cannot be estimated in terms of money saved by not incarcerating the offenders. Success or failure of probation should be determined by the probationer's ability to make successfully the transition from the relatively controlled environment provided by probationary aid and supervision, to self-controlled participation in normal social life. In essence, the answer to the question lies in whether or not supervision has helped to develop in the probationer desirable personality traits, inhibitions and resources, so that without assistance he can continue to adjust in society.

---

[1] The Advisory Committee on Penal Institutions, Probation and Parole to the National Commission on Law Observance and Enforcement. 1931.

Statistical measurements in relation to new arrests are in a limited way a measure of the success or failure of probation treatment in that they reveal whether or not the offender has reverted to crime. This is of prime importance if we recognize that in the probation system there is inherent the aim that society must be protected. From this premise it can be assumed safely that if a discharged probationer has not been rearrested for a period of years, then probation has served its function, at least in part.

It is extremely difficult to establish on the basis of statistics alone, a cause and effect relationship between probation and the fact that during a period of five or ten years after discharge, a probationer has not been rearrested. However, it is not too much to assume that a constructive probation treatment program, with its controls and restraints and its basis of social case work techniques, had had a major part in changing the criminal offender into an orderly, law-abiding person.

Authorities in the field of criminology have time and again pointed out that a proper gauge of success and failure in the probation field must be predicated upon a far-flung, individualized study of each probationer, over an intervening period of years after his discharge from probation. This, of course, is conceded.

However, a research project to determine the adjustment of probationers after their discharge, would require an elaborate, costly and time consuming process for which this Department has neither the additional staff nor the necessary funds. Therefore, of necessity, the study which we undertook was limited to a determination of whether or not probationers who were discharged in 1932 were convicted of new crimes during the period covered from their discharge until January 31, 1937, and a study of what services this Department rendered to the probationers in order to aid them to adjust, to change their attitudes and enlarge their sense of social responsibility.

Method of Study

For the purposes of the study, we selected those probationers discharged during the year 1932. This year was used because it gave us a leeway of between four and five years in which to study whether or not these probationers had reverted to crime.

In January of 1937, the original fingerprints of 331 probationers who were discharged in 1932 were taken from our case histories and cleared through the New York City Police Department, the Department of Correction of the City of New York, the Magistrates Court of the City of New York, and the Federal Bureau of Investigation of the Department of Justice. Correspondence was had with out of town law enforcement agencies to determine the disposition of the cases against those discharged probationers who had been arrested outside the jurisdiction.

When the ratio of success and failure had been ascertained, a study of the case histories in our discharged files was carried on for a period of several months to evaluate the services rendered the probationers and their response while under probation treatment. For this purpose a committee of probation officers was organized within the Department and to each probation officer was given a group of cases which had been supervised by other probation officers. No probation officer evaluated his own cases. The 331 probation case histories were distributed without regard to success or failure, and no probation officer was informed as to whether the cases which he was studying had been successful or had failed.

To facilitate this study, each probation officer was supplied with an outline in which the following phases of probationary supervision were covered.

Duration of the probationary period
Age groups by color and sex
Health problems (mental, physical, emotional)
Family and neighborhood situations
Economic and employment situations
Education
Recreation
Religion
Thrift
Attitudes towards social discipline
Future prospects

105

Of necessity some of the results were based upon the subjective interpretation of the examining probation officer. However, the results were then further studied and evaluated by the Chief Probation Officer and Mr. Elmer Reeves, the Case Supervisor who collaborated in the study. The cases were divided into success and failure groups, the statistics were compiled and classified, and an effort was made to see whether or not any correlation existed between the offense for which a defendant was originally placed on probation and the new conviction which placed him in the failure group.

Percentages of Success and Failure

Of the 331 cases studied, it was determined that 41 (12.39%) of the total had been convicted of new crimes. 290 (87.61%) had not been convicted of any new crime in any part of this country. In evaluating this 87.61% success percentage figure, we desire to point out that this Department regarded as failures those who had been convicted of even minor offenses, some of which can be regarded as crimes only in a technical sense. These latter included Intoxication (Suspended Sentences), Assault and Battery (Paroled), Annoying (Fined $10), etc., etc.

A study of the new offenses revealed that in 17 (41.46%) cases there existed a definite correlation between the offense for which the defendant was originally placed on probation, and the new crime which relegated him to the failure group. Ten (24.39%) of these offenders committed were convicted of a new crime within less than one year after their discharge from probation; 13 (31.71%) were convicted of new crimes during a period approximately between one year and one year and 11 months after discharge; 10 (24.39%) in a period of from two years to three years 11 months; 2 (4.88%) during a period of from three years to three years 11 months, and 6 (14.63%) reverted to crime after having been discharged for more than four years.

The Original Offenses

Each one of the probationers had been indicted for a felony. When placed on probation, 90 (27.19%) had pleaded guilty, or had been convicted of a felony and 241 (72.81%) had pleaded guilty or had been convicted of a misdemeanor.

106

149 (45.02%) of these offenders pleaded guilty to or were convicted of Petit Larceny. 32 (9.67%) pleased guilty or were convicted of Unlawful Entry and 32 (9.67%) pleaded guilty or were convicted of Assault 3rd Degree (Pugnacity), whereas 14 (4.23%) pleaded guilty to or were convicted of Assault 3rd Degree, involving sexual assaults. The remainder of the offenses ranged among Abandonment, Abortion, Assaults, Bigamy, Burglary, Criminally Receiving Stolen Property, Escaping from Lawful Custody, Extortion, False Financial Statement, Forgery, Larcenies, Robbery, Sending Annoying Letters, etc., etc.

Previous Court Records

Of this group, 245 (74.02%) were first offenders; 17 (5.14%) had previous juvenile convictions; 62 (18.73%) had previous adult court convictions and 7 (2.11%) had both juvenile and adult court convictions. However, included in the 62 adult court convictions are 9 Traffic Court offenses. 6 (1.81%) of this group who had been adjudged mentally defective and had been committed to the Institution for Male Defective Delinquents at Napanoch, New York, were placed on probation after they had been returned to this Court from that institution. Under the law, as at present constituted, mentally defective delinquents are no longer returned to the Court after commitment to this institution. One of this group had been found insane by a Lunacy Commission, was committed to Matteawan State Hospital, Beacon, New York, and when certified as recovered, was returned to this Court and was placed on probation on the then pending indictment.

Period of Probation

The period of probation in each instance ranged from 3 (0.91%) who were on probation for less than one year, to 50 (15.11%) who were under supervision for five years or more. The majority, or 243 (73.41%) were under supervision between two and four years. There is no marked difference between the period of probation of the success group and the failure group.

Age, Sex and Color Groups

When placed on probation, the age range of the success and failure group was between 16 and over 50 years. At the termination of probation, of the 290 probationers who were found to be successful at the end of five years, 128 (44.14%) were 25 years of age or under 23, (56.10%) of the failure group were 25 years of age or under. In the successful group, 252 (86.90%) were male, white; 17 (5.86%) female, white; 15 (5.17%) male, colored and 6 (2.69%) female, colored. In the failure group 35 (85.37%) were male, white and 6 (14.63%) were male, colored. There were no women in the latter group.

Mental and Physical Status

Two hundred and eighty-three (85.50%) of these offenders were examined prior to sentence either at the Psychiatric Clinic of this Court, or at Mental Hygiene Clinics which formerly cooperated with us for this purpose. Eight (2.83%) were found to be of superior intelligence; 171 (60.42%) of this group were found to be of average intelligence; 41 (14.49%) of dull normal intelligence; 29 (10.25%) of borderline intelligence; 33 (11.66%) feeble minded, and 1 (0.35%) was diagnosed as psychotic. After a commitment to Matteawan State Hospital, he was returned to this Court and placed on probation. The physical examination showed that 259 (91.52%) were normal; 9 (3.18%) were designated as being inferior; 2 (.71%) were characterized as confirmed alcoholics with pronounced physical deterioration, and 13 (4.59%) were found to be suffering from venereal diseases.

A study of the case records also revealed that a large number of probationers were suffering from severe emotional disturbances and tensions with concomitant attitudes of anxiety, frustration and inferiority. These were attributable to maladjustments in the home, economic insecurity and personality difficulties which had resulted in distorted behavior patterns.

At the inception and during the period of probation, this department was confronted with approximately 141 separate health problems. These were diversified and included pathological conditions which ranged from tuberculosis, gynocological conditions, venereal diseases, serious dental conditions, hernia, arthritis, glandular conditions, epilepsy, etc.

This Department, cognizant of its responsibility in the health area, secured or assisted in making available for probationers necessary services for the solution of their health problems. The study of the case records indicates that 507 distinct health contacts were made by this Department for the 331 probationers studied. This included contacts with clinics and hospitals, both for examination and treatment, interviews with private physicians, securing of dental care, prenatal care, post-natal care, referrals to diet kitchens, nursing services, making available summer vacations and convalescent care, etc.

At the termination of the period of probation, there were present 46 health problems which needed further attention. Accordingly, this Department contacted 45 agencies who undertook further health service. These agencies included the Association for Improving the Condition of the Poor, the New York League for the Hard of Hearing, the Board of Health Tubercular Clinic, Venereal Disease Clinics, the Veterans Bureau, various hospitals, Jewish Social Service Association, the Visiting Nurse Service, etc., etc.

Educational Status

The education of the group studied ranged from 12 (3.62%) who had had no formal education of any kind to 4 (1.21%) who had been graduated from recognized universities.

Two hundred and thirty-four (70.69%) discontinued their education either during or upon graduation from public school. Thirty-seven (11.18%) had failed to get beyond the fifth grade and only 56 (16.92%) were graduated. Seventy-three (22.05%) had attended high school, but only 7 (2.11%) were graduated. Only 21 (6.34%) had had any kind of vocational training.

The educational program of this Department not only endeavored to correlate the cause and effect relationship between education, training and employment, but also through stimulation and advice endeavored to broaden the cultural horizon of probationers through stress upon leisure time reading, discussions on current events, etc. Twenty-eight (8.46%) probationers were persuaded to continue with their academic training either at evening classes or through extension courses; 52 (15.71%) probationers engaged in courses for vocational training; 26 (7.85%) affiliated themselves with the New York Public Library, and in addition there is apparent in 131 (39.59%) cases the fact that the emphasis placed upon the educational development of the probationer, was productive of marked results.

Family and Neighborhood Situation

At the inception of the probationary period, 101 (30.51%) resided in areas which can be definitely characterized as slum. 142 (42.90%) resided in neighborhoods which were fair, whereas only 88 (26.59%) lived in desirable surroundings. Eighty (24.17%) of the homes of the probationers were very poorly furnished and 129 (38.67%) may be described as fair. Seventeen (5.14%) probationers were vagrants. Forty-three (12.99%) probationers were dependent upon charitable assistance and 87 (26.28%) lived on but a marginal income. The income of 131 (39.58%) were characterized as fair. Seventy (21.15%) had good incomes. The home life of a majority of these probationers was marked by domestic upheaval, congestion, friction, maladjustment and lack of parental understanding or control.

The emotional tone of the homes showed instability in 232 (70.09%) cases. In the case of 106 (32.02%) probationers, either parent was dead; in the case of 57 (17.22%) both parents were deceased. The broken homes in these cases appeared to be important contributing factors in the development of the delinquency patterns of these offenders.

The termination of probation revealed improvement in almost every phase of the probationers' home situation. At the end of supervision, only 64 (19.34%) probationers resided in slum areas; the homes of 135 (40.79%) were located in fairly desirable neighborhoods, whereas the neighborhoods of 132 (39.88%) were characterized as entirely desirable. The home furnishings had also improved, although 32 (9.67%) were still very poorly furnished and kept; the furnishings of 124 (37.46%) were characterized as fair, whereas 175 (52.87%) lived in comfortable homes. Despite the depression, and it must be remembered that those studied were discharged at its peak, a study of the economic situation of this group also revealed improvement. At the termination, only 23 (6.95%) were dependent upon charitable assistance, and 53

(16.01%) were living upon a marginal income. The incomes of 156 (47.13%) were fair, and those of 99 (29.91%) were good.

Although it is obviously difficult to satisfactorily measure emotional areas, the study reveals that at termination the home life of only 39 (11.78%) was unstable; 93 (28.10%) could only be characterized as relatively stable, but the family situation of 199 (60.12%) was evaluated as satisfactory and stable. At the termination of probation, the 17 (5.14%) who originally were vagrants, were no longer in this category.

In treating the problems emanating from the family situation, this Department throughout the period of probation functioned as a family case work agency. However, at the termination of probation, there were still present a number of family problems which this Department could not continue to treat, because its legal jurisdiction had terminated. Accordingly, arrangements were made whereby other agencies would assume at least temporary responsibility either upon a case work or relief giving basis. Seventy-three such agencies were contacted. They number among them the Emergency Home Relief Bureau, State Division of Parole, the Board of Child Welfare, the Institute of Family Service, Charity Organization Society, the Probation Department of the Family Division of the Domestic Relations Court, the Women's Prison Association, Bureau for the Handicapped, etc., etc.

Vocational and Employment Situation

At the inception of probation, only 21 (6.34%) had had any kind of vocational guidance or training. Eight (2.42%) had had no employment record prior to the inception of probation. The employment history of 84 (25.38%) was very poor, showing long intervals of idleness, lack of interest, and little capacity for sustained effort. Ninety-eight (29.61%) had established fair employment records from the standpoint of regularity and industry and the employment history of 136 (41.09%) was designated as good from the standpoint of regularity.

At the inception of the probation period, 226 (68.28%) were discovered to be vocationally maladjusted as manifested by blind-alley jobs, disinterestedness in employment, and lack of initiative. Eighty-five (25.68%) were well-adjusted industrially, whereas 15 (4.53%) had

111

made excellent employment adjustments. At the inception of probation, 212 (64.05%) were unemployed and 114 (34.44%) were working. Three (0.91%) were housewives and 2 (0.60%) because of old age were unemployable. The earnings of these probationers ranged from $2 to over $50 a week. Eighty-two (71.93%) of the employed probationers were earning between $15 and $35 a week.

At the termination of probation, only 42 (12.69%) were unemployed, whereas 276 (83.38%) were working at gainful employment; 5 (1.51%) were housewives, 2 (0.60%) were too old to work, one, an artist, was attending school on a scholarship basis, another was attending high school as a full time student and 4 (1.21%) were hospitalized.

In contrast to the employment records prior to probation, 287 (86.71%) probationers established fair or good employment records during the period of supervision. The employment record of only 30 (9.06%) during this period can be designated as poor. To offset the employment difficulties inherent in these cases, it was necessary to enlist the cooperation of numerous private and public employment agencies and vocational guidance services. Tests were conducted to ascertain the vocational aptitudes of probationers in order to facilitate their adjustment in industry. The efficacy of this approach is manifested by the results which reveal that at the termination of probation 41 (12.39%) probationers had made excellent adjustments, whereas the adjustment of 236 (71.30%) was characterized as fair or good. Only 41 (12.39%) were designated as industrially maladjusted. This maladjustment could not be overcome through the efforts of the probation officers because of resistances and circumstances beyond our control. At the termination of probation, 169 (61.23%) probationers were earning between $15 and $35 a week. 33 (11.96%) probationers were earning between $36 and $50 a week and 16 (5.80%) were earning more than $50 a week.

Recreation

The social investigations made by this Department prior to sentence revealed that the recreational activities of 182 (54.98%) probationers were disorganized. This disorganization manifested itself in excessive drinking, sexual promiscuity, gambling, poolroom and street corner loitering, etc. Thirty-five (10.57%) of this group were given to the regular abuse of alcohol. Only 2 (.60%) were members of any organized recreational group. The recreational habits of 128 (38.67%) were characterized as normal.

This group was increased to 292 (88.22%) at the termination of probation as a result of direction and assistance given to them. In contrast to only 2 (0.60%) who were members of organized recreational groups at the inception of probation, at the completion of the period of supervision, 64 (19.34%) were so affiliated. Among the organizations to which individuals in this group were affiliated were the Young Men's Christian Association, the National Guard, various fraternal organizations, community settlement houses, athletic organizations, etc. Only 1 (.30%) at the end of the period of supervision could be characterized as extremely intemperate. The extreme habits of 28 (8.46%) others, although not entirely eradicated, had been modified to a great extent.

Religion

This study, like other studies in delinquency, reveals most clearly how far those with delinquent patterns have drifted from the influence of their church. Eighty-two (24.77%) probationers had completely severed their connections with their church. The religious observances of 195 (58.91%) were highly irregular. Only 54 (16.31%) recognized the value of religion in their lives by regular observance of their religious duties.

At the termination, 162 (48.94%) were regular in their attendance at church. 139 (41.99%) were irregular in their attendance, but the study indicates that their vision had been enlarged with reference to the part religion played in their lives.

Of those who had become regular or irregular attendants at church, a large number had joined in the secular activities of the church through participation in organizations such as the Knights of Columbus, Catholic Boys Clubs, various centers and athletic activities. At the termination of probation, 30 (9.06%) had resisted all efforts to reawaken their interest in religious influences.

113

Thrift

The study further revealed that a majority of those who had been placed on probation possessed little if anything of material value; few carried insurance, and the great majority of them had no savings.

At the termination of probation the records revealed that 84 (23.38%) probationers had saved a total of $18,326.07; that probationers or their families carried $155,800 insurance; that 77 (23.26%) probationers had paid $73,721.63 in restitution and that 9 (2.72%) probationers had paid $14,267.25 in family support. In the cases of 114 (34.44%) probationers, the household management was improved through the medium of family budgets, controlled expenditures, curbing of extravagant purchases, etc.

Attitudes

At the inception of the probation treatment program, this Department was confronted with numerous conflicting attitudes with reference to social controls which had to be resolved before treatment could become effective. Of the 290 in the success group, 43 (14.83%) were definitely antagonistic; 118 (40.69%) were either indifferent or gave perfunctory compliance to the directions and advice; 129 (44.48%) were characterized as cooperative. In the failure group, 10 (24.38%) were definitely antagonistic; 24 (58.54%) were indifferent or gave perfunctory compliance and only 7 (17.07%) could be designated as cooperative.

At the termination of probation those in the success group can be placed in the following categories. One (.34%) antagonistic, 38 (13.10%) indifferent, and 251 (86.55%) cooperative. In the failure group we find at the termination 2 (4.88%) antagonistic, 20 (48.78%) indifferent, and only 19 (46.34%) cooperative.

Future Prospects

At the termination of the period of supervision, a "Discharge from Probation" is submitted to the Court in each case. This discharge presents the methods which we employed to change the probationer's attitudes and his social and economic condition, and the manner in which

114

he reacted to these influences. An integral part of the report is an evaluation of the growth of social responsibility on the part of the probationer upon which is predicated our opinion of his future prospects. The classification for these opinions are "guarded," "fair," and "favorable."

The 331 cases studied fell into the following classifications at the time of discharge.

Guarded	90	(27.19)
Fair	48	(14.50)
Favorable	193	(58.31)
Total	331	

It is significant to note that in 1932, of the 41 cases which subsequently were found to be failures, 22 (53.66%) were discharged as Guarded, 4 (9.76%) as Fair, and 15 (36.59%) as Favorable.

Conclusion

The important fact established by this study is that of the 331 probationers who were discharged in the year 1932, 290 (87.61%) did not revert to criminal activity. Thus it is apparent that the use of probation as a correctional discipline has been justified in these cases.

The fact that this large group was not convicted of new crimes is not sufficient evidence to predicate a hypothesis that they are all at present adjusted in a socio-economic sense. However, all adjustments are relative and no inflexible criteria have as yet been evolved to determine the adjustment of the so called law-abiding population, especially that part of it which has had no contact with case work or relief giving agencies.

Thus on the basis of the fact that these discharged probationers have not been rearrested, coupled with the indicated services of probationary treatment and their favorable responses, it is not too much to assume that the adjustment of these 290 is no different from that of the remainder of the law-abiding population into which they have been fused.

The limitations of this study prevent us from determining what factors and forces propelled the 41 failures toward further criminal behavior. The age, color, sex, background, economic and social situation show no significant variations from those of the success group. They were the recipients of the same type of services and restraints. Although the results of the study clearly indicate that their responses were not as satisfactory, nevertheless this variation does not appear significant enough to predicate definite anti-social behavior upon it. The answer can only be found through an individualized study of each one of these probationers and an evaluation of the influences which affected them, favorably or adversely after their discharge from probation.

It is our hope that at some time in the future we shall have the opportunity and the facilities to further this study so that it will encompass a detailed, individualized investigation into the lives of these men and women. The need of such a research program and the usefulness of its results are self-evident.

Chapter VIII

MANUAL FOR PROBATION OFFICERS

I. Training of Staff

No Manual for Probation Officers can be complete without a declaration of the basic principle that a department's executives are responsible for stimulating professional growth and for broadening the social vision of the members of the staff.

In the Probation Department of the Court of General Sessions this assumption of responsibility is not academic but is discharged through a planned program of education, training, intensive supervision and periodic evaluation of the work and progress of each officer.

1. Individual conferences with Case Supervisors during investigation of case and after submission of first draft of each pre-sentence report. (Division of Investigation.)

2. Individual conferences each week with Case Supervisors. (Division of Supervision.)
   (a) On cases presenting unique problems.
   (b) Analysis of case records.
   (c) Departmental procedures.

3. Correction and editing by Case Supervisors of each report before it is finalized for submission to the Court. (Divisions of Supervision and Investigation.)

4. Divisional Staff Conferences at weekly intervals.

5. Lectures at the office by specialists in allied fields.

6. Readings.
   (a) Suggested.
   (b) Prescribed.

7. Circulation of available literature, such as, magazines, pamphlets, bulletins, etc. on current trends.

8. Staff encouraged to attend courses at universities and schools of social work.

9. Staff urged to attend lectures given under professional auspices.

10. Staff allowed time to attend and participate in state, regional and national conferences in probation, social work and allied fields.

11. Integration of staff activities with other community social welfare programs.

12. Semi-annual ratings of each staff member based upon capacity, performance and professional growth.

II. INVESTIGATION METHODOLOGY

The use of social investigations in criminal courts represents the individualized approach to the offender and his offense, based upon an interpretation of the legal, social, mental and physical factors which illuminate his ethical concepts and explain his behavior patterns.

The Division of Investigation of the Probation Department of the Court of General Sessions conducts legal and social investigations to evaluate responsibility, motivation and personality, as an aid to the Court in sentencing the offender.

The investigations of this division portray, through presentation of the objective and subjective forces which were instrumental in shaping his past history and behavior, his potentialities for probation or institutional treatment.

To envisage the factors in the life of an individual, to conduct investigations which will comprehensively evaluate these factors and present them in such a manner that they will serve to portray the individual as a distinct personality, requires clear thinking, initiative and exacting effort.

The methodology of investigation is a step by step approach to the mechanics of investigation and also portrays the form in which the assembled data is to be submitted to the Court. The outline of procedure, however, cannot be effectively utilized unless the probation officer brings to his task a painstaking attention to detail, an outstanding uriosity and the ability to marshal facts and evaluate them in such fashion that they will present the individual in his true light.

The field sheet which is used by the probation officers has been developed to conform to the methodology of investigation and is designed to record through interviews and field investigations, the source material which forms the basis for the pre-sentence report. Copies of of these reports are forwarded to the institution to which the defendant is committed, to the State Division of Parole and the City Parole Commission.

Probation Officers assigned to this division should never lose sight of the grave responsibilities which are theirs. They must maintain an unbiased viewpoint, an impersonal attitude and a wise exercise of judgment. Accuracy of fact and of statement should be the primary objective because carelessness or indifference will do incalculable harm to all involved in these investigations.

With the usually adequate period of ten days to two weeks allotted by the Court as the normal time for the investigation of a case, comprehensive reports comparable to the best individualized case studies are possible. Haste and the possibility of errors attendant upon it are obviated and an opportunity is given to procure reliable and accurate information of the delinquent and his past life.

That all cases, whatever their relative aspects of uniqueness or commonplaceness may receive the same exhaustive consideration in investigation, the following outline of procedure has been drafted and the fundamental directions are to be scrupulously observed by the investigation officers.

A. Directions to Probation Officers

Immediately upon assignment of a case for investigation, the investigation should be initiated.

The indictment may be read between one and two P. M. daily in the Part in which the presiding Judge is sitting. Read the supporting affidavits from the Magistrates' Court which are filed with the court papers. Copy all relevant material on the Preliminary Investigation sheet.

Interview the Assistant District Attorney in charge of the prosecution of the case; obtain from him all the information at his disposal regarding the present case and any other complaints which may have been made regarding the defendant.

Interview the defendant, he may be seen in the Tombs between 9 A. M. and 5 P. M. daily and on Saturday between 9 A. M. and 12 noon. Secure an adequate social and criminal history. Defendants on bail are escorted to this office by the Court Attendants.

In all bail cases obtain a Clinic appointment from the Deputy Chief Probation Officer. In all cases prepare and forward to the Clinic within four days after pleading, an Outline of History with the proper attention to heredity, parental and developmental history and the personality traits and behavior of the delinquent. His school progress and industrial efficiency are important.

Include in the Outline of History a full account of the nature and circumstances of the present offense and a summary of previous delinquencies. Direct the defendant on bail to report at the clinic for examination—give him an admission card.

Secure from the Clinic the psychological, psychiatric and physical reports and evaluate each offender's development and behavior in the light of all the knowledge obtainable.

Have identifying information typed on Criminal and Social record, on Social Service Exchange slip, on Department of Health sheet, or Army and Navy clearance sheet and on the Alien Squad letter, and leave it with the record officer. The records will be searched and available data returned to you in 24 hours.

Secure institution, probation and parole reports including psychograms and details regarding previous arrests. Where girl complainant is in the custody of the S. P. C. C., see the agent at 2 East 105 Street.

Interview the complainant, arresting officer, witnesses, etc. Verify birth, death, marriage, citizenship and immigration records.

Visit the schools attended by defendant, see teachers, school nurses, attendance officers and other sources of information.

Visit defendant's places of residence, the home of his family, his landlords, neighbors, etc.

Communicate with all social agencies to which the defendant or his family is known and get social history. Wherever possible, obtain written summaries of their contacts.

In cases where the defendant has lived outside of New York for any period, contact the Social Service Exchange and write local authorities, probation officers and social agencies in other cities to conduct special investigations.

See present and previous employers. Verify information by firm's employment records. Evaluate legitimacy and opportunity, environment and other aspects of job. Fellow employees or neighbors may be able to furnish information in instances where firm has discontinued business and records are not available.

Obtain Army, Navy or Marine Corps or Coast Guard records.

Complete written reports in all cases as quickly as possible for correction by the Case Supervisors. The finalized reports must be submitted to the judges at least two days in advance of the date of sentence.

Every statement in the report must have been substantiated or the record must state the reason for the inability to do so.

The investigation report must be accurate, complete, fair and concise.

The average report can well be completed in from three to four pages.

B. CHANNELS OF INVESTIGATION

I. LEGAL HISTORY

PREVIOUS COURT RECORD

Under this heading the record of all previous appearances in Court of the defendant should be set forth with accuracy.

The precise month, day and year should first be given. Then the offense of which *he was convicted,* or to which *he pleaded guilty.*

121

The Court should be correctly designated, as for instance, Children'
Court, Magistrates Court, Court of Special Sessions, Court of Genera
Sessions, or in courts of jurisdiction outside New York, the name o
the City or County and State.

In the event that a former appearance in this Court is recorded
the name of the Judge before whom the defendant appeared should b
noted in parenthesis, beneath the name of the Court.

The disposition and the date of parole from institutions should b
accurately recorded.

In a Children's Court record, the offense is designated as Delinquen
Child, with the particular charge for which he was arraigned in paren
thesis under Juvenile Delinquency as (Burglary).

N.B. Arraignment as an Ungovernable or Neglected Child, on a
charge of Improper Guardianship, *does not* constitute " delinquen
child."

Abstract of Indictment

Under this heading include the date, hour and location of the offense
and state the complainant's name. Present the crime.

Offense

Complainant

The complainant's name, business and address should be given in a
single paragraph.

The time, date, place and manner in which the offense was
committed.

Complainant's allegations regarding offense, if he has any knowledge
of its commission and the defendant's arrest.

The name of the arresting officer; his precinct or squad; the arresting officer's account of the offense and arrest of defendant.

The number of offenders concerned; the number apprehended and
the facts regarding their arrest and disposition; the number unapprehended and the defendant's knowledge of them.

Discuss other indictments covered by plea.

Mitigating and Aggravating Circumstances

Was there premeditation, deliberation? Previous acquaintance with the complainant; motive of offense.

Acquisitiveness

Specific number of thefts, methods of commission; period over which thefts were committed; manner in which goods were disposed of; profit obtained thereby and disposal of funds; extent of injury of complainant. Has defendant assisted authorities by disclosing identity of confederates, the receiver of stolen property, etc.? Is the complainant covered by indemnifying insurance; has surety company settled with the complainant—is property unrecovered—can restitution be made?

Pugnacity

What is the extent of the complainant's injuries (time in hospital, number of stitches, permanence of disfigurement, cost, time lost from work). Was defendant the instigator of the offense herein, weapon used (describe).

Sex

Has complainant incurred a social disease or pregnancy? Age and mental condition of complainant; previous chastity of complainant. Disparity of racial origin, age and color. Provisions for care of child, if any.

Revolver

Description, calibre and manufacture of revolver; when and where obtained; loaded with how many cartridges, purpose and period of possession. Opinion of arresting officer as to the defendant's purpose of the possession of weapon.

For all types of cases

Has defendant previously been convicted of a similar offense; what was his intent? Does present offense constitute violation of probation, parole—has warrant been issued or lodged; the measure of culpability of defendant.

123

Attitude of Complainant

State the complainant's attitude regarding the disposition of the case. In sex cases the attitude of the girl's parents, if she is a minor, should be recorded.

II. Analysis of Environment

Personal History

Sources of information, age of defendant, racial origin.

Note: Natives of Latin-American countries are invariably classified as follows:

(1) Those of unmixed Spanish stock.

(2) Those of mixed Spanish and Indian origin.

(3) Those of mixed Indian and Negroid extraction.

Nativity, time in United States; time in New York City; citizenship; marital status.

Education and Early Life

Sources of information.

Schools attended (number or name of each); period, grade repeated or skipped; age at leaving; scholarship, deportment; truancy; response to discipline; speaks, reads, writes English;—special education (academic, vocational, cultural)—childhood ambition.

Mental and physical examination report during school year; mentality—superior, normal, defective.

Deviations—nervous disorder, psychopathic constitution.

Physical—superior, average, inferior.

Injuries—organic or functional disorders.

Amusements; early associates; habits, indulgence, repression;

Religious training and observances; age first delinquent.

Home life (attitude, traits, delinquencies, relation to adult career)— effective parental control. Broken home?

By whom was defendant reared? Under what circumstances?

124

Juvenile court or institutional record.

Note—All relevant data up to 16th year.

Sources of information.

Defendant's sequence, history of siblings, character of parents— broken home; loss of parents or others; cause; at what age; by whom reared.

Concerning the parents and the paternal and maternal grandparents, and the wife or husband of defendant, the following data:

> Name, date of birth, date of marriage, date and cause of death. Nativity, years in United States, years in New York City; citizenship, education; address; character and conduct, occupation and religious affiliations.

Health:

> Tubercular, epileptic, drugs, psychotic, alcohol, syphilitic, other hereditary influences.

Criminal Record:

> Date, court, offense, disposition.

Influence upon offender, etc.

Concerning other relatives, children, brothers, sisters, uncles, aunts, cousins, etc. the following data:

> Name, kin, living or dead, address, age, occupation, wages, mentality, physical conditions, social and economic status, criminality, attitude toward the defendant.

Defendant lives with family, wife, others, alone, owns home, rents apartment, lives in lodgings, permanency, transient.

Economic status of family—comfortable, average, poor, dependent, charitable aid. Income of family contribution of defendant. Does he support wife and children?

Unfortunate sex or marital relations. Progress, retrogression, solidarity; effect of conditions upon defendant.

125

Living conditions (home and neighborhood); number of rooms, rent, number in household, number of lodgers, moral conditions; present and previous residences of defendant; his reputation with landlord and neighbors; neighborhood conditions.

Summarize defendant's attitude toward family responsibility, position in group, etc. How do family account for defendant's delinquency.

Interested agencies (Social service exchange, family welfare, other social agencies).

Industrial History

Sources of information.

Occupation or trade; employed or unemployed at time of arrest; for how long. If employed, by whom, in what capacity, at what wages; have defendant's occupations been permanent, temporary, seasonal, full time, part time, skilled or unskilled; were the working conditions good; previous employments; nature, duration and reason for leaving. Explain unemployment intervals; how did he subsist—through relatives, loans, savings, thefts, etc.

Unnemployable—nature of handicap. Economically adequate.

Industrial training and age of beginning work; trade begun, trade completed, industrial ambition, position liked best, vocational maladjustment (specify); influence of daily work.

Thrift—savings, insurance, property.

Include army and navy, marine corps or coast guard service; regiment or ship, station; date of enlistment, discharge and rank.

(When employment is alleged by parents or relatives, or in places of doubtful character, ascertain validity of such employment.)
Note deleterious occupations and environmental menaces; defendant's character as an employee with reference to regularity, reliability, industry, efficiency and sobriety. Summarize and comment on employment record.

126

III. ANALYSIS OF PERSONALITY

PHYSICAL AND MENTAL

Sources of information.

State the findings of psychiatrist, clinicians and other physicians; is defendant physically normal, inferior; has he an unfortunate heredity, tuberculosis, social and cardiac disease.

Alcoholism, drug addiction, glandular disturbance—susception—duration of condition and prognosis.

Intellectual Capacity: (I. Q.) superior, average, retarded, defective; traits, interests, mental conflicts, psychoses, psychopathic; institutional commitments.

Is commitment to the Institution for Defective Delinquents at Napanoch or Matteawan State Hospital for the Insane recommended or indicated?

Sex abnormalities (particularly in sex cases).

CHARACTER AND CONDUCT

Sources of information.

Characteristics, temperament, attitude toward authority, sociality, aptitudes and interests; pathological traits; temperance, sense of responsibility, inclinations, conduct in relation to home, school, work, play, companions and community; impulses, urges, philosophy.

Emotions, sentiments and beliefs—Stability, positive, negative reactions, introvert, extrovert, complexes.

Attitude toward life—(Offense, etc.).

Recreation, Habits and Associates:

Recreation—Leisure, club membership, organized groups, athletics, dance halls, poolrooms, character thereof, saloons.

Habits—Alcohol, gambling, sex habits, others (specify)—(State degree, age acquired, present status, etc.).

Associates—Criminal associates, idling, characteristics of associates.

Religious Observances:

Name of church, location, pastor, denomination, membership, attendance (regular, occasional or discontinued); church organizations, etc.

Manner and Appearance:

Carriage, gait, expression, gestures, posture, cleanliness, neatness, affected, sincere, aggressive, humble, boastful, modest, enthusiastic, apathetic, forceful, weak, dignified, self-conscious, sullen, timid, irritable, ingratiating.

Circumstances and nature of previous offenses, causes thereof. Reaction to Prison life, parole and probation record. Police opinion (arresting officer, officer on post, detectives at precinct, other jurisdictions).

Etiological factors must be discussed basically and fundamentally as part of the Character and Conduct.

I. Subjectively (constitutional conditions, internal factors influencing the defendant's delinquency).

Beliefs, habits of thought, moral concepts, social tendencies, mental conflict, interests, defect, emotional patterns, stability. Derangement, deterioration, senile changes.

Consider and evaluate the elements of heredity, alcoholism, syphilis, neurotic tendencies, birth injuries, psychopathic constitutional inferiority, mental and physical defects, childhood diseases, affections of the nervous system, chorea, perversions, psychoses, unhealthy thinking and frictions with environment.

II. Objectively (environmental conditions, external factors, bearing on the anti-social development of the defendant).

Broken home; incompetent or indifferent parents; institutional rearing; harmful neighborhood influences, unwholesome recreation; idleness; lack of religious training; poverty; evil associates; defective education; inadequate supervision; deleterious occupations; unfortunate sex or marital relationships; economic failure; dependency.

In the vast majority of instances, a criminal act must be attributed to a number of antecedent, inter-related, causative factors, each one contributing its share toward the ultimate result, which is expressed in the anti-social conduct.

IV. Synopsis

Each investigation report must conclude with a few short paragraphs for ready reference, outlining the outstanding and pertinent facts of the defendant's social history and the present offense.

The following report of James West (the name is fictitious), illustrates the form and the content of a pre-sentence report to the Court:

INDICTMENT NO.	DATE FILED	INVESTIGATION FOR COURT		INVESTIGATED BY	CASE NO.
666666	Jan. 1, 1936			O.M.R.D.	88888

DEFENDANT	ALIASES (Court Name)	CODEFENDANTS
WEST, JAMES	Joe Smith Henry Carroll	John Smith

OFFENSE	PLEA √	INDICTED FOR	DATE OF PLEADING	DATE OF SENTENCE
Burglary 3rd Degree	TRIAL	Burglary 3rd Degree Petit Larceny Receiving	Jan. 1, 1936	Jan. 21, 1936

JUDGE	DISPOSITION
Hon. William Blank	

1—LEGAL HISTORY

PREVIOUS COURT RECORD

DATE	OFFENSE	COURT	DISPOSITION
June 12, 1928	Ungovernable Child	Children's Court	Children's Institution (Paroled July 3, 1930)
Oct. 1, 1930	Violation of Parole	Parole Board	Children's Institution (Paroled Nov. 25, 1932)

Abstract of Complaint and Indictment

On December 19, 1935 at about 4:00 A. M., West, accompanied b
John Smith and a minor, by forcing a door gained entrance to a roor
at 154 Third Avenue and stole a camera and wearing apparel of
total value of $36.50, the property of Edward Jones.

Offense.

Complainant: Edward Jones, who operates a curiosity shop at 15
Third Avenue, is the complainant.

Mysterious petty thefts had been occurring in the neighborhood o
the complainant's shop for a period of four months before the presen
offense. Because the entry had often been effected through unusuall
narrow openings and because quantities of material had been remove
in this way from many shops, the crimes were ascribed to three un
knowns characterized by the Police as the "three dwarfs." Jones th
complainant, decided to set a trap for the elusive intruders. He arrange
an electrical contraption leading from his shop to his living quarter
above.

Shortly after midnight on the indicated date, Jones closed and pad
locked the doors of his shop and retired for the night. About 5:0
A. M., the alarm sounded. The complainant ran to his store and foun
that the place had been entered through a small transom. The propert
mentioned above was missing. Jones began a search of the neighbor
hood. Shortly before dawn, he observed at the corner of 14th Stree
and Third Avenue an undersized boy, carrying a camera stolen fror
the shop. He was accompanied by two other youths. Jones telephone
the Police but by the time they arrived, the trio had disappeared.

The following day at about 3:00 P. M., Jones returned to the sam
locality and in a lunchroom on 14th Street near Third Avenue, appre
hended the undersized youth, who gave his name as Jack Smiley. Th
complainant summoned Patrolman William Church of the 13th Precinct
who arrested Smiley. On questioning Smiley, the officer learned tha
he had been living with James West and John Smith in a flat at 7
Keane Street. The officer proceeded to that address and arrested Wes
and Smith after a search of the flat disclosed part of the complainant'
property.

130

Mitigating and Aggravating Circumstances: Smiley, who was fifteen years old, but extremely undersized for his age, had escaped from the Children's Institution. He was returned there on December 26, 1935.

Known as "The Midget" to his companions, he admitted that he generally effected entry into places to be burglarized. He would crawl over the transom, squirm his way through narrow basement windows or worm his way through holes forced through walls. He would sometimes carry out merchandise himself, or, if possible, would open the doors so that his companions might aid in removing the property.

A search of the flat occupied by West, Smith and Smiley, disclosed some of the stolen goods. In addition a pawnticket revealed that Smith had pawned the complainant's overcoat for $4. There was also found a violin which the group admitted having stolen the same night from an apartment on the lower East Side. The flat occupied by the group had the appearance of a curio shop containing binoculars, cameras, pawntickets, travelling bags, watches and articles of clothing. The youths admitted that these articles had been stolen from various places.

The complainant sustained a loss of $4.37 to redeem his overcoat.

In the opinion of the arresting officer, John Smith is the most culpable of the group. Smith, profane in his language and vicious in his attitude, resisted arrest and was with difficulty taken into custody. Aged twenty-five years, he admitted that he had perpetrated similar offenses in Boston, Mass. He has a Children's Court record and has served a term in the New York City Reformatory.

West has been acquainted with Smith for about three months. They had met in a lunchroom. Smiley, previously known to Smith, had been with the other two about five weeks.

Attitude of Complainant: The complainant will be in accord with the Court's disposition of the case.

II. Analysis of Environment

Personal History: Eighteen years, eight months old and single, James West is a native resident of this city.

Education and Early Life: The defendant's mother survived his birth only about three months. Thereafter West was reared by his maternal grandmother until he attained the age of four years. He proved to be a burden upon his grandmother who, because of her age, was both physically and emotionally unfitted to rear a child. Accordingly, other arrangements had to be made.

The father had remarried about one year after the death of West's mother and subsequently manifested only a slightly veiled antagonism toward the defendant. It would appear that the father's rejection of West at this period was due, at least in part, to the fact that subconsciously he blamed West for the death of the mother.

The stepmother refused to assume responsibility for the defendant; first, because she was expecting a child of her own and, secondly, because West already at this time had acquired certain unrestrained habits and was regarded by his grandmother as unruly. As a result, the defendant was sent to a private boarding home. He remained here until he was six years of age. His foster-parents did not become attached to him, and thus, in this home too, his life was characterized by the absence of affection and interest. They state that he was recalcitrant and ungovernable. The father finally took him into his own home.

At the age of seven, West's rebelliousness became pronounced and he ran away from home on a number of occasions. Because of this, coupled with the Defendant's "insolence" in the home, the father had the defendant arraigned in the Children's Court on June 12, 1928. As an Ungovernable Child, he was committed to the Children's Institution.

During this period two other children had been born and the defendant's stepmother devoted her entire attention to her own children. Intense jealousy on the part of the defendant has figured prominently in his emotional development and has separated him from the other members of the household.

After spending two years at the Children's Institution, where his resentments found expression in deliberate breaches of discipline, West was paroled to his father on July 3, 1930. While at the institution, his father visited him but infrequently. Upon returning to his father's home, West reverted to his former rebellious attitude and he was returned to the institution three months later, on October 1, 1930. Reparoled on November 25, 1932, he again returned to his father's home. During this second commitment his conduct at the institution failed to improve.

Thereafter West attended Public School 999, Queens, and was graduated therefrom in June of 1933. His record for conduct and attendance was excellent, but he received relatively poor marks in his studies. He then attended the Vocational High School until October of 1934 when, at the age of seventeen, he discontinued his studies. His record at this school was generally satisfactory. It appears that he was making fairly good progress in subjects which enlisted his interest here until the father, uncompromising and severe, began to force West to register for courses for which West felt himself unsuited.

It is interesting to note that the defendant did not resent the impersonal authority of the school and appeared to adjust satisfactorily to discipline. He is remembered in school as a youth who responded very readily to interest, and worked hard to merit praise and the good will of his teachers.

Family and Neighborhood: The defendant is the youngest of three children, born of his father's first marriage. The oldest, a sister, aged twenty-two years and single, resides with her father and is employed as a file clerk for the Acme Bookbinding Co., 999 Broad Street. She earns $18 a week of which she contributes $10 to the maintenance of the household. The defendant's brother, David, has a previous court record and was sentenced to the New York City Reformatory on August 9, 1932 after pleading guilty to Unlawful Entry. For the past three years David has not lived at home. He is living in a rooming house on Chambers Street and has little contact with the rest of the family. By the defendant's father's second marriage there are four children, ranging in age from eight to thirteen years. The father is employed as a teacher of printing at the King's Vocational High School. He earns $220 a month.

For the past four years the family has occupied a comfortably furnished, well kept brick dwelling at 116-47 218th Street, St. George,

Long Island. The house, which is owned by the defendant's father, comprises six rooms and is valued at $8,000. The father has an equity therein of $5,200. In the neighborhood, which is desirable, the family bears a good reputation but the defendant is regarded as a headstrong, wayward youth, an impression which has been fostered by his parents.

The defendant's father is a positive, aggressive individual who demands unquestioned respect and obedience in his home. He is a good provider in that he attends to the physical needs of his family, but he appears to lack all concept of the emotional qualities which are essential in family life. He has commanded the respect of his daughter by his first marriage and that of the four children by his second marriage mainly through fear. The stepmother is not consciously aware that she favors her own children over her step-children. She is strongly attached to her husband and has adjusted her life to his mode of living, but her attitudes reveal that she resents the stepchildren because their presence recalls the father's first marriage.

In September of 1934, the defendant disappeared from his home and his whereabouts remained unknown until his arrest for the instant offense.

After leaving his father's home West lived for a short time in the home of relatives of his mother and in cheap lodgings or any place that afforded him shelter. For about six weeks prior to his arrest he had lived with the codefendants Smith and Smiley in the former's two room flat at 78 Keane Street, for which a rental of $11 a month was paid. These quarters were dirty, had no facilities for gas or electricity and contained but a few sticks of furniture. On the premises were found a number of empty food containers and the defendant admitted that the trio had secured food by stealing it from in front of stores in the early hours of the morning. At this address no information of value is obtainable concerning the defendants.

Because of the father's rigid adherence to a self-determined, strict code of conduct and his unyielding personality, the instant offense is a severe blow to his pride. The father however, is willing to allow West to live at home if the latter will receive uncomplainingly the stringent supervision to be imposed upon him, but since an early age West has displayed marked resentment against the home situation, and has preferred to live elsewhere, regardless of conditions and environment. It does not seem likely that the defendant will be able to adjust in the home of his father and stepmother.

Industrial History: The defendant has been in custody since December 20, 1935. He can furnish no verifiable employment. He claims to have had occasional employment at jobs such as dish washer, bus boy and painter's helper, but these by their very nature do not lend themselves to verification.

The same planlessness which characterizes West's social contacts is evident in his industrial history. At present he reveals no vocational interests.

III. ANALYSIS OF PERSONALITY

Mental and Physical: The defendant was examined at the Psychiatric Clinic of this Court. He was found to be of average intelligence and physically sound. He related a history of gonorrhea but claimed that this infection was now inactive. He also stated that he had sustained a head injury when he was about eight years old but further details of this are not available. However, an x-ray of the skull taken in 1928 was negative.

According to the examining psychiatrist, the defendant lacks emotional flexibility and reveals symptoms of a schizoid-neurotic.

Character and Conduct: James West's deterioration has been progressive. He considers himself an outcast and feels that all society is against him. Reticent, resistive and suspicious, he rarely makes friendly overtures and his features have assumed a mournful, discouraged cast.

Since leaving home in September of 1934, the defendant has associated with a disreputable element. He has spent much of his time in pool rooms, pin ball parlors, bowling alleys and cheap "coffee pots" along the Bowery. He has idled about street corners until the late hours of the night in the company of criminals and prowled the streets looking for places to burglarize or drunks "to roll." He has had occasional relations with women of the streets.

Undernourished and physically weak, West gives indications of being involved in serious emotional conflicts. He is extremely introverted and is given to brooding and morbidness. Aware that his life has been abnormal, he is baffled when he tries to explain it to himself. In many respects he presents a picture of complete negative reaction. He has an awareness of rejection, a sense of not belonging to anything or any person and an isolation from normal companionship. He has experienced frustration in achievement, he has no special interests and his wilfullness and rebelliousness are an outward manifestation of his feelings of inferiority, insecurity and self pity.

He has shown no ability to resolve his conflicts in a positive manner. He uses fantasy as an escape mechanism and there is every indication that he has withdrawn himself more and more from the realities of life. Essentially a hyper-sensitive person, his psychological processes have been crushed by a lack of understanding and affection. Although he has experienced satisfaction from sexual promiscuity and criminal activities, he also has experienced a deep sense of guilt.

West has attached himself to the co-defendant, Smith, and psychologically identifies himself with the latter, but he continues to experience frustration in his search for recognition and stability.

He is not deeply rooted in his rebellious anti-social ways. He realizes that he has been living outside the pale of acceptable social conduct and there is evident some struggle on his part for self-improvement and an unwillingness to choose crime as a definite means of livelihood. His tendency to form undesirable companionships has been more an expression of his longing for sympathetic human companionship than a desire to apprentice himself to hardened accomplices in criminal activity. This craving, coupled with a normal though misdirected adolescent sexual curiosity, motivated his associations with prostitutes.

The defendant's personality difficulties and his social problems do not appear so deeply rooted that they might not be solved or adjusted.

IV. SYNOPSIS

Aged *18* years, eight months and single, the defendant is a native resident of this city. His mother died when he was three months old and even at the age of four he was regarded as a behaviour problem. At the age of eleven he was committed to the Children's Institute as an Ungovernable Child and later returned for Violation of Parole.

Since September of 1934 his family has been unaware of his whereabouts. He has no verifiable employment and admits that he subsisted for the most part by criminal practices. At present, he manifests numerous personality problems.

In the instant offense, the defendant, Smith and a minor, who has since been returned to the Children's Institute from where he had escaped, burglarized the complainant's shop after having gained entrance by forcing the lock. They stole a quantity of personal property all of which has been recovered but the complainant spent $4.37 in order to redeem his overcoat.

In the opinion of the arresting officer, Smith, who pleaded similarly and is awaiting sentence by Your Honor, is the most culpable of the trio.

The complainant will be in accord with the Court's disposition of the case.

Respectfully submitted,

Irving W. Halpern,
Chief Probation Officer,
Attest: Court of General Sessions.

J. A. Walsh,
Deputy Chief
Probation Officer.

———————

III. Supervision Methodology

The Division of Supervision of the Probation Department of the Court of General Sessions functions at all times on the basic premise that its first responsibility is to protect the community from further anti-social acts by the individuals who have been placed under probationary supervision. To attain this objective, this Department functions as a social case work agency and as such maintains the ideology and

137

applies techniques consistent with accepted standards of social case work.

The supervision division of a probation department performs its functions, those of protection of the community and the rehabilitation of the individual in a unique setting and under conditions provided by legislative enactment and judiciary regulation, that set it apart from other social case work agencies. This setting and these conditions provide the authoritative tools in the probation field, which if used intelligently will react advantageously both to the community and the probationer.

This manual has been developed as an aid to probation officers of this Department so that they can more efficiently utilize case work techniques and processes in order to intelligently plan and carry into effect long range treatment programs for "the human being whose capacity to organize his own normal social activities may be impaired by one or more deviations from accepted standards of normal social life."[1]

Mechanical directions and outlines can only help to develop a constructive approach to the problems which each probationer presents. This manual must be used as a guide by the probation officer to the day by day performance of his duties. It is intended to be a step by step approach to a more organized method of evaluating and dealing with problems of adjustment.

The value of it is dependent upon what the probation officer brings to his profession especially the quality of his imagination and his ability to perceive and analyze the probationer's needs. Of paramount importance, too, is his ability to utilize community resources without which no probation department can function.

No tools have value unless the worker possesses the patience, sympathy and understanding to utilize them to the maximum extent. The probation officer's primary function is to mould personalities and to develop resources within the probationer which will help him in time of stress. The guidance which the probation officer provides must be constructive treatment toward the end that the probationer may be educated to know his own problems and to develop within himself the capa-

---

[1] 1928 Report of the Milford Conference.

138

cities to meet them. No mechanical or routinized effort can attain such an objective.

James S. Owens, former Director of Probation of the State of New York, in an evaluation of the capacities and equipment of those engaged in work with delinquents stated:

> "Obviously of initial significance is the professional equipment of the worker, his training, experience and that often amazing collection of individualized gifts, talents or defects which we group under the handy but infrequently defined heading of "personality." Should the worker be lazy or a time server by temperament his clients will by his lack of energy be deprived of many services which a more dynamic individual might have made available to them. Similarly a person lacking in imagination or having only a sketchy knowledge of his community's resources, and the etiquette of their use, may feel that all possibilities have been exhausted in a given case when a more alert worker might recognize at once an infinite variety of approaches that have not been as yet attempted. Specialized information, the spontaneously right reaction to a given situation, the intuitive feeling that the professionally proper thing to do is the prelude to disaster in specific instances, can all come only with experience and with the worker's growth of capacity to distill from his triumphs and errors the rare essence of tolerant understanding. They can come, moreover, only to the worker who accepts his job as a yardstick by which periodically to measure his own development of competence and who refuses to accept at any point the thought that any task he may have performed, might not have been done better. Experience when regarded solely as a description of length of service is valueless."[2]

A. TREATMENT

If we recognize that the probationer is no different from any other human being, then it is apparent that probation treatment is planned guidance. In planned guidance there is inherent an awareness of the probationer's problems and capacities as well as the skill to assist him to work them out in a constructive creative manner.

---

[2]James S. Owens, *Process in the Social Adjustments of the Delinquent,* Oct. 1936.

Although the fact that the probationer has come into conflict with the law may indicate his inability to make his own adjustments nevertheless, the probation officer must not assume overtly the responsibility of making them for him. It is of primary importance to recognize that the probationer's unwillingness to accept responsibility, his desire to shift his problems upon others may have been the basic cause of his conflicts. The test of the success or failure of treatment is not predicated on the probationer's responses to supervision but upon his ability to make the transition from supervised activity to normal life in society where he can adequately adjust.

The competent probation officer must possess an intellectual and emotional appreciation of the psychological conflicts of the probationer. In almost an intuitive way, since the mechanism for this has not been defined, he gains insight into the probationer's problems. The success or failure of treatment is the resultant of the action and interaction of the personalities of the probationer and probation officer. These constitute the dynamics of social case work.

Planned guidance implies understanding of and the capacity to use the case work skills of diagnosis, interviewing and treatment.

1. SOCIAL DIAGNOSIS is the interpretation of the findings of the social study, the explanation of the difficulty and its contributing causes.

  A. OBJECTIVES

    1. To describe and interpret the problems of the probationer in relation to his setting, with respect to:

      (a) Cause.

      (b) Contributing factors.

      (c) Effects.

    2. To bring to the foreground and insofar as possible to evaluate the relative significance of problems presented.

    3. To determine along what lines treatment is indicated.

      (a) Economic needs.

      (b) Environmental needs.

      (c) Emotional needs.

4. To see the individual problem as part of the entire cultural, environmental, psychological and physiological pattern.

    (a) To determine the probationer's treatability in relation to the possible direct treatment processes which may be utilized by the officer.

    (b) To determine what additional facilities, and what collateral agency services may be required.

B. ASPECTS OF SOCIAL DIAGNOSIS

1. Sociological—the knowledge of the responses with which probationer meets environmental conditions and forces such as family and home, school, health, church, employment, recreation, etc.

2. Psychological—the evaluation of the meaning of the sociological factors to the probationer and their effect upon his attitudes. How has he become oriented to these factors? What is his reaction to them, and what effects has this had on his present situation?

3. A continuous process—the recognition of the need for revision in the light of further understanding and new knowledge of either a factual or emotional nature.

4. Objective—the ability to appreciate the probationer's situation from his point of view, but without emotional involvement; awareness of the symptomatic nature of some behavior; viz., the fact that the probationer may drink to excess or shows an unwillingness to work are symptomatic manifestations of more basic problems, which must be attacked if the behavior is to change. The Probation Officer must be aware of the significance of outward manifestations and appreciate the sources from which they may come; such as:

    (a) Feelings of inferiority, hostility, resistance, etc.

    (b) Reluctance to accept plans.

    (c) Expressions of dissatisfaction.

    (d) Acute behavior reactions.

2. PLAN OF TREATMENT: The social diagnosis provides the basis upon which treatment is predicated. A treatment program to be effective must:

A. Be carefully planned.

B. Be based upon a thorough social investigation, a recognition of probationer's potentialities and limitations and a selective use of diagnostic material.

C. Be flexible so as to allow periodic revisions in the light of newly discovered data, and the progress or retrogression of treatment.

The media of treatment are:

A. Interviews with probationer and others.

B. Home and Collateral Visits.

C. Community Resources:
   (a) Mobilization.
   (b) Manipulation.

In formulating the plan of treatment the probation officer must:

A. Remove or ameliorate emotional pressures prior to attack upon psychological or emotional factors.

B. Concentrate upon immediate problem or problems, with awareness of possible latent problems.

C. Make the plan acceptable, at least in part to the probationer, and enlist, as far as possible, his cooperation in developing it.

D. Attempt to break down antagonisms on the part of the probationer or, if not possible, measure his resistance and meet them.

E. Utilize the constructive factors in the probationer's personality and situation; sublimate undesirable traits.

3. SOME ASPECTS OF TREATMENT: The ultimate aim of probation is to assist the probationer toward a more normal social adjustment by

developing him to his fullest capacity for self maintenance in keeping with approved standards of social behavior. Treatment may be divided into two general classifications:

A. Directive (Executive-Manipulation) primarily used to deal with needs arising from environmental difficulties. These may be resolved by:

1. Acquainting the probationer with community resources of which he can avail himself and instructing him in their uses.

2. Mobilizing necessary community resources for the benefit of the probationer.

B. Leadership (Personal Relationship) used to influence the probationer so that he will improve his social situation, develop sound ethical standards of conduct, change his attitudes and behavior.

1. Relationship between probation officer and probationer should be a dynamic process of free interplay of personalities.

   (a) Probationer should be helped to avoid too great dependence on probation officer.

   (b) Authoritative role should be submerged but not lost sight of.

   (c) Treatment must begin at the first interview.

   (d) Treatment must be directed toward basic problems and must be in accord with the social standards of the community. In addition, treatment should also be aimed toward enlarging the probationer's social vision and sense of community responsibility.

2. Acceptance of the probationer as a human being will help to:

   (a) Win his confidence and develop responsiveness.

   (b) Having him submit possible plans or solutions to his problems encourages his participation in the treatment program.

(c) Recognizing his accomplishments and providing further opportunities for his participation in the solution of his problem, makes each step a link in a total chain of treatment.

In initiating treatment the probation officer must:

A. Determine the genesis of the attitudes and behavior he is trying to change and their significance to the probationer.

B. Determine what qualities the probationer possesses upon which treatment can be based.

C. Gain an understanding of the probationer's thinking processes, emotional reactions and habitual responses and thus find the right psychological moment for making suggestions.

D. Make the plan or suggestions acceptable to the probationer and if possible have it evolved by him under the probation officer's directions.

E. Method—No specific method which guarantees perfect results has been devised. The probation officer must possess a flexible approach and be prepared to meet each personality reaction of the probationer with an offsetting one of his own. He must possess patience, sympathy, broad understanding and those qualities of personality which prove that he desires to help. He must control his emotions when his plans go awry and seek for causation instead of giving vent to impatience at relapses. The probation officer should always give the impression that he is never too busy or too tired to talk at length to the probationer. Probationer can frequently be reached through some person to whom he shows an attachment or by some concrete service performed for him or his family.

In his work with the probationer, the probation officer should endeavor to:

A. Establish Rapport—a satisfactory professional relationship between probation officer and probationer based on mutual respect, understanding, sincerity and confidence. This involves among other aspects, important psychological mechanisms of sublimation and transference.

1. Sublimation—the redirecting of some inner urge arising from a lower psychological level into some channel of interest on a higher level; viz., pugnaciousness is redirected into some form of athletic activity involving competition; desire for adventure manifested in burglaries, etc. redirected into vocational channels such as seamanship, aviation, etc.; desire for recognition seen in gangster affiliations redirected into sports, mechanics or active participation in club activities.

2. Transference—the building up in the probationer of confidence and respect for the probation officer to such a degree that he transfers to the probation officer feelings of deep loyalty and respect and thereby accepts the leadership and guidance of the probation officer.

B. Help develop Insight—understanding by the individual of the motivating factors behind his behavior; although insight does not necessarily solve a problem, nevertheless, understanding of the causes of conduct is sometimes effective in forestalling recurrent deviations of the same type.

1. Applicable—To individuals who have the intellectual capacity and are accustomed to think before responding to stimuli.

2. Inapplicable:

   (a) To individuals who respond to stimuli without thought. (Here the use of substitute responses and compensations is indicated.)

   (b) To individuals who have built up a defense mechanism for inadequacies, the breakdown of which may strip them of the courage to face reality. Where the defense mechanism has no serious implications, the probationer may be aided to modify it. Where it will result in conflicts with accepted standards of conduct, and the probation officer is unable to cope with it, the assistance of a psychiatrist must be secured immediately.

C. Permit self direction—an intelligent and discriminating modification of the approaches outlined in this manual is to be applied to that small group of probationers who appear to be capable of making their own adjustments.

4. INTERVIEWING: The medium of direct approach to the probationer is the interview, the method whereby much of the information used in planning is secured and through which most of the results of treatment are insured.

A. In interviewing the probation officer must:

1. Always bear in mind that his approach to the probationer must be individualized.

2. Approach the probationer's standards of morality and his cultural setting with tolerance and understanding.

3. Maintain an objective but sympathetic attitude towards the probationer's problems.

B. Every interview must have a specific objective and be an integral part of the entire plan of treatment.

C. Each interview is an opportunity to study the probationer, his ambitions, interests, traits, likes, dislikes, attitudes, prejudices, etc., and to evaluate his reactions.

1. Encourage the probationer to discuss his own life and problems freely in order to release emotion.

2. Discuss situations related to the major problem, touching upon it and gradually leading into it.

3. Avoid direct questions if dealing with unpleasant subjects which are likely to elicit an unfavorable or negative response; secure the least painful information first.

146

4. Do not ask questions extraneous to the story which is being unfolded by the probationer; questions which follow the general trend of the story may be interjected.

5. Avoid obvious note taking in the presence of the probationer, with the exception of imperative factual data; such as, addresses, dates, etc.

D. In securing information from collateral sources the probation officer should:

1. Obtain all relevant information.

2. Explain the need for the information requested.

3. Encourage the probationer to aid in the selection of sources to be canvassed.

4. Encourage the probationer to secure certain information personally.

E. To impart information to the probationer:

1. All requests for information should be complied with and given at the probationer's level of understanding.

2. Probationary and legal requirements should be interpreted impersonally and objectively.

3. Painful information should be imparted tactfully, only after the probationer has been prepared for it.

F. Setting of Interview:

1. Privacy is essential.

2. Mingling of probationers while awaiting interview should be avoided.

3. Probationer's hours of employment, domestic situation and other factors should determine the time and place of interview.

4. If probationer is unable to adjust himself for the interview in the Probation Department, other arrangements for prolonged interviews should be made.

G. Points to be observed in interviewing:

1. Lessening the emotional tension by placing the probatione at ease.

2. Discussing topics of interest along the lines of the proba tioner's past experiences.

3. Keeping discussion at probationer's level of understandin and manifesting personal interest in his problem.

4. Assuring the probationer that all matters which do not affec the community safety will be treated as confidential informa tion.

5. Permitting the probationer to lead the discussion but guidin it, thus maintaining a control so that the interview will, a far as possible, follow the plan which has been develope for it.

6. Recognizing and favorably commenting upon the progress an the accomplishments of the probationer.

7. General attitude of the probation officer: he should be courte ous; refuse to take offense; should not raise critical issue immediately; treat all plans of the probationer, as long a they are sincerely offered, as rational; he must maintain pois when confronted with excitability; he must not withdrav from problems; his interrogation must be designed to releas the probationer from the fear of making revelations; he mus create a non-judgmental atmosphere.

B. DEPARTMENTAL PROCEDURES

When the Court suspends sentence and places a defendant o probation he is accompanied by a Court Attendant to the offic of the Deputy Chief Probation Officer in charge of Division o Supervision who interviews the probationer.

1. INITIAL INTERVIEW BY DEPUTY CHIEF PROBATION OFFICE Since the Court Hearings and the period of uncertainty whic has preceded it and the presence of excited relatives some times charge the situation with emotion, this interview is a brief as possible.

A. Content of Interview with Probationer

The Probation Card is filled out and given to probationer. An explanation is given him of the rules of probation which are on the card. He is given definite instructions as to the time and place of his reports. He is informed that the probation officer will visit the home within 48 hours and therefore it is advisable for the probationer to acquaint members of his family with this fact and with the name of his probation officer. It is explained that the maximum period of probation is entered on his card since the Court has the power to extend any period named at the time of sentence to the maximum permitted by law. The probationer is told that a review of his probation record will be sent to the judge before he is discharged, and that the length of the probation period depends upon his progress and adjustment.

B. Complainant

The complainant is again interviewed if he accompanies probationer. The amount and terms of restitution if ordered by the Court are discussed.

C. Assignment

In general probationers are assigned to officers in whose district they reside and to those of the same religious faith. In exceptional cases an officer especially equipped to handle particular problems will have a probationer assigned to him regardless of district boundaries.

D. Probation Officer's procedure

(a) In cases which do not require immediate contact with the probation officer, the probationer is assigned a reporting date within the coming week.

(b) If the probationer is being permitted by the Court to leave the city or if he is homeless, he is referred immediately to the probation officer to whom he is assigned. If he is without funds, the probation officer must arrange for food and shelter. Agencies cooperating in this type of service are the Prison Welfare Department of the Salvation Army, the Men's and Women's Prison Associations, the Municipal Lodging House, the Bureaus for the Homeless and the Men's Service Division of the Emergency Relief Bureau; for adolescents under the age of twenty-one, the Newsboys' Home and the Children's Aid Society. (See Directory of Social Agencies.)

Where the probationer and his family are without funds and transportation must be provided, arrangements may be made through the Division of Transportation of the Department of Public Welfare and the Division of State Aid of the State Board of Social Welfare.

An especial effort is to be made in cases of homeless or unattached probationers and those residing outside the jurisdiction of the Court to secure names and definite addresses of relatives and friends who may be reached in an emergency.

E. Mechanics

All the material which the Investigation Division has secured is given on the date of sentence by the Deputy Chief Probation Officer to the Case Supervisor who keeps a record of each new case and reviews it one month from the date received. The Case Supervisor turns all of the material over to the Probation Officer after noting any matters requiring immediate action and discusses them with the officer within a few days after the case is received.

2. INITIAL STEPS BY PROBATION OFFICER

A. Mechanics

(a) Read carefully all the material already in the case history.

(b) Consult the investigation officer in order to secure from him any additional impressions or suggestions for follow up which he may have.

(c) Fill out field sheet for the field book.

(d) Fill out the card registering the case in the finger-print file at Police Headquarters. (This Department will then be notified immediately should the probationer be rearrested.)

(e) Secure any additional information necessary for a complete understanding of the probationer and secure all data which could not be procured prior to sentence. If letters which the investigation officer has written have not been replied to, letters must be written again if no answer is received within a reasonable time. If the schools were closed at the time the investigation was being conducted, the school record should be secured as soon as it is available and interested school authorities are to be contacted, etc.

(f) The report of the Psychiatric Clinic of the Court is to be studied carefully and note is to be made of any physical or mental condition needing treatment. The psychiatrist who examined the probationer in the Psychiatric Clinic must be consulted in all cases in which clinic follow up has been recommended or in all cases in which probation officer desires further study or advice by the psychiatrist.

(g) Take any immediate action indicated by "Order of Probation," the Deputy Chief Probation Officer and Supervisor.

(h) After considering carefully in the light of all information available, determine method af approach to

151

the probationer and his immediate problems. This must be subjected to modification from time to time.

B. Initial Home Visit

(a) Unless there are exceptional circumstances the first home visit must be made forty-eight hours after the time that the probationer is placed under supervision.

(b) As the first home visit will be the initial meeting of the probation officer and the probationer's family, it is of primary importance for the officer to use it, as far as possible, for establishing a friendly relationship with the family.

(c) The interview need not be lengthy. Circumstances may be such that a very brief interview will appear advisable.

(d) The interview should be casual and friendly in tone and calculated to put the members of the family interviewed at ease. The probation officer as soon as possible should give the members of the family adequate insight and the necessary perspective with respect to the aims, objectives and functions of the probation officer and the Probation Department. If they choose to discuss their attitudes towards the probationer, his offense and court experiences, let them do so, if it seems to be furnishing them a needed release from tension. Probation officer must be careful not to be drawn into partisan or controversial discussions.

(e) Probation officer is to be cautious not to let his official position be known to strangers, if persons other than the members of the family are present.

(f) Probation officer is to advise family that the visits will continue from time to time over the entire probationary period.

(g) Without becoming domineering probation officer is to make clear that strict compliance with probationary regulations will be expected.

(h) If probationer is present, it is usually not advisable to enter into any lengthy discussion with him until the time of his first report.

C. Initial Interview with Probationer

(a) Interview occurs within one week from the placement on probation.

(b) There should be no suggestion of haste and the probation officer should aim first at putting the probationer at ease. If he needs to let loose his antagonism and resentments or if he needs to justify himself, let him do so.

(c) Before the interview is terminated probation officer is to give probationer an understanding of probation and clear up any misconceptions he may have.

(d) The probationer is to be made to realize that probation is neither a system of espionage nor of paternalism. Probation officer must try to bring the probationer to see that he is an adult and as such is expected to be self-directing, that if the Court had not believed he was capable of self-direction he would have been given custodial treatment. He is being given probationary treatment which is a period of demonstration of his ability to function acceptably as a free citizen. The probation officer is the person representing the Court and Society to whom the demonstration is to be made and therefore it is necessary that personal report be made to the probation officer and that the probationer's daily life at home, at work and at leisure be open for review. It is a legal requirement that he conform to probation regulations. The probationer will be credited for good performances and the Court will be informed when it seems desirable for the probation period to be terminated.

(e) Probation officer is to have the probationer understand that probation officer is to be used as the probationer needs his services as guide, adviser and friend but that the probationer's performance on probation and the credit therefor is to be the probationer's alone.

(f) It is advisable to show the probationer the Court Order of Probation if it contains any special Court orders (restitution, family support, etc.). The probationer's plans for carrying out these directions should be discussed.

(g) The penalties for non-compliance with the requirements of probation should be discussed but not stressed at this time, viz., court hearings, bench warrants, arraignment and commitment.

(h) Although the probationer may show little insight as to his basic problems at the time of the first interview, his being able to do so in the future may depend upon the probation officer's approach at this time.

(i) The immediate goal of the first interview is the establishing of a foundation for future contacts. Only a beginning can be made in the first interview. The building of the confidence of the probationer in his probation officer must go on during the whole period of supervision.

3. RESTITUTION, REPARATION, FAMILY SUPPORT[3]

In all cases of probationers who have been directed by the Court to make restitution, reparation or payments in family support, use the following procedure:

A. General

(a) All payments are made to and disbursed only by the bookkeepers.

---

[3]Refer to Section Recording Form No. 1 and No. 2.

(b) Read the sentencing minutes. If these have not been transcribed and it is important because of the circumstances of the case for the Department to know immediately what was said in the Court, ask the court stenographer to read back the minutes. Probation officer must copy the pertinent data for the record.

(c) The probationer is to begin restitution payments as soon as possible. He should initiate these regardless of whether or not all the details concerning restitution have been settled or not.

(d) If the Court does not indicate the total amount of restitution and to whom it is to be paid, this Department determines it. Obtain from the beneficiary a statement giving in detail his losses and the amount of restitution he claims. Verify his losses. Secure bills for repairs or for treatment for injuries received, statements from employers as to time lost, etc. Discuss these matters with the probationer and determine his ability to pay. Notify the beneficiary as to the rate of payments and secure his attitude, in writing if possible, regarding the rate suggested.

(e) Submit a letter to the supervisor for the Court recommending the amount of restitution to be paid and the rate of payment (if the Court order sets the total amount of restitution it will be unnecessary to notify the Court of the rate of payment).

If the beneficiary is unwilling to accept the decision regarding the amount of restitution and arrangement for payment, arrange a meeting of all the interested parties. If no compromise agreement can be reached, submit a letter for the Court narrating fully what steps have been taken by this Department to effect a compromise and request a date for a court hearing. Notify all the interested parties to be present at the hearing at which time the Court makes its determination.

B. Family Support

(a) In family support cases it is imperative that payments be made regularly. If a probationer misses even one week's payment and if it is determined that he is unable to make the payments, take up the matter of leniency with the recipient. If a probationer is able to pay and refuses to do so, discuss the necessary steps to be taken with the case supervisor. It is a good plan in family support cases to induce the probationer, when he is able to do so, to put on deposit with the bookkeeper, additional amounts to insure payments if he should later be unable to meet his obligation. If there is a bond to insure payments it is necessary to have a Court order to draw upon it. Such an order must be requested from the Court, if after a thorough investigation it seems unlikely that the probationer will resume payments.

(b) If the Court specified a date for the discharge of a probationer who has been ordered to make family support payments, where desirable, notify the Court that the period of probation is about to expire and request an extension of the probationary period to the maximum (in cases of abandonment the time may be extended to the seventeenth birthday of the youngest cnild).[4] When no further extension is possible because the maximum period of probation is about to expire, advise the probationer's wife that she may file a petition for support in the Court of Domestic Relations and help her take the necessary steps. Include in the Discharge from Probation the fact that another Court will continue to supervise the probationer.

(c) Since it is probationary regulation that a probationer support his family, the probationer's wife is not advised to petition the Court of Domestic Relations

---

[4] Code of Criminal Procedure—Section 933.

for a support order during the period in which this Court has jurisdiction. Such an order may be initiated in this Court by the Probation Department regardless of the nature of the offense for which a probationer is under supervision. After discussing the family situation with the case supervisor, submit a report to the Court stating the reasons for requesting a family support order and recommending the rate of payments.

In cases involving the support of children born out of wedlock, it is generally advisable to aid the mother to bring paternity proceedings in the Court of Special Sessions where a support order may be made for the support of the child until its sixteenth birthday.

C. Suspension, Reduction, Irregularities, etc.

(a) In cases in which the probationers, who, because of reduction of income, unemployment, illness or some other verified cause, are unable to meet their restitution payments over a period of three weeks, discuss with the beneficiaries the matter of reduction in rate or a temporary suspension of payments.

If it appears probable that the probationer can resume payments within three weeks and the beneficiary is willing to wait, it will be unnecessary to acquaint the Court with the probationer's failure to meet the payments. However, if the probationer cannot resume payments for more than three weeks, obtain a statement in writing from the beneficiary as to his attitude and request the Court for a reduction or suspension of restitution payments for a specified period. Include in the letter to the Court the attitude of the beneficiary. A probationer's primary responsibility is toward his immediate family. If it is verified that payments of restitution would cause his family to live below the level of the minimum budget

157

determined by this Department, request the Cou
for a suspension of payments. Money given a pr
bationer or his family for relief is not to be used f
restitution.

(b) In cases in which a defendant has been placed on pr
bation for the primary purpose of making restitutic
and after about six months there seems to be no po
sibility of his complying with the Court Order, di
cuss the matter with the beneficiary and if he wishe
request a Court Hearing.

(c) The beneficiaries must be kept informed of the re
sons for any irregularity of payments and must I
immediately notified of any important developmen
such as the issuance of a Bench Warrant, commi
ment for a new offense, etc. If the probationer
brought before Court for Violation of Probation, tl
beneficiary must be notified of the date of hearin
prior thereto. The attitude of the beneficiary towar
the probationer must be incorporated in the repo
to the Court.

D. Discharging Probationers

(a) If restitution has not been liquidated six months be
fore the end of the probationary period and it aj
pears unlikely that the probationer will be able t
meet his obligations, the probation officer must mak
an effort to adjust the matter with the beneficiar
Media such as confession of judgment, settlement fc
smaller amount, waiving of restitution, etc. may t
utilized. If such an adjustment is not possible, re
quest the Court to hear the case about three montl
in advance of the expiration date. Indicate in th
request to the Court the efforts which have been mad
to effect an adjustment. After the case supervisc
has secured a date of hearing from the Court, proba
tion officer is to notify and see to it that all inte
ested parties are present at the hearing.

(b) When applying to the Court to discharge a probationer include a request for permission to return to the probationer papers, deeds, notes, or any other security which may be held by the Department.

E. Filing

(a) The originals of all orders from the Court having to do with restitution (letters, probation histories, discharges, etc.) must be filed with the bookkeeper and must under no circumstances be placed in the case folder. Notations are made on the carbons of such letters which are included in the case record as to the date they were signed by the Judge, etc.

4. MAIL CASES

The probationer who is either temporarily or permanently residing outside the jurisdiction of the Court and with whom or with whose family the probation officer has no personal contact is classified as a mail case. This Department does not transfer probationers to Probation Departments in other jurisdictions. It always retains official custody.

Contact is kept with such cases by correspondence. Request a probation officer in the locality in which the probationer resides to give personal supervision. If a probation officer is not available, enlist the aid of a social agency or a person of recognized standing in the community to help in the supervision of the probationer. It is advisable to request supervision by the probation officer or agency which was contacted in the course of the investigation or by an agency which has previously been interested in or has knowledge of the probationer or his family. In writing to request supervision mention briefly the reasons for so doing and when the officer or agency has agreed to accept responsibility for supervision send a complete summary of the record.

Supply the probationer with the mail report blanks. Give him an explanation of how they are to be filled out and the frequency with which they are to be mailed to this Department. Have the probationer sign an agreement to return to the jurisdiction of the Court upon demand of the Probation Department. Explain to him that he will be required to report to a local probation officer who will aid him in his efforts to effect an economic and social adjustment. Inform him that this Department will write that officer requesting the latter to accept his personal reports and countersign his mail reports.

Write a letter to the sentencing judge requesting permission for the probationer to reside outside the jurisdiction of the Court.

He is not permitted to leave the city until the request has been granted.

Answer promptly any questions the probationer may ask on his mail reports. Acknowledge them at least once in four weeks. Write as often as necessary when there is any crisis in probationer's affairs. Commend the probationer for improvement in his condition and for regularity of reports. Remember that probationers need encouragement and will lose interest in a one-sided correspondence. If the probationer fails to report, write for an explanation within one week.

Request the local officer or cooperating agency to report upon the probationer's progress once in six weeks.

When probationers desire to leave this jurisdiction for vacations of not more than two weeks, which have been granted them by their employers, discuss their request with the case supervisor. In the majority of cases it will probably appear that it is not necessary to obtain Court permission.

5. Transfers Within the Department

Since in the main probationers are assigned to probation officers according to the district in which they reside, when a probationer moves from one district to another he is generally transferred to the officer into whose district he has moved. However, the following exceptions are made.

160

A. Probationers who are to be discharged shortly.

B. Probationers whose residence in the new district will be of brief duration or those whose plans are known to be unsettled.

C. Probationers who will probably be reporting by mail for some time, although their families have moved into a new district. In this classification are boys in the Civilian Conservation Corps and seamen.

D. Probationers with special problems whose plans of treatment would be disrupted by a transfer at that particular time.

In isolated instances the probation officer may feel that he is unable to successfully treat the problems of a particular probationer because of factors such as, subtle antagonisms and resentments the probationer has developed. In these instances the case may be transferred, upon the direction of the case supervisor to another probation officer.

Transfer Procedure

When planning a transfer give full consideration to the effect the transfer will have upon the probationer. He has become accustomed to a certain probation officer; he is used to his methods and requirements and a working relationship has been established between them. To cut this off abruptly sometimes with no explanation often has a damaging effect upon the probationer and he may interpret the change as indicating a lack of interest in the Department in him and his problems. Therefore, the transfer procedure is to be carried through carefully with a full understanding of its implications:

A. Verify the probationer's new address.

B. Read over the case record and supply any lacking factual material aod see that directions of the Case Supervisor have been carried out.

C. Have the case record pasted and put in good order.

161

D. Bring the case dictation up to date and either include characterization of the probationer, a brief statement as to the situation and the method of treatment felt advisable (diagnostic statement) or a new case analysis.

E. Give the case record to the Supervisor with the field slip and the "Notice of Change" slip attached.

F. Acquaint the probationer with the *probability* of transfer and the reason for it.

G. The case supervisor reviews the case and writes a memorandum to the officer to whom the case is transferred and also gives a transfer notice to the probation officer making the transfer.

H. Upon notification of the official transfer by the supervisor notify the probationer to report at a time when the officer to whom the probationer is being transferred will be present. Introduce him to the new officer who notifies him of the time he is to report. If it is not possible to arrange for a personal introduction, write the probationer to report at a time designated by the new officer, or notify him personally when he is to report and write the name of his new officer and the time he is to report on his probation card.

I. Discuss the case with the officer receiving it and be sure that the new officer is made cognizant of the various problems inherent in the case and that he understands such details as the best method of verifying employment, where to find members of the family at home, etc.

Transfers during Vacation Periods

Obviously when transferring an entire case load for the vacation period, it is impossible to carry through this entire procedure. However, it is most important that:

1. Each probationer be told of the transfer for the vacation period and that his record will be carefully scrutinized by his officer upon his return from vacation.

162

2. Each probationer's card be marked with the name and receiving day of the substitute probation officer.

6. TERMINATION

In the main the period of probation is terminated either by discharge from supervision or commitment to an institution for Violation of Probation. Isolated cases may be closed for reasons such as death, the unwillingness of the District Attorney to effect the return of a violator to this city, etc. However, under no circumstances may a case be closed without the explicit permission of the Court.

A. Procedure to be followed in Discharging.

Probationers are discharged at the expiration of the period of probation specified by the Judge, unless circumstances indicate the need for an extension of the period until the maximum permitted by law. Extensions may be requested in order to provide further opportunity for treatment, to insure support payments or to give the probationer more time to liquidate his restitutional obligations. If no period has been designated, the probationer is discharged at the end of the maximum period permitted by law unless there are exceptional circumstances, such as:

(a) When the probationer has made a satisfactory social and economic adjustment.

(b) When the probationer should be rewarded for his achievements on probation.

(c) When further supervision would be detrimental to the probationer.

In discharging a probationer before the expiration of the maximum period, the effect upon co-defendants also on probation must be considered.

Maximum Period of Probation

The maximum period permitted by law in a misdemeanor is three years. Since July 1, 1933, the maximum period in a felony case is "not beyond the maximum time for which he might be sentenced."[5] In abandonment cases the period is until the seventeenth birthday of the youngest child. If the probationer pleaded guilty to the "attempt" to commit a crime, he may be kept under supervision for a period which is not more than one half the longest term to which he may have been sentenced for the crime (applicable to felonies and not misdemeanors).

Under no circumstances is a probationer to be promised a discharge prior to expiration of the probation period. He may be told, however, that if his record justifies it, the matter will be taken up with the supervisor and with the Court. False hopes of an early discharge are not to be held out.

Restitution

No probationer is to be discharged until a satisfactory adjustment of restitution has been made. If no agreement can be reached regarding any unpaid balance of restitution, a court hearing must be applied for some months in advance of the expiration date.

Preparing the Report

1. The fingerprints are to be cleared. If the probationer has been residing outside the jurisdiction of the Court, the prints are to be cleared with the Police Department of the city in which he lives or if there is a criminal identification bureau for the city, the prints are to be cleared at the state capital and also in this city.

2. All discharges must be submitted to the supervisor one month in advance of the expiration date.

3. The case record is to be read carefully. All pertinent information or verifications which are found to be lacking are to be secured.

4. A final report is to be secured from a clinic in cases in which the probationer has been under treatment for venereal or chronic disease or for a mental condition.

---

[5] Code of Criminal Procedure—Section 933.

5. The social agencies actively interested in the probationer or his family are acquainted with the probationer's imminent discharge. If the probationer or his family will need the services of a social agency after probationary supervision terminates, a suitable agency should be interested in follow-up care and the probationer and his family should be persuaded to accept the services of the agency.

6. If Court action (Domestic Relations, Paternity Proceedings) is indicated, take proper action.

7. Notes under the headings covered by the discharge form should be made or the case should be briefed so that material for dictation can be readily found. All information must be up to date. The first draft of the discharge should be read by the probation officer before it is submitted with the case folder with completed dictation to the case supervisor.

8. The case is reviewed by the supervisor and the discharge is edited and then submitted to the sentencing judge for his signature.

9. When the application for discharge has been signed by the judge, the probation officer is given written notice by the case supervisor.

   The probation officer then notifies the probationer by letter of his discharge. This letter may either be mailed to the probationer or handed him when he reports for a last interview. In many cases a final interview for a frank expression of what probation has meant to the probationer will be found of interest and help both to him and the probation officer. Note should be made of it in the case history. The probationer is to be encouraged to come back and see his probation officer on a friendly basis. Probation officer should offer to render post probation treatment whenever necessary.

10. In restitution cases in which the full amount has not been paid, the original discharge is to be filed with the book-

keeper and a notation made on the carbon copy of the date the judge signed the original and mention made of the fact that the original is in the bookkeeper's files.

Mail Cases

In discharging probationers who have been reporting by mail, secure a final report and recommendation from the probation officer or agency who have been supervising the probationer at his place of residence. This agency is to be notified when the discharge is signed by the Judge. The summarized form, instead of the customary form for discharge, may be used in mail cases.

Preparing Cases for Closing

All material is to be pasted in proper order in folder. The Termination Slip is to be filled out and attached to the folder and the case submitted to the case supervisor.

B.   Procedure to be Followed with Violators.

Violations of Probation: A probationer may be committed to an institution by the Judge who placed him on probation either at a hearing or at an arraignment for Violation of Probation. Hearings are usually requested because of the probationer's failure to comply with a condition of his probation when the failure is not of such a nature as to necessitate the issuance of a Bench Warrant. Arraignments for Violations of Probation must be preceded by the issuance of a Bench Warrant which is signed by the sentencing judge upon the request of the department. Bench Warrants for Violation of Probation are issued for three causes:

> (a) New arrest.
>
> (b) Misconduct.
>
> (c) Absconding.

Warrants are executed by the Police Officers assigned to this Department.

1. *General*

If a probationer is arrested for a new offense the probation officer is to secure full information regarding the circumstances and apply immediately for a Bench Warrant for Violation of Probation.

Exceptions may be made with the approval of the case supervisor or Deputy Chief Probation Officer regarding minor offenses, such as traffic violations, peddling without a license, etc. in which cases, a report is to be submitted to the Court that no warrant be issued.

In certain other cases of arrests in which it appears the probationer may not have been guilty of the offense charged, the Court is requested to hold the matter of the issuance of a Bench Warrant in abeyance until the new case has been disposed of. If the probationer is found not guilty, the Court is requested not to issue a Bench Warrant. If found guilty Warrant must be requested at once. In cases of misbehavior and non-compliance with the rules of probation, the probation officer in consultation with the case supervisor will decide if a Bench Warrant should be requested. Without threats but simply by a statement of the situation the probationer must be brought to the understanding that the inevitable consequence of serious misbehavior will be a referral of his case to the Court.

When a probationer has been notified that his misconduct if continued will necessitate the issuance of a Warrant, the Warrant must be issued if there is no improvement.

In many cases, especially in those in which the probationer is lax in reporting, it is advisable after consulting the case supervisor to have the notification made by a letter to the probationer and a time limit set.

A probationer is to be considered an absconder and a Bench Warrant applied for if he has not been heard from for two weeks and he cannot be located.

Every effort is to be made to locate a probationer through relatives, friends, social agencies, etc. both before and after the Warrant is issued.

The fingerprints must be cleared to determine if there has been a new arrest.

2. *Applying for the Warrant*

Probation Officer is to fill out the warrant application and submit it to the case supervisor with the case record, being sure that the dictation is up to date. The Judge then is requested to sign the application which is then returned to the supervisor.

After the record has been entered in the Bench Warrant docket, the warrant officer secures the Warrant from the Clerk of the Court. He then consults with the probation officer and files the warrant in the institution in which the probationer is confined or he accompanies the probation officer, if the latter knows where the probationer may be found.

In the cases of absconders, the clerical division registers the probationer as "Wanted" both with the New York City Police Department and with the Bureau of Identification, Department of Justice, at Washington, D. C.

The officer must make continuous efforts to locate absconders until a five-year period has elapsed. If in that time after following all possible clues there is nothing learned regarding the probationer's whereabouts and periodic clearance of the fingerprints has been made the Court may be requested to grant permission for the case to be closed in the Probation Department and the Warrant filed in the office of the Clerk of the Court. The case may be reopened if the probationer is ever rearrested on another charge or his whereabouts discovered.

3. *Preparing the Report*

(a) The probation officer must initiate a new investigation and become fully informed as to the probationer's activities, conduct, etc.

(b) The probationer is interviewed. Information is secured as to where he has been and his activities while an absconder. What is his explanation for violating probation? What is his present attitude? What are his plans?

(c) A letter is written to the Court setting a date for hearing.

(d) An appointment is made for the probationer's reexamination in the Psychiatric Clinic and a letter sent to Clinic giving a report of the probationer's behavior since the original examination.

(e) The fingerprints are recleared. If the probationer was an absconder, the prints are cleared in the localities where he has resided.

(f) The probationer's home is visited and information as to the family's present circumstances, their attitude toward the probationer and their plans for him are secured.

(g) Information about employment held by probationer while he was an absconder is investigated and verified and any promise of employment he may have are verified.

(h) Data are secured from parole departments if probationer has recently served a sentence. What was his record at the institution? Did he have any examination while there and what is the period he will be under parole supervision?

(i) The content of the report to the Court must make clear whether or not the probationer should be continued on probation. The report is given to the supervisor three days in advance of the date of hearing.

C. Channels of Probation Treatment

Since the probation officer, as a social case worker, is concerned with human relationships and the problems that arise out of them, he is involved in an area not only philosophically but technically elusive. At the inception of supervision, the probation officer has been furnished a body of information about the probationer, his offense, his family, neighborhood, his early life, education, employment history, etc. which has been secured and evaluated by the Division of Investigation. Thereupon he is immediately beset with a number of questions; how shall he interpret this data? Which are the more urgent of the many apparent problems? What are the assets, the liabilities, the treatability, the prognosis or outcome?

This Department has developed a useful and practical method in carrying forward treatment processes by utilizing a schematic analysis which places emphasis on the following eight channels or areas of social activity:

1. Discipline.
2. Health.
3. Family and Neighborhood.
4. Employment.
5. Education.
6. Recreation.
7. Religion.
8. Thrift.

The application of therapy in these channels must not be stereotyped or rigid. The needs of each individual probationer, emotional level, intellectual equipment, social and cultural plane, etc. are the differentials which indicate the nature of the treatment to be applied.

In the utilization of these channels, the probation officer's approach is that of the case worker in any agency setting. However, the Probation Department of the Court of General Sessions must function not only as a case work treatment agency but must always remain cognizant of its responsibilities to the community as a crime prevention and law enforcement agency. Thus there has been evolved in the Probation Department of the Court of General Sessions a methodology of treatment which is peculiar to itself and which to some extent is based upon statutory and judicial mandate.

Statutory enactments and rules of the Court and Probation Department provide for:

Reports of the probationer.

Home visits by the probation officer.

Employment Contacts by the probation officers.

Conditions of Probation set by the court.

Conditions governing restitution, family support, etc.

Violation of Probation, etc.

A. MECHANICS

1. Reports of the Probationer

   (a) Objectives and Value of Personal Reports

       1. As a measure of securing personal contact and interplay of personality between the probationer and probation officer.

       2. As a measure of discipline and oversight. This aspect has two facets, each somewhat reflecting the other: the disciplinary (control) and treatment (educative) process.

          In the probationer's reports the probation officer has a definite and constructive tool for influencing human behavior.

          The use of this tool requires a high order of skill and should become the probation officer's key to that mysterious, complex, perhaps quite disorgan-

171

ized, mental and emotional world of the probationer. Unless used with understanding the process of reporting may become a dispiriting ordeal
to the probationer and thereby defeats its purpose.

(b) Occasion and Frequency of the Report

1. Probation Officers are on duty two nights a week
to receive probationer's reports.

2. The probationer is told to report to his probation
officer in a room set apart, at a prearranged hour
and day of each week. While this schedule is basic,
in certain situations exceptions may be made.
After a detailed study of the problems and after
a conference with the Deputy or Case Supervisor,
written permission may be obtained to require the
probationer to report more or less often, depending on the exigencies of the treatment process.

(c) The Printed Report Card Records

1. A brief resume of the conditions of probation.

2. The period of probation.

3. The name of the probationer and probation
officer.

4. The hour and day of reporting.

5. Space for probation officer's notation of probationer's report.

   This card which remains in the probationer's possession, serves as a reminder of his reporting obligation, and his "receipt" marking its performance.
In this respect the probation officer too has a duty,
that of keeping this continuing periodic appointment which should also have the dignity, obligatory character and prerequisites of any social or
business appointment.

(d) Non-personal Reports

1. Mail

The court may give permission or direct the probationer to report by mail if he resides or is employed permanently or temporarily in a distant jurisdiction. In such cases:

(a) Probation Officer verifies probationer's reason for leaving this jurisdiction by direct communication with relatives and through request for investigation by a local probation department or other cooperating agency. A request is made for the local agency to accept personal reports and countersign mail reports and a summary of the case is forwarded.

(b) Probationer must sign agreement to return to this jurisdiction upon request.

(c) Letter is written to sentencing judge requesting permission for probationer to reside outside court's jurisdiction.

(d) Probationer is supplied with mail report blanks, and given explanations and directions for filling these out including the information regarding the frequency of reports, requirement of local supervision, the avoidance of routine report, this Department's interest in the probationer's problems and offers of aid and advice.

(e) Probation officer should make periodic and prompt replies to probationer's letters. If probationer fails to report, write for explanation within one week.

(f) Communicate with local agency for report on probationer's activities at least once every 3 months.

173

2. Telephone or Other Reports

Telephone reports or reports by relative or friend are unacceptable, except as means of explanation for a temporary condition; such as, illness, exigencies of employment, etc. They must be verified by the probation officer within 24 hours.

(e) Failure to Report

1. When probationer fails to report at the scheduled time, the probation officer must visit his home within 24 hours.

2. If the probationer's whereabouts is unknown:

    (a) Reclear fingerprints and Social Service Exchange immediately.

    (b) Make complete reinvestigation of all of the probationer's recent activities, i.e., home, relatives, place of employment, associates, etc.

    (c) If, within a reasonable period (not later than 2 weeks) the probationer is not located, after a conference with the case supervisor, an application for a Bench Warrant may be made to the court.[6]

2. The Home Visit

(a) Objectives and Values

The home visit emphasizes the personal nature of probation officer's work. How else may the probation officer gain an appreciation of the feelings, attitudes, values, relationships, living conditions, etc.—that are part of the "personality in trouble," whom he undertakes to help constructively. It must be recognized that the family situation of which the probationer's problem may be but one symptom, may require as

_____
[6]Refer to Section "Termination of Probation."

much or more attention and treatment as the individual probationer. The probation officer must therefore be keenly alert to the physical set-up, the emotional atmosphere and the intra-family relationships of which the probationer is a dynamic part. Only in this way can the probation officer fully understand the nature and intricacies of the stimuli and forces which shape the personality of the probationer and to which his behavior may be but a normal response.

(b) Frequency

By Department rule the home is to be visited at least twice a month. If the situation requires intensive treatment or if a probationer has failed to report, additional visits are necessary. Visits may be reduced to one a month after a conference with and the permission of the case supervisor.

3. Employment Contacts

(a) Objectives

The probationer is expected to be gainfully employed. Since his industrial adjustment has direct bearing on his social adjustment, the supervision of the probationer's employment activities is a major responsibility of the probation officer. The following questions must and can be satisfactorily answered by judicious and skillful investigation: Is the probationer satisfied with his job? Is he suited to it and does it offer opportunities for advancement? How is he regarded by his employer? by his fellow workers? Are there any occupational hazards, or objectionable practices or stimuli implicit in the probationer's job situation, such as, unusual temptations to asocial conduct, drinking, stealing, gambling, etc.

(b) Frequency

Rules of the department require at least one employment visit or verification per month.

175

(c) Method

1. If employer is aware of probationer's court status, the probation officer should interpret to him this department's program and objectives, and can frequently elicit that type of interest which will aid the probationer in his employment situation.

2. If the employer is unaware of the probationer's court status, probation officer, with the aid of the case supervisor, must deal with the situation upon an individual basis. The problem of whether or not to inform the employer must be decided on grounds that involve knowledge of all factors such as the probationer himself, his offense, his previous employment, his present position, etc.

   (a) The probation officer must visit the place of employment to note the externals such as the location and set up, and make direct unmistakable verification of the probationer's employment by observing him either coming to, from or at work.

   (b) Without disclosing the probation officer's direct interest in the probationer in question, much can be learned by arranging an interview with the probationer's employer, foreman, personnel director, as part of the technique of uncovering employment possibilities for unemployed probationers.

   (c) Establishment by the probation officer of contacts with trade associations, unions, better business bureaus, investigation departments of banks and insurance companies and such organizations as Dun and Bradstreet are particularly useful where the probationer is an officer of a corporation, or conducts his own business.

176

(d) Wage Verification are made by inspection of weekly wage check or pay envelope at time of probationer's personal report.

Wage verification becomes an exceedingly important issue when the court directs that restitution be made, or obligates the probationer to make family support payments, or where budgeting, household management, thrift, savings, are outstanding problems.

3. Miscellaneous

If the probationer is a salesman, his salesbook will record his earnings. If in business for himself inspection of his account books, bank book and financial statement will show his probable income.

4. Contacts for Vocational and Avocational Training

(a) For the vocationally untrained or misfit

In this group, the probation officer often notes either the probationer's indifference or hostility to training suggestions unless their usefulness in securing employment is very apparent. Here it is advisable to encourage the development of avocations which might help further training or work adjustments, particularly where a probationer shows interest in mechanics, a musical instrument, etc. Training in these as an avocation can be secured at trade or vocational high schools, W. P. A. or adult education courses, extension courses of universities and in numerous private trade schools. The vocationally untrained or misfit probationer may gain valuable insight into his real capabilities by means of a vocational testing series given by trained consultants at the vocational consultation services.

(b) For the probationer who is comparatively well adjusted vocationally

177

The probationer who is satisfied with his position should be encouraged to enlarge the boundaries and scope of his knowledge and skills by attendance at schools for courses both of a cultural nature and those related to his work.

5. Relationship with Other Community and Social Agencies[7]
   The real interdependence existing between probation and nearly every institution and social agency of the community necessitates the development and maintenance of mutually cooperative attitudes in order to avoid waste of time and effort. Towards this end:

   (a) The probation officer should know what services to expect of any given agency, its jurisdiction, scope and limitations.

   (b) The probation officer should be familiar with all community resources, particularly those in the district to which he is assigned.

   (c) Referrals to agencies should be carefully considered and adequately prepared. In referring persons to other agencies the probation officer must pave the way for the agency's service by fully acquainting the prospective client with the function of the agency and by informing the agency of the proposed visit. If necessary submit a detailed summary of contact. Probation officer is not to content himself with the mere referral but is to make every possible effort to see that the objectives of the referral are attained.

Cooperating agencies are utilized

1. For information

   (a) The Social Service Exchange and its registered agencies provide essential social data and clues to further information.

---

[7]Probation Officer is to utilize the Directory of Social Agencies, the Directory of Probation Officers of the United States, Inter-City Agency Directory, etc.

178

(b) Police and other governmental agencies are used for criminal and official investigation, identification and verification of vital statistics, etc.

(c) The probation officer must be fully aware at all times of the probationer's conduct and activities. This knowledge can come only from constant, painstaking and thorough investigation. In addition to utilizing the services of available agencies, the probation officer must seek information and verification from those persons, in addition to the family, who come into direct contact with the probationer in his daily activities. However, unless circumstances demand an official approach the probation officer must make his inquiries among tradesmen, neighbors, friends, co-workers and others who are in a position to furnish tangible information concerning the probationer in a manner which will not jeopardize the probationer's position in the community.

2. For Treatment

(a) Agencies for Specialized Service

Where a case presents a problem for the solution of which a particular agency has special facilities or personnel, the probation officer should make contact with this agency, discuss the problem with its intake representative and make the necessary arrangements for advisory service or referral.

(b) Department of Public Welfare (H. R. B.)

Since a large percentage of probationers or their families are in some way dependent on public relief, the probation officer should know the mechanics and functioning of the Home Relief Bureau. Cooperative relationship with the staff of the district offices is of great value and can best be accomplished by personal contact or conferences on individual cases carried

179

jointly. Through exchange of information and discus
sion of the case, duplication of effort is avoided,
more adequate plan of treatment is evolved, and mor
effective social planning will result. Mutual confidenc
between the Department and the Home Relief Burea
is essential. The probation officer is expected to dis
close to the Home Relief Bureau all pertinent factua
information in his possession concerning the proba
tioner and his relatives; such as, places of residenc
employment, earnings, financial resources, etc.

B. CHANNELS

1. DISCIPLINE

To subject probationers to the normal regimentation whic
makes for orderly life is of course the essential task fc
the Probation Department, but further than that, the prc
bation officer must, in the development of his program o
discipline, bring about results which develop resource
within the probationer. The development of a program o
discipline which will inculcate habits of industry, restrain
consideration for the rights of others and the developmer
of an attitude of obedience and acceptance of normal code
of conduct, represent fundamental objectives. These ob
jectives will not be attained, however, through any mecl
anized approach to the problems of those on probation c
by any routinized methods of dealing with them. Th
probation officer must bring to the probationer a servic
which is far-reaching and enduring. To do this, it is neces
sary for him to study the probationer as an individual; t
learn to what influences he reacts; to know how to mee
his needs; and to substitute understanding for force an
scientific knowledge for aimless meddling.

To achieve this the probation officer must utilize purpo
ive, impersonalized authority and discipline. The proba
tioner should be brought to recognize that the source c
authority is society; that it functions, in his case, throug

180

the court and the medium of the probation officer. The probationer must be brought to recognize that if he is to live a normal, well adjusted life, it is necessary that he conform to certain definite authoritarian requirements, not only insofar as his relationship to probation is concerned but also and most important as it affects his life in the community.

In dealing with the facet of discipline the probation officer must never lose sight of the fact that the aim is not repression but the effecting of real and permanent changes in the habits and attitudes of the individual and the family.

This obviously cannot be gained by mere rigid disciplinary requirements such as routine reporting and overt compliance adduced only because of fear of consequences of misbehavior. In using authority the probation office should base his approach upon the following interrelated data:

1. Authority in the life of the probationer
   (a) How has the probationer reacted to authority in the past?

      In interpreting factual material concerning the life experience of the probationer, in order to exercise a purposive authority and discipline, the probation officer must consider:

      1. Offense
         (a) Was it committed alone?
         (b) Was it committed with others?
            1. Was the probationer the leader or follower?

         (c) Motivating factors
            1. What did the offense mean to him in terms of satisfying his needs?
            2. Was the motive immediate or underlying?

3. What are the possibilities of another
offense being committed; how good a
probation risk is he?

2. Placement on Probation

(a) Attitudes of probationer

1. Is it only an escape from incarceration?
2. Will it glorify him with his group?
3. Is it a disgrace?
4. Does he sense an opportunity for self-develop-
ment?
5. What needs does the probationer recognize in
himself and to what extent can capacity for this
recognition be developed?
6. Does he show any feeling of personal responsibility or does he project his guilt upon his
environment or others?
7. Does he say or imply that if he had a job or
if he had his physical needs supplied adequately
he would not have committed offense?
8. How does he react to probationary regulations?

(a) Has he an intelligent appreciation of their
purpose?
(b) Is he inclined to accept them without question?
(c) Does he fight against every restriction of
what he believes is the liberty to which he
is entitled?

(b) Probationer's recognition of his needs:

1. Economic level

(a) Can he understand the cause and effect
relationship between training, preparation

for employment and his economic situation?

(b) How has the depression or relief affected him?

(c) Does he look upon probation as an extension of the relief set up; does he consider probation as just another welfare agency that will supply material wants?

2. Emotional Level

(a) Has he a sense of frustration? Does he feel that his desire for adventure, for experimentation, for finding out things for himself is blocked?

(b) Has he a feeling of security, of understanding with his family and others, or the reverse?

(c) Family Situation—Treatment may often have to be directed toward parents and other members of the family in addition to the probationer. Often it may be necessary to relieve tensions in family relationships before anything can be done to treat probationer.

3. The Disciplinary Aspects of Probation

(a) These are manifested in certain requirements imposed by statute, by the Court and by the Department. It is incumbent upon both probationer and probation officer to adhere to these regulations and of prime importance that their purpose and value be understood.

1. Reports.

2. Home visits.

3. Employment contacts.

4. Family Support Payments.

5. Conditions of probation as prescribed by the Code of Criminal Procedure.

6. Other conditions of probation which may be specifically set by the court, viz., not to drive automobile; remain away from particular neighborhood; not to annoy wife, etc., etc.

4. Imposition of Authority

(a) The application of authority is based upon the analysis and interpretation of the data outlined above. Its effectiveness is dependent upon the understanding and insight of the probation officer. If the probation officer is confronted with a disciplinary problem, with which he is unable to cope, he must discuss the situation with the case supervisor.

The latter after a perusal of the case record, an interview with the probationer, and if necessary with members of his family may:

1. Make recommendations regarding the situation.

2. Reassign the case to another officer if the disciplinary problem appears to be a manifestation of an emotional conflict between the probationer and his officer.

3. If the probationer has absconded, outline the steps necessary to discover his whereabouts and fix the period for the re-investigation.

4. Direct the officer to request the issuance of a bench warrant.

184

2. HEALTH

The physical and mental health of the probationer determine to a large degree both his capacity and will to respond to probation treatment. The responsibility of the probation officer with respect to problems of physical health is well stated by Dr. Maurice J. Karpf when he says:

> "The case worker should be prepared to recognize the manifestations of the common diseases and should also know the elements of their treatment and prognosis; should know something about the causes of these diseases; should be informed on the relative contagiousness and infectiousness of the diseases as well as the means for carrying them from person to person; should have at least rudimentary knowledge of principles of hygiene and some knowledge on resistance and immunity."[8]

The implications inherent in physical disorders are relatively obvious and the diagnosis of physical pathology is well established by medical science. In the realms of the mind and the emotions the probation officer is confronted with problems which cannot be resolved as easily. The diagnosis and proper evaluation of those personality traits which play a large part in shaping the behavior patterns of offenders require extended and searching inquiry. The psychiatric approach to these problems has been welcomed by this department. In order to develop plans of treatment which will be practical and which will have constructive results, every person on probation must be examined either in the court clinic or by an independent psychiatrist. The processes of mental and behavioristic growth are confusing to those without specialized training and cannot be positively determined as consecutive steps even by the psychiatrist. The probation officer in order to determine the factors which motivate these processes, should seek the scientific aid which the psychiatrist offers.

[8]Karpf, Maurice J., *The Scientific Basis of Social Work.*

Physical examinations of probationers for the determination of physical capacities and of physical limitations
and ills are also conducted in the Court Clinic. In physical conditions may lie, to some extent, the answer to
behavior patterns. In a sense of inferiority induced
by physical handicaps and diseases, may lie the germ of
an offender's gangster growth.

The probation officer must guard against arbitrarily imposing his own pet notions of mental and physical health
upon the probationer. The necessity of treatment, based
upon medical authority, must be presented on the basis of
the probationer's understanding, interests, ambitions, needs
and desires. Unless the probationer's condition is a menace to others in the community or he is mentally incapable
of self-direction, he has the right to decide for himself
whether he desires to submit to operative or medical measures. The probation officer's task is to help the probationer
and his family to develop insight into their health needs
and to give definite aid in procuring medical diagnosis and
treatment.

A. The problem of health, mental or physical, is an underlying factor responsible for many disturbances in
   conduct.

   1. Though some individuals suffering from poor health
      or mental ills are able to adjust in a relatively satis-
      factory manner, others, for a variety of reasons, do
      not. Hence their maladjustment may result in:

      (a) Vocational instability or vocational incapacity

      (b) Poor judgment, resentment against life, com-
          pensatory devices of anti-social character.

      (c) Discouragement and a desire to live intensely
          leading into delinquent conduct (cardiac and
          tubercular cases).

      (d) Commission of anti-social acts in order to se-
          cure sense of power (use of revolver, etc.)

186

B. The probation officer must attempt in every way to help the probationer improve habits of personal hygiene, to correct physical disabilities and to bring to bear available resources to alleviate mental or emotional difficulties whenever they appear. This he must do by persuasion, by utilization of health agencies and by the distribution and interpretation of pamphlets on health and hygiene which are available in this Department. This approach is effective at times in aiding probationers to become happier, more responsible and socially well-adjusted citizens, viz.:

1. Inculcation of simple habits of hygiene results in improved health and outlook.

2. Removal of skin blemishes results in gaining of self-confidence and self-reliance.

3. Removal of defects in hearing or speech increases self-confidence, promotes vocational efficiency and eliminates excessive introversion.

4. Obtaining of artificial limbs makes probationers more secure and often economically self sustaining.

5. Care and instruction to cardiac and tubercular sufferers result in more hopeful probationers, capable of performing designated duties in selected vocations.

C. Psychiatric Clinic

At the inception of supervision the probation officer has in his possession a detailed report from the Psychiatric Clinic which presents the psychiatric diagnosis, the intelligence rating, the physical and neurological diagnosis and where necessary recommendations for treatment.

1. If the report needs clarification the probation officer must confer with the clinic as to an interpretation of the findings and elaboration of recommendations.

2. Conference must be held with examining psychiatrist to determine whether or not the diagnosis in full or in part should be divulged to or interpreted for the probationer.

3. If probation officer discovered a pathological condition, mental or physical, which escaped detection at the time of the initial examination, a conference with the psychiatrist preparatory to reexamination is held.

4. Psychiatric treatment may be arranged for at the clinic

D. Other Heal Agency Resources

Since the physical limitations of the court clinic do not permit an extensive treatment service the manifold health agency resources of the city should be utilized.[9] More often than not the probationer or his family have only a vague realization of the available treatment and preventative resources simply because of lack of knowledge. The probation officer's task must be one of education and persuasion in order to overcome obstacles arising out of fear and ignorance of the principles and practices of mental and physical hygiene.

1. The probation officer can teach habits of personal cleanliness and simple hygiene measures such as ventilation, cleanliness in the home, washing of hair, cleaning of teeth, etc.

2. The indicated procedures for referrals must be followed and the probation officer must check on the progress of the treatment by letter or personal contact with the agency. Where a serious health problem exists calling for intensive service, a conference with the social service department of the hos-

---

[9]See Directory of Social Agencies.

pital or agency used is arranged, a summary of the record is forwarded and the problem followed to its conclusion; a written report from the cooperating health agency must be made part of the case record.

3. The probation officer can meet the immediate health needs of the probationer and his family by referrals to mental hygiene, dental, medical, and venereal clinics, conveniently located hospitals, the Department of Health, visiting nurse services, etc.

4. Follow-up psychiatric care may be secured at agencies such as the Neurological Institute, the Vanderbilt Clinic, the New York Hospital, Lenox Hill Hospital, Bellevue Hospital, etc.

5. This Department makes available summer camps for under-privileged children of probationers through Fresh Air Funds of newspapers, lodges and family service agencies. Probation officers must keep records of those children who can be benefited by this service.

E. It is not possible to outline procedures of treatment to cover all of the many and diverse health problems which the probation officer will meet. However, the following examples should provide necessary assistance.

1. Family health work—It should be emphasized that the interest of this Department in problems of mental and physical health is not restricted to the probationer but includes all members of his family. The probation officer should:

   (a) Improve standards of health and habits of hygiene where necessary.

   (b) Secure prenatal, confinement and post-natal care where necessary.

189

(c) Enlist cooperation of visiting nurse services, clinics, hospitals, diet kitchens, etc.

2. Venereal Diseases

   (a) Education of probationer and family to the danger of venereal infection.

   (b) Pamphlets regarding these diseases are to be given to the probationer and their import and value discussed both as a preventative measure and an aid in cure.

   (c) Examinations to determine whether or not an individual is infected may be secured at the Psychiatric Clinic of the Court, the Venereal Disease Clinic of the Board of Health, various hospitals, etc.

   (d) Treatment must be secured for infected probationers either through their private physicians or through the venereal disease clinics of the Board of Health or at city or private hospitals.

   (e) Special attention must be given to families of probationers who suffer from a venereal disease. Probation officer must explain to the probationer the necessity of exercising care so that others do not become infected. He must be persuaded to inform his immediate family of his condition. If he refuses to do this the aid of the treatment agency must be enlisted for this purpose. As a last resort probation officer must himself acquaint the members of the family with the probationer's condition.

   (f) Arrangement must be made for examination of those members of the family who may have been infected and when necessary, treatment must be secured for them.

3. Probationers refusing out-patient treatment for contagious or infectious diseases must be institutionalized.

4. Tuberculars or others suffering from chronic ailments should be subjected to periodic examinations and necessary treatment must be secured. The probation officer has a responsibility to see that families and others are protected from contagion.

5. Physical disorders, such as encephalitis, which are characterized by behavior symptoms and personality changes must be kept under careful probation and medical observation.

6. The physically disabled or those suffering from various forms of mental diseases or emotional tensions often require special vocational counselling and training. This may be obtained from organizations such as the Institute for Crippled and Disabled, the State Department of Social Welfare, the W. P. A. Consultation Service, the New York Adult Education Council, etc.

D. Procedure Prior to Discharge

1. Prior to discharge, re-examination in the Psychiatric Clinic of the Court or at another clinic, is secured to ascertain whether or not successful progress has been made in treating the disability. If continued treatment is advisable, follow-up care with some outside agency is to be arranged prior to discharge.

2. Probationers, on discharge, are to be urged to keep in touch with their probation officers. The interest of the probation officer in a case must not cease upon discharge and, in many instances, the probation officer may be able to render effective and continued aid to the man or his family, thus insuring the permanency of the adjustment effected.

3. FAMILY AND NEIGHBORHOOD

Through the family we trace the roots of the individual. His family usually represents his place in the social scale and the influences which are thrown about him in his family life are as far reaching as any other contacts which he makes. His social codes find their bases in this fabric and to a large extent he gives expression in his daily life to the influences which play upon him in these relationships. The attitudes of parents, friction and discord, lack of sympathy and understanding, neglect and antagonism both subtle and apparent, all have their place in the making of the offender.

Family disorganization, congestion, economic incompetency, poverty, lax behavior, or a broken home, are problems to which every probation officer must actively apply himself if he is to have any hope of changing the mental attitudes which result in behavior patterns conflicting with the law.

Each probationer is a part of a unit and that unit is the family. To meet the needs of the family, to bring about an adjustment of its problems, is to bring about the solution of some of the probationer's problems. To build up the family economically and socially means the rendering of a similar service to the probationer. With this building up process which must be educational and practical, the entire family is aided to develop a higher sense of group responsibility.

The probation officer must at all times recognize that he is working on a family case work basis. He should utilize all the agencies and individuals that can cooperate in his work with the family—from the Social Service Exchange to the patrolman on the neighborhood beat.

The probation officer's work in the Family and Neighborhood area may, for reasons of clarity and simplicity, be divided into two phases, (a) psychological and (b) material and economic. The psychological aspect pertains to

192

the development of attitudes conducive to the acceptance and carrying through a plan of treatment. The probation officer at this stage already has considerable data on the family set-up, their attitudes toward each other, toward the probationer, toward social institutions, the apparent and submerged difficulties and the nature and extent of conflicts among the group. The probation officer is in a position to act impartially as guide, friend and adviser in the effort to resolve these problems and conflicts. The probation officer should at all times be aware of his limitations. In problems which necessarily require special treatment which he is unable to provide, he must enlist the aid of the best qualified special services and expert advice that are available. In addition to further interpreting and continuing the investigation initiated, the probation officer in entering into the family situation should recognize:

A. Psychological Level

1. The acceptance or rejection of the Probation Officer: What emotional tensions, preconceptions and prejudices are present because of the probation officer's authoritative position?

2. The probationer and his family

   (a) Does the probationer assume his rightful place in the family group; is he submissive or domineering; does he recognize his responsibilities; can he assume them; how does delinquency affect probationer's status in group?

   (b) Are there present any undue tensions in the home? Is there present disintegration and overt or concealed antagonism; is it a closely knit, affectionate group; are there problems arising out of conflicting ideologies; is there present undue conflict between foreign born parents and native born children, etc.?

(c) Are there present problems originating from mental or physical health and what is their effect on the probationer and his family?

(d) What, if any, is the effect of the physical conditions of the home upon the probationer or the other members of his family?

(e) Are any other members of the family delinquent and what is the effect upon probationer and the family group?

(f) Do the cultural and social standards of the group make for difficulties in environmental relationships?

(g) If the probationer lives alone, how is he affected by isolation?

B. Economic and Material Level

1. The neighborhood—Its quality; influences for good and evil; racial complexion; housing; crowding; gambling; prostitution; inadequate play space for children, etc.

2. The Household

(a) Economic status; comfortable, average, poor; dependence upon relief.

(b) Income and contribution of probationer.

(c) Living conditions; number of rooms, rental, number in household; number of lodgers.

(d) Reputation and social status of family.

(e) What social service agencies are ar have been interested in the group.

(f) Probation officer must make opportunities to meet all the members of the family group including lodgers and also note both casual and habitual visitors to the home.

194

C. Treatment

1. Problems on Psychological Level

   (a) Probation officer must relieve and overcome tension precipitated by his authoritative position through the influence of his personality, his offers of help and his performance of concrete services for the family group.

   (b) Problems emanating from the family situation must be resolved on an individual basis.

2. Problems on an Environmental Level

   (a) Where desirable and practical induce change to better neighborhood.

   (b) Where not practical for family to move.

      1. Join with authorities in effort to eradicate objectionable features.

      2. Help the probationer to gain insight into the deteriorating influences of part of his environment so that he will restrict his activities to the desirable features.

   (c) The probation officer must be thoroughly acquainted with the recreational, religious, health, employment and social service resources of the neighborhood so that he can utilize these resources for the material improvement of the probationer and his family.

   (d) Through inexpensive outlays by the family the probation officer can effect improvement in the appearance of the furnishings and in other ways make the home atmosphere brighter and more congenial.

   (e) In carrying out the foregoing the probation officer must give practical consideration to the economic status, aesthetic standards, cultural level and emotional tone of the family.

4. EMPLOYMENT

We have found that many probationers are mechanically apt and require only the guidance and stimulation of interest to accept the training which will fit them for competition in industry. Vocational testing, vocational guidance and job referral represent available services that should not be overlooked. Probation always has the grave problem of unemployment to cope with. Every effort must be made to place in trade schools those who can profit by special training not only as an aid toward economic adjustment, but also to prevent probationers from loitering about the streets in idleness. For the probationer to be self-supporting and economically adequate is of primary importance to him as well as to the community. Regular employment of a satisfying nature is a character building discipline.

The probation officer must have knowledge of the employment possibilities in the city, the opportunities for vocational training, the techniques of industrial adjustment and the methods which must be utilized in job hunting. The responsibilities of the probation officer are:

A. For the employed probationer

1. In analyzing the probationer's job and possibilities therein, the probation officer must be cognizant of the relation of the probationer's past employment history and periods of unemployment to his present situation; is the probationer's occupation permanent, temporary, skilled or unskilled; are the working conditions good; is his wage commensurate with his work and ability; opportunities for advancement; relationship with fellow workers, etc.; the evaluation of the probationer's reaction to his job is of primary importance.

196

2. The probation officer must make every effort to remove the probationer from blind alley jobs which may develop frustrations, antagonisms and rebelliousness. Every effort must be made to see that the probationer is employed in a position suited to his capabilities and temperament and which possesses opportunities for advancement. In developing plans toward this end the probation officer must not arbitrarily impose his ideas upon the probationer but must permit the latter to follow his own inclinations to a reasonable degree. If the probationer is permitted to experiment, he will eventually accept the probation officer's plans more wholeheartedly—especially if he has had part in their development. The probationer must be informed of the facilities for vocational training and persuaded to pursue courses in public or private schools (Refer to Education) in order to broaden his opportunities for employment and to enhance his value to his present employer.

B. For the unemployed probationer

1. Technique of Job Hunting

The probationer's involvement in criminal behavior, subsequent emotional stress, the strain of incarceration, court process, loss of caste, and severe drain on his and his family's limited financial resources often creates in him a sense of frustration, helplessness, and bitterness. These may lead to sloth and confirmed economic incompetency. The major problem is to create in the probationer a desire for gainful employment and the material and emotional satisfaction which it brings. Most probationers, not unlike any unselected group of the general population, are lacking in the ability to attack a problem efficiently, planfully and with adequate knowledge of the factors involved.

197

In job placement the probation officer has an opportunity to help the probationer analyze his problem in an objective way.

(a) What marked personality problems does the probationer present? How do they affect his employability? How can they be mitigated?

(b) Has the probationer any outstanding skill or interest that can be capitalized?

(c) What material resources, family or business connections are available?

(d) How can he utilize the public and private employment agency resources.

(e) Does the probationer know how to apply for a job at a department store, a factory, an insurance company, a transit corporation, or a local retail establishment?

(f) When any kind of a job is urgently needed does the probationer know how to determine when and if an industry or trade has its peak demand for workers?

(g) What is the best way of canvassing prospective employers?

(h) Should the probationer create his own job, i.e., go into business for himself even in a limited way?

(i) How can he be made more employable?

(j) When employed what methods must be used to make him more valuable to an employer?

5. EDUCATION

It is well known that education materially affects the personality of an individual, broadens his outlook and gives him understanding. The education of those with whom the probation officer deals is at best fragmentary and in many

198

instances, the probationer has not even completed the grammar school grades. To deal adequately with his needs, it is often necessary to stimulate his interest in a world outside of his limited vision or experience, while to establish him as a productive social unit often requires training and at times re-education.

It has been shown that those who are placed on probation are not so much anti-social as they are non-social. This attitude has been due to their lack of appreciation of their obligation to their fellows. The awakening of a sense of responsibility is an educational process for which many approaches are available.

The educational handicaps which have been found present among probationers and which are present of course in the population as a whole may be grouped into three classifications.

1. Mental defect.

2. Personality disorders.
   (a) Undesirable behavior patterns are frequently concomitant with meagre educational achievement.
   (b) The deviate personality is frequently maladjusted educationally and possesses hazy reality contacts.
   (c) Nervous blockages are frequently an indication of educational failure caused by or resulting in lack of initiative, feelings of inferiority, etc.
   (d) Environmental impingements, such as fatiguing employment, unusual, irregular hours of work, family needs, etc. often militate against educational progress.

3. Educational Background
   (a) Poor preparation due to the incidence of truancy, absence from school due to illnesses, court appearance, family difficulties, etc.

199

(b) Lack of adequately developed habits of concentration and thinking, with resultant confusion discouragement and fatigue.

(c) Over-valuation of personally formulated experience.

(d) Lack of interest in and capacity for further formal education.

(e) Lack of parental interest in or indifference to formal education.

(f) Misguided ambitions frequent in delinquent areas and families.

The Probation Officer's task is:

1. To help the probationer develop insight into his educational and vocational lacks or needs and to awaken in him a desire for education to further vocational or cultural aims.

2. To interpret to the probationer the opportunities for further educational training along the lines of his interests and abilities.

3. To realistically present the greater employment opportunities available to those with adequate education and specialized training.

4. To enlist the aid of those who can influence the probationer to participate in an educational program designed to meet his needs.

5. To provide the probationer with concrete services to assist him to attain his objective.

In planning an educational program for the probationer, the probation officer must bear in mind that it is to be based upon the probationer's own capacity and interests and that its aim is two-fold:

1. To further the probationer's academic and vocational development.

2. To inculcate in the probationer favorable habits and traits such as concentration and perseverance towards the completion of a program in order to attain a definite objective.

Furthermore the probation officer must be cognizant of and be prepared to meet obstacles to further education such as the following:

1. Community, school and family attitudes resulting from the stigma of crime, etc.
2. Feelings of discouragement and disgrace due to offense and consequent defeatist attitude.
3. Economic necessity and long or unsuitable hours of employment.
4. Unless tactfully handled the probation officer's contacts with school authorities may militate against probationer's adjustment as the latter may thereafter be regarded as a potential problem.
5. Multiplicity of conditions and circumstances such as over-age., family responsibilities, etc.

A careful evaluation of the probationer's past educational progress precedes any attempt at planning an educational program. This study must include the probationer's failures and their causes, his aptitudes and capacity; his interests and desires; his handicaps and limitations.

The problem of further education is not limited merely to formal schooling. Planning educational programs may be divided into the following three broad categories, which in whole or in part can be made applicable to all probationers.

1. Informal
   (a) Aiding the probationer to affiliate himself with civic and cultural groups; having him attend lectures, forums, discussion groups, etc.

(b) Urging the probationer to read books, periodicals and magazines and discussing these with him.

(c) Having the probationer join the New York Public Library.

(d) Preparing reading lists for the probationer which are suited to his mental capacity and related to his interests.

(e) Utilizing the services of the Reader's Adviser of the New York Public Library to develop reading interests and prepare lists for the probationer.

2. Formal[10]

(a) Board of Education: day and evening public schools for academic and vocational training.

(b) W. P. A. Program, classes in academic, cultural and vocational courses.

(c) Civilian Conservation Corps Education Classes.

(d) Private Commercial Schools.

(e) Universities—both for collegiate and technical study as well as for extension courses.

3. Counselling Services

(a) Adult Education Council.

(b) Board of Education.

(c) W. P. A. Educational Counselling Service.

6. RECREATION

The quest for new experience and for adventure to offset the humdrum and often depressing influences of home environment, appears as one of the impelling influences which drive boys and young men to associate with disorderly companions in groups or gangs. The desire for association

---

[10]Consult Bulletins provided by the Division of Supervision and utilize the services of the Adult Education Council of which this Department is a member.

with those who are congenial and whose codes of conduct are more or less similar to their own, also impels them to participate in the recreation which they find desirable.

Commercialized forms of amusement, such as the undesirable poolrooms are so often the congregating points for groups from which delinquents are recruited. Centers of commercialized amusement, where low standards of conduct are tolerated, have in a large measure influenced and weakened the offender before he appears in the court. A program of spare time activities which has value in building character and which serves to enlarge the social consciousness of the probationer must be substituted. To be effective it must be an interesting and satisfying substitute for the glamour and lure of the unwholesome recreational activities from which the probationer is to be diverted.

It has been the objective of the Probation Department to drive home to the community through constant repetition, the thought that as the youth of the community is conserved through supervised and properly directed leisure, so will this city profit by removing the influences which contribute to the development of delinquency. The probation officer should remember that monotony, loneliness, routine jobs and isolation from normal social activities distort the personality and may predispose probationers toward asocial conduct. The misuse of leisure time is often due to the probationer's ignorance. He should be brought to realize that recreational outlets which are creative and socially desirable can provide him with interest and a maximum amount of satisfaction.

A. Any recreational program for the probationer must be based upon the following interrelated data:

    1. Community recreational resources.

    2. The probationer's interests, resistances, needs and inner capacities in relation to the community resources.

3. The probationer's familial, vocational and social adjustment.

B. A planned recreational program must revolve about the following three essentials:

1. Determination of the recreational needs of probationer:

   (a) Does he find sufficient outlet within the family circle for desirable recreational activities?

   (b) Is he lonely and does he feel unwanted?

   (c) Does he withdraw from social or group activities?

   (d) Has he any hobbies or particular interests, viz., stamp collecting, music, mechanical pursuits, athletics, etc.?

2. Awakening in the probationer an awareness of his needs, a desire for their satisfaction and concretely aiding him:

   (a) By informing probationer of the existence of community resources with which probation officer must be thoroughly familiar.

   (b) By persuading him to avail himself of these facilities.

   (c) By making personal contacts for the probationer.

3. Redirection of harmful activities into socially accepted channels:

   (a) By consulting probationer's own tastes and inclinations.

   (b) By breaking down old behavior patterns through providing new contacts and associations.

(c) By suggestion and arousing curiosity.

(d) By inducing experimentation in new types of recreation.

C. The Probation Officer can and must be of assistance to all probationers and, where possible, to members of their families in either developing or fostering recreational programs based upon individual and group satisfactions. He can approach this problem through one or more of the following facets:

1. Reading—those probationers capable of deriving satisfaction from books can be directed to make a fuller use of the public libraries with whom we have a working arrangement or be encouraged to develop desirable reading habits. Reading lists should be supplied either by the probation officer or by the Reader's Adviser of the New York Public Library.

2. Neighborhood Settlement House or Recreation Centre—here the probation officer must often accompany the probationer but not before he has prepared the ground by a confidential discussion with the club leader or director of the Settlement House or Recreational Centre, cautioning him about disclosing the probationer's status and arranging for a personal interest in the probationer's recreational problem.

3. Hobbies—these may be fostered through bringing to the attention of the probationer organized groups, such as stamp collecting clubs, hiking groups, athletic associations, sportsmen's clubs, aviation mechanics, civic organizations, etc.

4. Church—through church memebrship manifold recreational facilities are available, such as, dramatics, athletic activities, cadet corps, dances, etc.

205

5. National Guard—enrollment herein provides desirable supervised outlet which includes discipline and athletics, as well as social activities.

6. Athletics—playgrounds, gymnasia, public school evening recreational centers, neighborhood teams industrial, labor and union athletic leagues, etc.

7. Miscellaneous—the probation officer should be aware of, and in touch with, the vast recreational facilities not mentioned above such as the theatre and concerts, both private and W. P. A. fostered; the radio, public lectures, educational programs, open forums, museums, etc. For the younger members of the probationer's family, the probation officer must utilize, in addition to the foregoing, neighborhood outdoor facilities such as parks and play streets, etc.

7. RELIGION

The church has been justly called one of the most important agencies of social control, discipline and education which exists in the community. Our surveys reveal that the age of offenders has been slowly descending through the years, and in recent years the graver crimes have been perpetrated by youthful offenders. The majority of these offenders have drifted away from the influence of the church for a variety of reasons. To bring them back to this constructive influence has been the every day problem of the probation officers.

To enlist the aid of the church is to bring to the probationer a more far-reaching influence than casual church attendance. It involves a recognition of the traditional authoritative role of the church as the interpreter and arbiter of the moral law. In addition to religious influences, probationers derive benefit from participation in the diverse activities which the churches today are providing.

Only by knowing the particular spiritual and religious needs of the probationer and his family as well as the religious resources and activities within the community, can the probation officer effectively aid the probationer.

The probation officer may help develop in his probationers a sincere appreciation of religion through personal contact with the religious leaders of the different faiths. By drawing within this orbit those probationers who can be induced to respond, the desired ends may be attained.

8. THRIFT

Crimes of acquisitiveness are an invasion of the property rights of the community. Generally speaking, those who commit this type of crime have no consideration for the property rights of others because they possess so little of material value themselves. To teach them to conserve their earnings so that their sense of security can be developed, is to give them a feeling of confidence and responsibility plus the knowledge that possessions honestly acquired are entitled to those safeguards which the state, through its laws, throws about every person.

However, before they can be taught to conserve their earnings, those on probation and their families must be taught to make a wise allocation of them.

The family budget is nothing new. It has been utilized with good effect by every social agency dealing with family problems. A proper disbursement of income has far-reaching effects upon the stability of family life and upon the mental attitudes of those who make up the family group. The unwise dissipation of income and the mortgaging of future earnings mean that a period of stress will some time appear.

The development of security means the building of resources. This Department urges that such resources be created in each case through savings accounts and life insurance. In addition, the development of habits of thrift is a tool in self discipline and education which is of primary importance.

Although it is apparent that a large number of probationers are unable, because of economic insecurity, to save large sums, even minimum wage earners, excluding of course recipients of relief, can be taught to save systematically even if the sums saved are themselves meagre. In developing this channel of approach the officer must take extreme care to correlate it with the adjustment process as a whole and weigh carefully the probationer's temperament, his needs and his economic level. If the probation officer's approach is tactful and planned, he will find that compliance which may have been based initially upon obedience will be translated into an active interest in personal finance management, carrying with it the satisfaction of achievement.

The objectives of this channel are:

1. To aid the probationer to gain insight into his need for saving and to make him aware of how he can establish some form of financial reserve, no matter how small.

2. To assist the probationer to utilize his income in the manner which will best satisfy his needs and at the same time afford him with the maximum possible satisfaction.

3. To prevail upon the probationer to live within his income by curbing extravagant habits, gambling, unnecessary installment purchasing, etc.

4. To develop feeling of security based upon some form of financial reserve.

5. To develop feeling of responsibility by having the probationer so arrange his expenses as to take adequate care of his responsibilities.

6. To develop a respect for the property rights of others by having the probationer acquire some assets, no matter how limited.

The thrift program utilized by the Department and which is applicable to all probationers in whole or in part can be divided into three categories:

1. Management.
   (a) Household.
   (b) Personal.
2. Savings Account.
3. Insurance.

The probation officer can best inculcate habits of thrift by:

1. Reasoning on the bases of social and economic improvement, future security, future educational activity, purchase of necessary wants such as furniture, etc., establishment of own business, desire to provide for dependents, etc.

2. Finding more desirable uses for moneys hitherto expended indiscriminately by appealing to vanity or pride, such as, saving for clothing or particular object.

3. Developing of budgets, both personal and family.

4. Utilizing services of cooperating agencies, such as the family service departments of Catholic Charities, Jewish Social Service Association, the Institute of Family Service, etc. which deal specifically with problems of household management.

5. Utilizing pamphlets, publications and budgets issued by social agencies, banks, and insurance companies.

D. RECORDING

Case recording in a Probation Department is social case recording with the added factor that it is official documentation. The purposes of case recording are as obvious as the businessman's bookkeeping system or the scientist's records of experiments.

The case record to serve the purpose for which it is intended must contain tangible, vital information. It must clearly reflect the status of a case at certain period, the general objective conditions and also must portray the probationer as an individual personality, the problem area, the plan of treatment and its progress. "The primary purpose of the case record is to improve the quality of service to the client and to help us understand him and his situation."[11] The following objectives are basic in this Department:

1. To record performance or non-performance of obligations created by law, such as: probationer's reports, record of home visit or employment verification, restitution and family support payments or other specific Court Orders.

2. To provide statistical data as required by law or for administrative, criminological or social research purposes.

3. To portray the techniques which the probation officer uses in diagnosis and treatment; and to provide a gauge by which the quality of his service can be improved.

4. To provide a basis of efficient, rapid and useful direction and evaluation by the supervisor of the probation officer's work.

---

[11]Gordon Hamilton, *Social Case Recording.*

5. To be used as an educative tool for the probation officer and the Department and to help develop a body of knowledge which will aid society to formulate programs for crime prevention and treatment.

Methods of recording vary according to the type and aim of human activity sought to be recorded and each has problems peculiar to itself. Recording in a Probation Department has its unique problems. One has already been mentioned—what may be termed its legalism. Others are found in the varying and complex problems of administration, personnel, economy, etc.

Cases cannot be selected nor discharged at will. Hence, the case load of the department at all times consists of probation types which vary from the offender capable of self direction under supervision to cases that require intensive long range treatment. All must be supervised and records of probationary treatment must be kept through the appointed periods of probation which vary from two years to five years or more, averaging three years.

Furthermore, there are "conditions of probation" that must be satisfied by the probationer and recorded by the probation officer, as for example personal or mail reports, home visits, and employment verifications, payment of restitution, etc., etc.

In the light of the limitations and problems briefly mentioned above, this Department has been constantly experimenting in the interests of greater efficiency, improved methodology and advancing standards of social work.

One of the earliest forms of case recording used in this Department and elsewhere was the "chronological entry," a diary type, recording events and facts as they happen. The advantage of this type of recording consists in its simplicity and its adaptability to almost any type of social work. Its advantages are most apparent in an agency with a highly selective case load and intensive administrative supervision, where services are highly diversified and cases are "active" for relatively short periods of time. The objections to the chronological entry type of recording carried over a protracted period of time is that it often creates a

211

confusing record, and a collection of a considerable mass of usually unselected data of insignificant content. In probation agencies where repetitive data is obligatory and case loads are heavy, the chronological method presents the danger of creating the mechanical repetition of a formula.

The last ten years have witnessed changes in definitions and outlook in social work and practices. Although treatment has always been the main objective, the variations in recording practice were based on the weight given to the factual data, to diagnosis or interpretation, to family relations and to the actual treatment process. Attempted orientation of records toward a truer and more pragmatic focus is still going on. This Department has tried to give one form of expression to this dynamic process in its recording method.

The first step was the development of the preliminary investigation techniques and the format of the report to the Court—a sequential topically arranged social and legal history which includes an interpretation of the various personality and environmental factors which combined to create conflict with society.

(Refer to Investigation Methodology.)

Since it was felt that the chronological method of dictation was inadequate, a committee consisting of the members of the staff of this Department was organized in the Fall of 1934 to study the problem of case recording. The result was the formulation of an outline to be used as a guide and aid to the probation officer in organizing his material before and as he records it.

Since the outline is not to be followed mechanically, a periodic summary narrative form was decided upon as providing a degree of flexibility for presentation of a coherent, integrated picture of fact or event in logical sequence, with an opportunity for interpretation and diagnosis.

Experimentation revealed that the monthly summary, for the purposes of this Department provides an individualized, more coherent, better integrated record. With the outline before him the probation officer should be stimulated to, and reminded of not only the immediate problem, but periodic reformulation and re-evaluation of plan of treatment, adequacy of process, and the play of the personality on personalities involved within the total milieu.

Another problem the solution of which was sought primarily as a measure of economy, is the satisfaction of the statutory requirements (reports, visits, etc.) by their representation by a simple code placed at the head of the periodic summary. To simplify somewhat the problem of executive supervision and case reading, significant changes, factual or diagnostic, are to be emphasized by underlining. For the same reason, marginal headings are used to indicate for the sake of clarity, certainty, and emphasis, facts of legalistic import such as new arrests, Court hearings, etc. After long experimentation, a new outline was devised for the Initial Entry which marks the point of departure from the investigation record to the supervision case history, bearing in mind that both are parts of the integrated whole.

The initial entry is to be used as a transition entry to indicate the inception of treatment. It must be written one week after the probation officer has had his initial interview with the probationer. Its primary purpose is to record the probation officer's recognition of the human and environmental material with which he is working.

The data included is based upon the preliminary investigation, conferences held between the supervision officer and investigating officer, and the two or more contacts which the supervision officer has had with the probationer and his family during the first week of probation.

The material which is to be included in the eight channels of probationary treatment should be blocked and recorded succinctly and in this section there is no need to report the analysis of the investigating officer. The probationer's situation as related to the eight channels of treatment should be recorded insofar as possible by utilizing brief, factual data.

The analytical summary and tentative plan of treatment must be *supplemented* and enlarged upon by a case analysis, which is to be written three months after the inception of the period of supervision.

Each case record is reviewed by the case supervisor at the end of the first month, the review being incorporated into the written record. The original plan of treatment is revised periodically, usually at intervals of three to five months, through the medium of the case analysis which tabulates:

> (a) The problems.
>
> (b) The causal factors.
>
> (c) The plan of treatment.

These case analyses are approved by the case supervisor who aids in their formulation during the weekly individual conference with the probation officers.

Outline for Initial Entry

Probationer's Name   Case Number
Home Address
Employment

I.   Probation status

     A. Offense.

     B. Disposition and maximum period of probation.

     C. If sentence deferred, indicate date of next hearing.

     D. If codefendants are involved, give names, case numbers, pleas or convictions and disposition.

     E. Notes special conditions of probation; e.g., restitution, terms, permission to leave jurisdiction, etc.

     F. Note any letters or applications which have to be submitted to the Court.

II.   Probationer's situation

     A. Personal History.

     B. Brief summary of investigating officer's characterization.

C. Channels of probationary treatment:

    1. Discipline.

    2. Health.

    3. Family and neighborhood.

    4. Employment.

    5. Education.

    6. Recreation.

    7. Religion.

    8. Thrift.

D. Note any social agencies which are actively interested in either the probationer or his family at the present time.

III. Analytical Summary

A. Positive Factors (Assets).

B. Negative Factors (Liabilities).

C. Additional factual material needed.

D. The tentative plan of treatment (Objective and subjective phases).

OUTLINE FOR PERIODIC (MONTHLY) SUMMARY

Probationer's Name   Case number
Home Address
Employment:

Illustration of Summary Heading

Date of Dictation

SUMMARY FOR NOVEMBER 15th to DECEMBER 16th, 1934:

R: Nov. 15, 22, 29; Dec. 6, 13; HV: Nov. 20, Dec. 12. EV: 12
OC: 3, T. 12, L. 3

SUMMARY for Nov. 1 to 30, 1934: R: 7, 14, 21, 28. HV 2, 19.
EV. 0; O.C. 8. T: 10. L: 4

SUMMARY for Dec. 5 to 14, 1934: R: 6. H.V. 7, 10, 11, 13.
E.V. 2. O.C. 12. T: 9. L: 6

EXPLANATORY

a. Summary should cover a period of approximately four weeks, except as noted in paragraph "h".

b. Give months or dates of period covered.

c. Explanation of code:

R: Reports—Personal (or MR, Mail Reports): Give dates of reports during period.

HV: Home visits: Give dates of visits during period.

EV: Employment Verification or Visit: Give dates.

OC: All other contacts (Visits or Interviews only): Give number.

T: Telephone received and made: Give number.

L: Letters—received or sent: Give number.

BODY OF SUMMARY:

d. Organization, accuracy, completeness, economy (brevity) should be directing principles in dictating the summary. Also, the Probation Officer should make an attempt to maintain a correct balance between the factual and interpretive matter of the record. He should keep in mind that a wholly factual record may not be a true record nor one that is truly indicative of the Probation Officer's efforts.

For example: An incomplete record of, or the omission of, the details of an illuminating interview or the failure to interpret an event or a series of events or record of facts will often result in a distorted picture of a particular case. In the organization of material the following plan must be followed:

1. Home situation: Give names of persons interviewed, relationship and interest.

(a) Description of changes in home situation:

    1. The present as compared with that noted in last summary.

    2. If new address, how does new home and neighborhood compare with former, and reasons for moving, rental paid.

    3. Note changes in composition of household group, new boarders, births, deaths, marriages.

    4. Health problems newly developed and Probation Officer's efforts to solve them.

    5. Economic problems newly developed and Probation Officer's efforts to solve them; total family income.

    6. Agencies interested, nature and extent of their current interest: relief bureau, crime prevention bureau, religious organizations, clinic, etc.

(b) Other changes:

    1. Changes in attitude of family members toward each other.

    2. Changes in attitude of family members toward probationer.

    3. Changes in attitude of family members toward Probation Officer.

2. Personal situation:

    1. Regularity of reports with explanation of deviations.

    2. Changes in personal appearance.

    3. Citizenship.

    4. Employment visits and verifications: In recording this note persons interviewed, character of fellow employees, conditions of work, adjustment to job; wages, how verified.

5. If unemployed, his job seeking technique, mental attitude, dependence, Probation Officer's efforts on his behalf and the probationer's response.

6. *Health*—Current Problems:

   Physical problems.

   Mental Hygiene problems as indicated by the probationer's general conduct and response to probation.

   Social adjustment.

   What the probationer or probation officer has done toward resolving these problems; the probationer's responses.

7. *Thrift*—How probationer manages his fiscal affairs, budgeting of income and expenditures, installment purchases, extravagance, regularity and amount of savings, insurance, benefit society, property accumulation. Describe Probation Officer's efforts and probationer's and his family's response.

8. *Leisure Time*—How occupies and Probation Officer's estimate of the value to probationer. Describe Probation Officer's efforts to effect a more desirable change in activities and associations; what plans suggested or organized, outlets, schools, etc. contacted and probationer's response.

9. *Personality Development*—Note changes in probationer's development of better understanding of his responsibilities (individual and social), and his effort to shoulder them.

   In evaluating personality and in interpreting attitudes the probation officer must bear in mind the need for seeking for causation and not confusing symptomatic behavior with causation. The probation officer's analysis of the personality with which he is dealing must recognize that the probationer is the sum total of his inheritances and life experi ences. Unless the probation officer understands the motivating factors behind behavior he cannot perform his work which does not merely encompass the changing of objective factors but is based upon his ability to mould and change personality.

The case record must depict the probation officer's recognition that he is dealing with a living human being. In providing an integrated picture of the probationer, the probation officer in addition to relating objective data, such as physical appearance, physical deformities, manner of speech, etc., must base his analysis upon the probationer's temperament, attitudes, interests, inclinations, emotions, sentiments, beliefs, adjustments, social outlook, acceptance of responsibilities, etc.

3. General Problems:

Probation Officer should denote the degree of progress and success achieved in resolving the probationer's general problems; reasons.

e. In Summary *underline*
1. Significant changes in Civil status such as new home or employment address, birth, marriages, etc.
2. Significant factual items in social status, as earnings, hospital contact, family welfare contacts, savings, etc.

Underlining is most efficiently used when used most sparingly.

f. Devote separate paragraph to family support and restitution status—preferably at end of summary.

g. *Headings:* The only headings to be used in the margin are significant probation, court, or police changes in status, viz:

Deferred Sentence: Date.

New Arrest: Date, officer, etc.

Bench Warrant: When issued, judge, etc.

Violation of Probation: Date submitted.

Probation Histories: Date submitted, nature of his tory, etc.

Letters to the Court: Date submitted, nature of con tacts, and purpose.

Court Appearances: Name of court, date judge, dis position, etc.

Transfers to New Officers: Date and name.

Closing entries:

ILLUSTRATION OF HEADING:

Letter to Court

On December 4, 1934, an Application To Establish Terms Of Restitution was signed by Judge Blank. Original on file wit bookkeeper.

New Arrest

On December 10, 1934, Smith, at 10 A.M., in front of 489 Sev enth Avenue was arrested by Detective Jones of the 5th Squa charged with stealing a Ford Sedan, the property of one Henr Robinson of 75 West 89th Street. At a hearing held at the Fift District Magistrates' Court, Smith was held in $2,500 bail fo the Grand Jury.

h. When a significant event occurs requiring immediate dictatio such as a new arrest, court hearing, or for any other reasor the dictation should be a summary covering the period fror the date of the last entry until the date of immediate dictatior

---

The following excerpts from case records clearly illustrate no only the type of dictation which is required, but also indicate insofar as possible during the limited periods recorded, the tech niques used in the adjustment process.

    1. JAMES WEST

      a. Initial entry

      b. 4 Months' Dictation

      c. Case Analysis

      d. Case Review

WEST, JAMES   #88888

Home Add.: 16-83 Eastern Blvd.,

                 Rossiter, Long Island.

Unemployed

INITIAL ENTRY

?/28/36 I.   PROBATION STATUS

On December 19, 1935, at about 4 A.M., West, accompanied by John Smith and a minor, by forcing a door, gained entrance to a room at 154 Third Avenue and stole a camera and wearing apparel of a total value of $36.50, the property of Edward Jones.

The day following the theft, West and Smith were arrested in their two room flat at 78 Keane Street. A search of the flat disclosed part of the complainant's property. A pawn ticket was also found indicating that Smith had pawned the complainant's overcoat for $4. The complainant sustained a loss of $4.37 which he expended in order to redeem his overcoat.

West and Smith admitted having perpetrated three or four other similar burglaries. Smith was regarded by the Police as the more culpable of the two defendants.

On February 21, 1936, following his plea of guilty to Burglary 3rd Degree, West was placed on probation by the Hon. William Blank for a period of five years.

On April 9, 1936, the codefendant, Smith, who has a previous court record, was sentenced to Elmira Reformatory.

221

When Smith appeared for sentence, he did so with a contemptuous sneer at the Court and spat loudly on the Court-room floor. He was characterized by the Court as the "toughest" defendant seen since Gerald Chapman. After being sentenced Smith spat again, winked at a court attendant and stalked off.

Smith's adherence to the "underworld code," his bravado and contempt for authority, all had their part in influencing West, dependent and highly suggestible, to participate in criminal activity. Subjected to unsympathetic and rigorous discipline throughout his life, West's resentment against authority culminated in the instant offense. Essentially a follower, West had attached himself to the dominant codefendant whose self sufficiency and positive revolt against all restraint, he deemed worthy of emulation.

This tendency toward hero worship and West's traits of dependency and suggestibility can be utilized to advantage in the process of adjustment.

The minor, who was living with the youths and who was implicated in the offense, was committed by the Children's Court to the Children's Institution on January 20, 1936.

II. PROBATIONER'S SITUATION

Aged 18 years, eight months and single, the probationer is a native resident of this city.

The Court report submitted by the Division of Investigation shows that since an early age West has given unmistakable evidence of serious emotional conflicts. He has become extremely introverted and is given on occasions to brooding and morbidness. At this time he is a shy, distrustful youth who has developed a feeling that every one is endeavoring to oppress him.

1. *Discipline:* A neurotic child and allegedly a disciplinary problem to his relatives at the age of four—committed to private boarding school at that age—wayward and re-

bellious at the age of seven—arraigned in Children's Court as Ungovernable Child when eleven years old—a former inmate of Children's Institution.

2. *Health:* (a) Physical Health: Had gonorrhea about a year ago—claims this infection was inactive—head injury at an early age—circumcision performed at Children's Institution—x-ray of skull and Wasserman in 1928 were negative—physical examination at Court Psychiatric Clinic essentially negative.

Mental Health: (b) Intelligence Quotient at age of eleven .96—at that time was not suffering from any disorder—case record at Children's Institution, however, states West was psychopathic and shut-in type with possible psychopathic traits that must be carefully guarded against—eneuresis—intellectually normal.

Examination at Court Psychiatric Clinic shows probationer lacking in emotional flexibility—psychiatrist feels that West only recently has shown any tendency to adjust —a schizoid neurotic. Psychiatrist desires to re-examine West in August.

Sexual Life: (c) While at the Children's Institution West was characterized as one of the worst masturbators that has been observed there but apparently was broken of the habit—recently sexually promiscuous.

3. *Family:* Mother died when West was three months old —reared until six by maternal grandmother—father remarried but stepmother was unsympathetic—father lacked understanding—was strict and tyrannical—West recently a vagrant.

4. *Employment:* Has no verifiable employment—has little vocational training—appears to lack special interests— shiftless and apparently lacking in ambition.

5. *Education:* Truant at the age of eleven. Received some education at Children's Institution. Later attended P. S.

147, Queens—was graduated therefrom in June, 1933—poor marks in studies. Thereafter attended Jamaica Vocational High School short time—discontinued studies—lost interest in subject of auto mechanics.

6. *Recreation:* Unorganized—associated with disreputable element—consorted with criminals—frequented poolrooms and pinball parlors—petty gambling—occasionally intemperate.

7. *Religion:* Of the Roman Catholic faith—has drifted away from church—very infrequent attendance.

8. *Thrift:* No interest in savings.

No social agencies interested in the case.

III. Anayltic Summary

(a) Positive Factors: (Assets)

1. Good health.
2. Although neurotic and immature, he is of average intelligence.
3. Father offers to pay fee at employment agency.
4. Father in comfortable financial circumstances—offers home.
5. Grammar school education—some vocational training.
6. Father's home located in desirable environment—removed from places where West formerly resided.

(b) Negative Factors: (Liabilities)

1. Schizoid neurotic—psychopathic tendencies.
2. Undernourished—physically weak.
3. Past associate of criminals and disorderly characters—frequents disreputable places of amusement.

224

4. Sexually promiscuous—infected with gonorrhea about a year ago—allegedly cured.

5. Reared in a broken home—has never received adequate affection or understanding.

6. Lacks adequate vocational training or specialized interests in the industrial world.

7. Attitude toward life morbid and lacking in hope—distrustful and antagonistic towards supervisory discipline.

(c) *Additional Factual Material Needed:*

(1) Further information is required regarding the probationer's family history and the interrelationships existing in the family circle.

(2) Information is required regarding the various factors responsible for the probationer's present emotional condition.

(3) As the probationer is inclined to be very reticent and secretive, further information is needed regarding his real attitude towards the problems that confront him and towards his past experiences.

(d) Tentative Plan of Treatment:

(1) Strong efforts will be made to secure employment for the probationer.

(2) Efforts will be made to secure a satisfactory home for the probationer. If he becomes discontented at his father's home and continues to evidence his inability to adjust there, other arrangements must be made.

(3) Efforts will be made to substitute more wholesome outlets for the probationer's present interest in undesirable companions and unwholesome forms of amusement.

(4) Attempts will be made to awaken in the probationer some hope and interest in life and especially
some desire to improve himself vocationally and to
secure adequate industrial training.

(5) An attempt will be made by this Department to
give to the probationer that interest and understanding as well as a desire to help which he has failed
to receive in his own home or from those with
whom he has been associated.

(6) Probationer will be urged to resume his interest in
his church activities.

(7) Probationer is to be re-examined at the Psychiatric
Clinic during the first week of August 1936—or
sooner if necessary.   HOO:RN

4-3-36 Summary from February 21st to March 31st, 1936.

R.: Feb. 25, March 3, 10, 17, 24; H.V.: Feb. 24, March 9, 22 ;
L (1); O.C. 2

West when arrested had been leading a transient life on the
lower east side, living with disreputable companions in cheap
flats and lodging houses. After being placed on probation he returned to the home of his father and stepmother. Although West
never was able to get along with his father or stepmother he was
persuaded to give residence here one more trial. He is entirely
dependent on his father for support.

The father, a printing teacher at the Benton High School owns
an eight room comfortably furnished, well-kept one family brick
building in Rossiter, L. I., which is valued at $8,000. He has an
equity in the home of $3,200.

The probationer's father is a slender, fiery, overly-aggressive
individual who appears egocentric and authoritative. His profession as a teacher has imbued him with what appears to be an
inward conviction of infallibility; he is easily irritated if any of
his edicts in the home are questioned. Unless his children obey

him without question, he develops rages which he follows by corporal punishment.

The stepmother is a neat, tidy woman of short stature, quiet and self contained. She seems unemotional, practical and calculating, and faces life with severe logic. She is opinionated, but not in a loud or offensive way. Realizing her husband's craving for power, she tries to give him every outward evidence of respect and obedience, and accomplishes any personal ends required by shrewd indirection.

Others in the househod include the probationer's sister, aged twenty-two, who is employed as a file clerk. Yielding by nature and possessing a quiet disposition, she has acquired the technique of living fairly harmoniously with her father and stepmother.

The probationer's only brother, who is a former inmate of the City Reformatory where he served a sentence for Unlawful Entry, resides in a cheap hotel on Chambers Street and works as a laborer. His father states that he was always rebellious in the home. He has little to do with the family and when interviewed by the P. O. he manifested no interest in West and refused to discuss himself or the family.

Four children are the issue of the probationer's father's second marriage. They range in age from eight to thirteen and all attend school.

These children appear to have always been favored over the offspring resulting from the elder West's first marriage. They were privileged to eat in the dining room while the probationer was forced to eat in the kitchen. When there was a division of opinion between the probationer and them, their word was generally accepted as the truth.

The entire situation, with its conflicting personalities, its diverse urges for power and domination, is fraught with danger as far as domestic harmony and constructive influences are concerned.

According to the father and stepmother who were interviewed on the occasion of the home visits, West keeps to himself and seldom engages in conversation with any members of the household. Probationer's father is utterly pessimistic regarding the future of the probationer He cha.racterizes the probationer as shiftless and desirous of shirking his responsibilities. He regards the youth hopeless as far as employment is concerned. He indicates a willingness, however, to donate the employment fee to any agency which can secure a position for West.

The probationer on the occasion of his reports was soft-spoken and quiet in manner and always well attired. He volunteered little information regarding himself and answered questions put to him in monosyllables. His recent experience appears to have confirmed his feeling that the world is against him.

The probationer is a blackhaired, brown-eyed youth with a long face and listless manner. At times he gives the impression of being in a slight stupor but he occasionally shakes himself out of this lethargy long enough to answer questions in an abrupt fashion. He is thin, and does not appear to be very strong. His height is five feet eight inches. He is awkward and there is a suggestion of furtiveness about his manner.

Venereal Examination

He was sent with a letter to the Board of Health requesting that a Wasserman test and a smear be taken and that a report be sent to this Department. On February 26th West submitted to these tests. A report was received indicating the examination was negative.

West is unable to adjust to his home and desires freedom from its restraints. This desire for freedom has been apparent in the probationer's general attitudes and is obviously a reaction to his unhappy early experiences at home, in institutions and in the community.

Some attempt has been made to make him realize the disadvantages of leading a vagrant existence and to have him discontinue associations he has made with the undesirable element in poolrooms and street corners.

Because of his inner discontent, West shows little interest in recreational activities and no ambition for vocational training or additional education of any kind.

Effort has been made by the P. O. to create in the father and stepmother some sympathetic understanding of West's problems, without success. The father is adamant in his refusal to see any good qualities in his son and it is obvious that he would be only too glad to see the probationer out of the way, even though in prison, where he could not be a reminder of parental failure. The stepmother, interested almost exclusively in her own children, seems only too glad to abide by the decision of her husband regarding West.

The P. O.'s efforts to change West's attitude toward his unfriendly family were also futile. It was pointed out that his stay in the household need not be permanent, but that it was better than leaving at this period when he was unemployed. Attempts were made to aid West gain insight into the personality and attitude of his father and stepmother. It was brought out that the father is accustomed to obedience and attention in his school; that he craves absolute obedience in the home; that the stepmother has her own four children making constant demands upon her time and that he could not expect too much from her. He was urged to make every effort to lead a quiet inoffensive life in the home and to avoid antagonizing his father and stepmother.

It was then pointed out that a good job might be the solution of West's immediate difficulties, that if he were working steadily, he would be self-maintaining and need no longer subsist on the charity of unfriendly relatives. Probation Officer offered to do everything he could to aid him secure work, so that he might shorten his stay in an unhappy environment. The probationer was also urged to seek employment himself instead of sitting back hopelessly to await the aid of others. He was given specific directions and employment contacts were made for him which he followed half-heartedly and without success. An effort was made to give the impression that the Probation Department was interested in his welfare and was doing everything possible to aid in his readjustment.

West continues to be apathetic. Accustomed to harsh and unsympathetic treatment he seems unable to grasp, as yet, that the P. O. is interested in his welfare and West is apparently in fear of him. His intense emotional reaction towards his family and his feeling of being unwanted are the basic causes to West's negative responses to supervision. HOO:RN

4-5-36 Case discussed with Supervisor at conference (See review on file).

5-6-36 Summary for April 1936

R.: Apr. 9; M.R.; Apr. 14; H.V.: Apr. 7, 20; O.C. (3) T. (1) West is stil unsociable and reticent and there appear some signs of an increase in his nervousness and tension. He intimated that he found life with his father and stepmother unbearable.

The father seen on the occasion of the home visit on April 7 was so intense in his expressions of antagonism that P. O. was forced to recognize the immediate need of removing the probationer from his home, even if temporarily.

P. O. visited the City Employment Agency and found that the only available position was a farm job at Bowling, N. Y. which paid $30. a month and maintenance. Bowling is near enough to New York City so that the P. O. can make personal visits to the farm.

Although West has had no farm training it was believed that he should accept this position so as to remove him from his impossible home situation. The matter was discussed with the Case Supervisor and although the possibilities for failure were recognized, it was felt that circumstances necessitated this step. When the probationer reported on the 9th after a discussion of the factors involved he expressed his willingness to accept the job. His attitude clearly reflected his lack of enthusiasm for the work; it is apparent however that he is willing to do anything to get away from home. P. O. telephoned West's father who was overjoyed at the prospect of the probationer's departure.

Permission to leave Jurisdiction

Permission to leave jurisdiction of the Court was secured from Judge Blank on April 9, 1937. West left the city on April 11th.

A mail report was received on April 14th stating that he found the work very hard but that he hoped to get used to it. On the same date that this mail report was received, however, West telephoned the Department and stated that he had been discharged because of his inexperience in farm work and that he would return to this city and report. He stated that he would not return to his father's home as he felt ashamed and humiliated for his failure to hold the job and did not want his father and other members of the family to ridicule and laugh at him. He asserted in his telephone call that he would be living with his maternal aunt, Mrs. Mack at 666 Chambers Street.

As West failed to report in person thereafter, Mrs. Mack was visited. The home is located in a dilapidated tenement house. The flat consisting of four rooms was poorly furnished and gave evidence that its occupants were living in poverty. Mrs. Mack stated that the probationer had not slept at her home although he had visited her since his return from Bowling.

The probationer's aunt is an obese, garrulous, friendly woman. She seemed interested in the probationer and his activities but seemed afraid that too much interest on her part might obligate her to give West material aid or a permanent home.

Mrs. Mack found great enjoyment denouncing the probationer's father and stepmother. The aunt, living in poverty, seemed jealous of the luxurious environment in which she felt the West family resided in Rossiter. She launched accordingly into one enthusiastic tirade after another against the stepmother. She pointed out that the probationer as a child had been dressed in rags. He had eaten left-overs, and was forced to sit in the kitchen. He was denounced on one occasion for talking too much and on another occasion for being too glum, etc. No constructive assistance can be expected from her.

Subsequently a visit was made to City Employment Agency which had sent the probationer to Bowling, but they were unable to give any information as to West's present whereabouts. The director informed P. O. that West had left the job of his own accord. According to the employer, West was unfitted for farm work.

Mr. and Mrs. West were then visited. They were not surprised to hear that probationer had absconded and could offer no clue to his whereabouts.

Bench Warrant

Inasmuch as further efforts to locate him were unsuccessful and as he had given false information concerning his residence with Mrs. Mack a Bench Warrant was requested and was issued by Judge Blank on April 30th.   HOO:RN

6-3-36 Summary for May 1936

R.: May 29; L. (1); Telegrams (2); O.C. (11); T. (1);
H.V.: May 31

West's fingerprints were cleared in this city and in Washington. He has not been rearrested. Another visit was made to the home of his aunt at 666 Chambers Street. Mrs. Mack and several other relatives of the probationer were interviewed here. They had not seen or heard from West but they gave further information regarding the probationer's family background which indicated strongly how disagreeable a time West must have had as a child.

Probationer's father and stepmother were communicated with. They stated that they had not received any word from the probationer. The father is quite indifferent and almost glad that his son has absconded.

New Arrest

On May 6th, information was received from the police that the probationer had been arrested again. He had been arrested by

Motorcycle Patrolman John Doe at 2:30 A. M. at 52nd Street and Third Avenue, with three codefendants as they were riding in a stolen Essex sedan, the property of John Lant of 888 East 82nd Street. The case appeared in Felony Court but was adjourned for one week.

After learning of the probationer's whereabouts, P. O. telephoned the stepmother and informed her of the probationer's recent arrest. She was requested to appear at this office with the probationer's father.

When the father appeared for a conference, his attitude was that the probationer got himself into trouble and that it was up to him alone to get out of it. He refuses ever again to have West in his home or to aid him in any way.

On May 12th, P. O. interviewed Motorcycle Patrolman John Doe. According to the officer, the probationer had been living with one of the codefendant's, Raymond Edwards, in a furnished room at 777 East 82nd Street. Edwards had never been arrested before while the other two codefendants, Rosario Costa and John Rodgers had records for Burglary and Assault. It was the opinion of the arresting officer that Costa, who was driving the automobile at the time of the arrest actually stole the car, valued at approximately $25. The charge in Felony Court will be Petit Larceny.

Discharged in Felony Court

On May 17, after another adjournment, the case was disposed of in Felony Court. Costa was held for Special Sessions while the probationer and the other two codefendants were discharged. Our warrant having been lodged against West, he was remanded to the City Prison for future hearing as a violator of probation. The date was set for May 25th.

Interview in City Prison

The following day West was interviewed in City Prison. He stated that after losing his job on the farm he accompanied Edwards whom he had known for several years, on a three day

233

hitch-hiking trip to Asbury Park in order to look for work. Following this he remained entirely within the confines of this city, residing in numerous "flop houses" on the Bowery, namely, The Winsett, Royal and Morrison Hotels, where he paid about thirty cents nightly for lodging.

After returning to this city he secured work selling the Onward Magazine for a Mr. Burke at 785 East 12th Street and earned $15 weekly for the last two weeks.

Probationer stated that he had done no wrong and was innocent when arrested. He claimed that he and Edwards were on their way home when Costa and Rodgers pulled up with the car and offered to drive them here. West insists that he did not know the car was stolen and says that this was borne out by the fact that the charge against him was dismissed.

West insists that he will not return home to his parents but wants to live with a friend, James Dalton, in some furnished room. "I would rather live in a Bowery flea bag than in Rossiter with my father and stepmother in their beautiful home," he said. P. O. subsequently verified the fact that probationer had resided at the hotels mentioned. On May 18th, a telegram was sent to the Chief of Police of Asbury Park. It was ascertained that West had not been arrested while in that city. The three codefendants substantiated West's story.

A visit was made to the office of Mr. Burke who after some persuasion said that he would be willing to reemploy West. After West's background was discussed, Mr. Burke manifested a sincere interest in the youth.

Reexamination

Another examination was arranged at the Psychiatric Clinic. The report which was received from the psychiatrist, indicated little change in the probationer's condition. The psychiatrist felt with the P. O. that continued residence with the father tended to accentuate the probationer's neurotic traits. He also felt that ability to earn some money would relieve the probationer's neurotic tendencies. It was mentioned that the probationer's present job, selling a "liberal" magazine at fairly good pay, would increase his self-confidence in many ways.

The psychiatrist noted that when the probationer was previously examined he had an Intelligence Quotient of .96 whereas at this examination he achieved an Intelligence Quotient of 110 which borders on a superior score. The only explanation the psychiatrist offered for this change was that formerly emotional factors had held him back. The psychiatrist felt that continued contacts in the clinic at about two months intervals and an arrangement whereby West could continue to support himself and live away from home in a good environment would aid in West's rehabilitation.

Continuance on Probation

On May 25th after a Violation of Probation Report had been submitted to the Court giving details as to the present status of the case, West was continued on probation on the recommendation of the Chief P. O.

P. O. had luncheon with the probationer who is now without funds. West seems to have developed a much more friendly attitude toward the Probation Officer and towards supervisory discipline. The recent investigation seems to have impressed West with the fact that this Department was treating him fairly and that the P. O. had some sympathetic insight into his predicament. West now appears to realize that association with undesirable companions is constantly leading him into trouble.

West was enthused when P. O. informed him that he could return to work immediately. He seems greatly stimulated by his new job. At luncheon he indicated his interest in the labor problems of the country and the fact that he has become alert to various movements and thoughts to which he previously paid no attention. Probationer stated that his new mental awakening also had renewed his interest in religion. He states that he intends to visit his old church, St. Peter's on Warden Street, with greater regularity in the future.

235

He was informed that this Department is interested in helping and not persecuting him, and in order that plans for his future might be developed and carried through, he would have to report with regularity.

West was then accompanied to the office of the Onward Magazine, Mr. Burke greeted him cordially and offered to advance him $10. which at the P. O.'s suggestion was reduced to $5. The probationer's friend, Dalton, who made quite a good impression upon the P. O. was also there and offered to share his furnished room with West until the latter was settled.

New Address

Dalton lives at 444 Gray Street, an undesirable neighborhood. The subject of moving to another neighborhood was discussed with the boys who willingly agreed to follow the P. O.'s advice.

On May 26, P. O. with the aid of Mr. Burke secured a room for the boys with Mr. and Mrs. Weston at 7788 Warwick Avenue, Man. The boys moved there on May 27th.

The new home of the probationer is located in a desirable section. The apartment house is clean and no loiterers frequent the street corner nor are there undesirable places of amusement in the immediate vicinity. The probationer and Dalton each pays a monthly rental of $10. Their quarters are part of a five-room apartment which is leased at a monthly rental of $50. by the Westons who are editorial workers for a trade magazine. They have no children or other lodgers. Their apartment is furnished in good taste.

The Westons were not advised of the fact that West is on probation and they regard the Probation Officer, who they know as a social worker, as merely being interested in West who has had family difficulties.

One report was made by the probationer thereafter. He likes his home and enjoys his work. He does not feel that this job offers any great future but at the same time it enables him to earn a livelihood.

The alert interest which West now has in life is reflected in his personal appearance. The lethargy which he formerly had is disappearing. His eyes are brighter, he is more spontaneous and not quite so self-absorbed and introverted.

7-8-36 Summary for June 1936

R.: June 1, 7, 14, 22, 28; H.V.: June 2, 30; E.V.: June 11, 14, 25; O.C. (3)

"I am beginning to feel more like working and amounting to something," West said on his first report. The probationer is gaining in energy and ambition. His physical condition has improved as has his general outlook. During the month he has averaged $18. a week, and Mr. Burke who was interviewed on three occasions continues to be satisfied with the probationer.

West appreciates the fact that so many employment visits are made. He is beginning to rather like close supervision. "I like to have somebody take an interest in me," he said. "Why, Dalton had a friend who used to come up to see Burke all the time and I used to wish someone would do the same about me." West likes his new home and has already become attached to the Westons who on the occasions of the home visits informed the P. O. that the two boys are getting along splendidly. A close friendship continues to exist between West and Dalton who frequently accompanies the probationer to this office.

Dalton is a serious self-reliant manly chap who is twenty years of age. He is frank and fluent, dresses neatly and appears genuinely interested in West. He has had some high school education and possesses considerable intellectual curiosity. He is Mr. Burke's star salesman and averages about $25. a week. As yet little information has been secured about his background, beyond the fact that he was born in St. Paul, Minnesota, was orphaned at the age of 12, was reared by a maternal aunt until he was 18 years of age when he came to this city. Because of the strong and beneficial influence which Dalton exerts over West, P. O. has decided to work with both boys insofar as possible.

The admiration and loyalty which West formerly had toward hoodlums appears to be in the process of being transferred to Dalton, the Westons and the P. O. Recognizing the ever-present danger of accentuating the probationer's dependency, the P. O. during the past month has endeavored to impress West with the fact that it is necessary for him to solve his own problems and that he is intellectually capable and possesses the necessary insight to do so. The need of developing self reliance and maturity in West had been discussed with Dalton and Mr. Burke. Both seem to have gained insight into the probationer's situation and personality. If the probationer remains with the Westons, this aspect of the case will be presented to them.

Dalton realizes that selling magazines offers little opportunity for advancement. West appears to be coming to that conclusion. However, neither youth possesses any definite idea of what vocation he desires to follow. Accordingly, P. O. discussed with them the need of preparation for employment. The values of vocational testing were presented and as both boys showed interest, P. O. arranged to have them tested at the Boys Vocational Department on July 6th.

West lacks wholesome recreational outlets. He has shown interest in his church. Feeling that this interest might also be utilized in developing a recreational program, in addition to religious interest, P. O. interviewed Father Stewart of St. James' Church. P. O. was advised that the Catholic Boys' Club in the parish appeared to suit the probationer's needs. The organization's activities include athletics, library facilities and open forums and lectures on current topics.

When this subject was discussed with West he showed great interest especially in the cultural activities of the organization. Accordingly, on June 23rd, West was accompanied to the rectory where he was introduced to Father Stewart. The interview was productive and West is to attend the next meeting on June 29th. He asked permission for Dalton to accompany him. This was, of course, granted.

Although West is earning approximately $18. a week, he finds it difficult to meet his expenses. He is aware that money slips easily through his fingers. P. O.'s discussions on this subject had had some results, as West stated that he has been giving small sums to Dalton for safe-keeping since he feels the latter possesses more sound judgment and a greater sense of responsibility than he himelf.

This phase of the case was presented to Mr. Burke who stated that he, too, had noticed West's inability to budget. He promised to do his utmost to counsel the probationer along these lines.

On the occasion of his last report for the month the P. O. again broached to West the problem of budgeting and saving. This time West was quite receptive and actively assisted in the development of a budget (on file). As a result, the probationer agreed that there appeared to be no reason why he could not save regularly $2. each week. The uses and advantages of banks were again discussed with him, and he was finally persuaded to institute a savings account at the Canal Bank on Wednesday when he is paid. The probationer's sincerity and interest were manifested by his voluntary statement that he intended to start his account by depositing $4. which Dalton has been keeping for him.

West was reminded to attend the meeting on June 29th and to bear in mind his appointment at the Boys' Vocational Department on July 6th.   HOO:RN

Name: WEST, JAMES
Date: July 1, 1936   Case No. 88888

CASE ANALYSIS

I.   PROBLEM

1.   The probationer is vocationally maladjusted.

2.   The probationer's leisure time activities are disorganized and undesirable.

3. The probationer has little concept of money management.

4. The probationer presents a personality problem which is characterized by emotional imbalance and social inadequacy.

II. CAUSAL FACTORS

1. West was neglected as a child. His father and stepmother showed little interest in his hopes and aspirations, and by their indifferent attitude brought on feelings of insecurity. As a result, the probationer found himself unable to concentrate on any planned vocational program. Lacking incentive, he made no progress in school along either academic or vocational lines.

2. West during his formative years was more interested in escaping from a disagreeable domestic situation than in securing recreation within the home circle. Lacking direction and failing to develop wholesome interests, he attached himself to disorderly youths whom he met on street corners and in poolrooms, where he sought recreation. Admiring the freedom and self sufficiency that these youths appeared to possess, he endeavored to emulate their activities and became a victim to petty gambling, sexual promiscuity, drinking, street corner loitering, etc.

3. Throughout his life West has been deprived of little luxuries and even necessities which he deemed essential to his happiness. His home situation, developed in him a hopeless attitude toward life. Feeling deprived and being unable to conceive that at any time he could earn an income sufficient for his wants, West spent what money he earned recklessly and in a manner which he thought would give him the maximum amount of satisfaction. Not only has he failed to establish any form of financial reserve, but he feels almost incapable of ever being able to do so.

4. West's personality developed in a broken and unsympathetic home atmosphere with little of the natural parental affection that was his due. One of the results was the creation of undesirable habitual attitudes and a sense of inadequacy which affect him as a social personality. His conflicts are expressed in his inability to make an adequate social adjustment; a feeble rebelliousness toward the existing social order; as well as an intense craving for acceptance by people about him and a too ready responsiveness and suggestibility to any sign of interest.

III. Plan of Treatment

1. Arrangements have been made to have West submitted to psychological tests, as a result of which he will be advised regarding his industrial capacities and possibly be placed in a suitable position by the Boys' Vocational Department. Once the probationer's industrial capacities have been determined, courses will be suggested to him on the basis of the results of the vocational testing series and after conference with the New York Educational Council. Then arrangements will be made to enroll him in a vocational school. The aid of The Readers' Advisor at the New York Public Library will be enlisted so that West may have proper and interesting material to read. West may need considerable persuasion to accept the idea and plan of vocational training. To overcome long established inertia, intensive supervision will be required. After West's acceptance of plans, he should be held strictly accountable for the performance of the various steps initiated.

2. Recognizing the absence of any creative direction and planfulness in West's leisure time activities and noting his favorable response to the activities of the Catholic Boys' Club, P. O. will further stimulate Father Stewart's interest in the probationer, since West's need for encouragement is apparent. The P. O. will continue an intensive

interest in the probationer's recreational activities and through advice and material assistance aid him develop a new satisfying and socially acceptable philosophy of leisure time activity. The stimulation received from these contacts should be reflected in an awakened interest in more desirable social and religious experiences including athletics, group discussions, perhaps hobbies, etc.

3. West has given evidence of having gained some insight into his need for budgeting and saving. After he has opened his savings account, P. O. will demand regular deposits no matter how small. P. O. will continue to develop and supervise the budget which has already been initiated. By means of these processes, P. O. may be able to provide West with a recognition that the security which he craves may in part be secured through systematic savings and the resulting development of a financial reserve.

4. A satisfactory home, regular employment, interesting and offering possibilities of advancement, and the sympathetic interest of adults will aid the probationer to acquire a sense of security and of being wanted. Material progress ought to result in the loss of West's feelings of inferiority and frustration. Social contacts and social prestige will resolve a number of personality problems which are upon an emotional level. Close supervision is required but care must be taken to curb West's dependent traits. The recommendations of the Court's Psychiatric Clinic will be followed and West will be referred there for treatment at regular intervals.

HOO:AM

July 5, 1936 *Case Review by Supervisor*

Case dictation to June 30, 1936 noted. Your treatment of the case indicates a grasp of the problems involved. West appears to be responding favorably to supervision. However, it is obvious that any adjustment which the probationer may appear to have made during the short period of supervision is still superficial and extremely precarious. His unhappy life experiences and deep feelings of inadequacy and insecurity are reflected in his emotional imbalance, his inability to conform to routine, his lack of insight into the drives which result in his erratic behavior and the difficulty he has in focusing thinking and action upon a definite objective.

Understanding of the drives and impulses which express themselves in West's behavior and personality may be gained from an analysis of his history. It must be recognized, however, that West's behavior is compounded not only of unconscious impulses but is in part the result of conscious needs and situations in which he became involved by a combination of external factors. His frantic search for affection is reflected by his ready attachment to whoever will associate with him and his constant seeking for new objects since no one has given him the affection and security which he craves. This drive, the unconscious search for a mother substitute, is also manifested in wanderlust, the probationer's inability to remain in any setting for a protracted period.

Another aspect of West's conflicts is his relationship with his father and the latter's consistently tyrannical attitude. There has been developed in West, the child and adolescent, a parental hatred which should have been displaced in the course of normal development. Instead it has become intensified as a result of West's life experiences. We are not as yet prepared to describe the components of the father's attitude toward the son. Further interviews should be had with the father in order to make efforts to resolve the conflict. West has continued to encounter rigid and uncomprehending parent substitutes in foster homes, institutions and among relatives. By the same token, he projected unto these parent substitutes hatred of and resistance to authority. His inability to adjust has expressed itself in wayward behavior and unhappiness which finally culminated in criminal activity.

For an extended analysis too little is yet known of the probationer's emotional history with reference to his relationship to his father, stepmother and others who were responsible for his rearing. Much of his recent behavior, as we know it, is

243

still indicative of his strong sense of inferiority, insecurity and disorganization. Other evidences are his associations with toughs, criminals, or even "radicals" whose poise and self assurance he envies and desires to emulate.

For any effective treatment a secure stable home with at least a minimum of adult interest and affection must be provided. P. O. should assume the role of a parent substitute but must exercise care lest West transfer his hatreds and not his affection. At the same time, P. O. must be wary lest a too sympathetic approach intensify the probationer's dependent traits.

The major problem is to provide West with insight into his situation and to have him recognize that he cannot hope to find that type of parent substitute which he seeks and to sublimate drives in this direction into constructive channels. An effort to resolve the problem of disorganization should be made by organizing the probationer's activities and requiring conformance to routine in the hope that this type of program will assist in the organization of West's thinking processes. The P. O. must continue his contacts with the Psychiatric Clinic.

REW:SI

II. Henry Foster

2 Months Dictation

The summaries record the progress of the case during the fourth and fifth months of supervision. In the case record they are preceded by the preliminary investigation report to the Court, the initial entry, and three summaries each of which cover a period of one month.

Fostor, Henru   Case No. 86342
Home Address: 87 Burry Street
Wife's Home Address: 34 Burry Street
Employment: Irregular

R.: 6, 13, 20, 27; H.V.: 12, 19, 23; E.V.: 12, 13; O.C. (5) T (3)
On the 10th P. O. received a telephone call from Mrs. Foster requesting an interview, preferably at her home. An appointment was made for the 12th. The home was visited on the 12th. Mrs. Foster and her sister-in-law Mrs. South of 883 Devine Avenue, were present. The flat was clean and neat. The living room, where the interview was conducted is somewhat overfurnished with a complete dining room set which is polished and dustless. Mrs. Foster, the probationer's wife, as always, was neatly groomed and cosmeticized; her voice is somewhat shrill, hard, and her speech slightly and softly accented. Her sister-in-law is a matronly, earnest, well meaning housewife type. Mrs. Foster unhesitatingly broached the subject of the interview. She apologized for her deception of the P. O. admitting that her sister-in-law, Mrs. South, prompted the calling of this interview. *The probationer no longer lives with her*—hasn't in fact been living there for perhaps two months, except for an occasional visit. She couldn't stand him any longer. His drunken debauches were intolerable. He never struck her, but would come home in a filthy drunken condition and urinate on couch and floor. He had been an alcoholic for "years." His own relatives knew of this condition but avoided the matter. She never disclosed this to her own relatives and family for reasons of pride and shame until about two years ago, when, while she was in a hospital undergoing an operation, Mrs. South, who was taking care of the children, found the probationer in a "drunken, dirty" stupor.

Her brother, Mr. South, and herself tried to change him by pleading, getting jobs for him, putting him in business, etc. but without success. They approached his relatives, who unmistakably and definitely washed their hands of him and under no circumstances will have anything to do with him. She could offer no explanation for his alcholism, except that he might have developed the habit during service in the Army. She spoke well of his relatives as respectable, hard working people. She recalled that all of his jobs were secured through relatives. He worked hard, earned good wages, adequately supported his family and to some extent controlled his drinking, usually taking off a day or two for his drinking sprees. Since he is, as a rule, quiet and unassertive, few people knew of his drinking and since he worked with friends or relatives, there was always a tendency to "protect him." The probationer was generally uncommunicative and unaffectionate except when drunk when he blabbered about his love for her and the children. To the outside world he was polite and affable.

During the depression he became worse, couldn't work regularly, lied about his job and earnings and indulged more and more in drinking. He turned over his bonus money, about $700. to her. Much of it went for medical care, the balance for living expenses. Her own relatives, a brother living in Albany and Mr. South aided in keeping the home together supporting her and her children. One relative in 1934, borrowed money and endeavored to establish, with the probationer, a window shade business. During the first week the probationer smashed the car in a collision and the business had to be given up. In Feb. of 1935 the probationer came home one day drunk and muttered something about having enough money "soon." With a premonition of evil she pleaded with the probationer throughout the night to disclose his activities, but to no avail. The arrest for the instant offense followed shortly. She has no love or confidence in the probationer and wants no more of him, except to have him support her and the children. She is at the end of her rope. Her relatives are no longer able to aid her; his relatives, all of whom she has already seen, are also unable to help her and furthermore want no part of him.

P. O. suggested she make immediate *application for relief* which, however, for reasons of pride, she hesitates to do.

Mrs. Foster pleaded with P. O. to do "something" about the situation, perhaps "scare" or "lecture" the probationer who now lives at *87 Burry Street*.

P. O. visited this address. This is an old four story tenement with two railroad flats on each floor. These flats have been converted into "roomers." According to the landlady, the probationer has, during the past two months, occupied a room on the fourth floor, paying $4.00 a week. His reputation is good.

P. O. visited the Acme Millinery Shop at 5th Avenue and 49th Street and the Bernheim Hat Store at 883 West Avenue. Without disclosing his official position, P. O. learned that the probationer is still known at these stores but is not a regular employee. At the former store the probationer is employed as "extra"; at the latter he works but intermittently.

When the probationer was seen at the subsequent interview he described his situation as unchanged, working week-ends at the Acme Millinery Shop and earning $5 to $7 a week. He denied ever drinking and stated that he is living with his family until P. O. disclosed the contrary information. The probationer then admitted living at 87 Burry Street. He spoke little, merely giving brief responses to questions. He hinted his wife nagged him, and because he didn't earn enough she "locked the door on me." His only other extended comment was to the effect that when he earned good money he was a good husband: when he was down and out "she throws me out." When P. O. pointed out that this was untrue and that the reason for his difficulty was alcoholism he made no comment except to deny that he drinks.

Reexamination

P. O. explained again the functions and purposes of the psychiatric clinic and urged him to submit to examination and treatment. P. O. discussed the case with Dr. Blank and made an appointment for the 20th. P. O. also invited probationer's wife to be there. She came on the 20th accompanied by Mrs. South. Both were extremely nervous and fearful of encountering the probationer.

Dr. Blank submitted a report on the 22nd (on file). He stated: "The outlook in general is not at all encouraging but we will see the man again and will make every possible attempt to assist him." Dr. Blank agreed to see the probationer regularly each fortnight.

In briefly reviewing and analyzing this case, it is readily apparent that Foster presents a more or less typical alcoholic problem. In general terms, the man, during his adult life, has been involved in deep and severe inner conflicts which have disturbed the normal balance between masculine and feminine impulses. The drinking is one of the outward masochistic expressions of this conflict. He is struggling to be normally masculine. He wants to be punished, he drinks, he lies, commits a crime, does not support his family and when sober is restitutive. His wife has found an outlet for her masculine impulses, "lectures," her drinking husband, dominates the household, etc. There is also some evidence to show that the wife, even in courtship, was the aggressive partner.

It is doubtful, whether Foster can acquire insight into his problem and there is considerable danger of disturbing whatever precarious adjustment has been made. A disciplinary approach may create more serious problems. It is furthermore doubtful if P. O. will fare better than the wife or relatives since the probationer has thus far defeated their efforts. Too much help will have a tendency to confirm and intensify the probationer's irresponsibility, and may encourage his infantile wish to defeat P. O.'s and others' intentions.

It seems therefore important for the time being that P. O. should attempt to gain some acceptance of the existing situation by both the probationer and his wife. The probationer is to be encouraged in whatever constructive impulses he possesses, for example, the desire to be gainfully employed, to gain the affection of his children, etc.

If possible, the help of a sensible male friend or relative such as Mr. South, should be secured in order to aid the probationer in working out his problems.

At subsequent interviews with the probationer's wife and Mrs. South at the home and at this office, these problems were discussed and it was decided to have Mr. South communicate with the P. O. in the near future for an appointment at some convenient time.

Case Conference

On Feb. 25th, 1936 the case was discussed at conference with case supervisor.

4/4/36 Summary for March 1936

R.: 4, 11; T.R.: 18; M.R.: 24, 31; H.V.: 7, 19, 25; E.V.: 21, 28; O.C. (8)

A convenient date and time for the conference with Mr. South, the probationer and his wife was finally set for March 11th at 3:00 o'clock. In the meantime on the 7th, the situation was fully discussed with the probationer's wife at her home. She asserted that it was hopeless and futile to attempt to effect any reconciliation between them, that she had no love or affection for the probationer, that all she wants is to "make" him support his wife and children. She admitted that at one time Foster was a good provider and that he had some tolerable qualities. She finally agreed to make some effort to adjust their differences and accept him in their household provided the probationer refrained from drinking to excess, and treated her respectfully.

The probationer was also seen alone. His reaction was less positive. He seemed to agree too readily to the P. O.'s plan. However, the gist of his response was the repeated affirmation that his wife doesn't want any part of him.

On the 11th Mr. South arrived about half past three, Mrs. Foster and the probationer somewhat later. Mr. South is a short, meticulously attired, middle-aged salesman, affable, well-mannered and articulate. He appears to be a solid, middle class family man type, intelligent and mature in outlook. There appears to be no question of his sincere interest in the plight of his sister, the probationer's wife. At the same time, he appeared to show considerable insight into their problem, that both sides played a part in the development of the situation as it exists today. Mr. South described in some detail his own and the family's efforts in behalf of the probationer during the last two years.

Since both Foster and his wife protested their inability to com
to an adequate solution, the following *working plan* was agree
upon by the P. O., Mr. South and the Case Supervisor; first
an effort is to be made to persuade both the probationer and h
wife to accept the situation as it exists. Second, relatives wi
be requested to contribute to a fund of from $50. to $100.0(
Third, part of this fund to be used by the probationer and h
wife to move their household to another neighborhood, and th
remainder for the purchase of necessary wearing apparel for th
wife and children. Fourth, P. O. and relatives are to make a
intensive effort to secure employment for the probationer c
regain a job for him with one of his former employers.

This plan was presented to the probationer and his wife individe
ally, and then together. Considerable effort was required to pre
vent the probationer and his wife from quarrelling and squal
bling, as the wife persisted in accusing the probationer c
lying about some more or less immaterial incidents in the pas
The probationer's wife was highly emotional and couldn't re
strain her weeping provoked by the probationer's "delibera
lying." The probationer appeared to be well controlled, almo
apathetic. His ready acquiescence only too obviously lacked sin
cerity. Before he left the interview he asserted that he hope
to get a job very soon. Until the planned reconciliation is e
fected, Foster is to make an effort to support his family.

At the end of the conference Mr. South seemed to be qui
discouraged since he had made an almost heroic effort and ha
high hopes of accomplishing something more tangible than th
perfunctory acquiescence of the probationer and the emotion
reaction of the wife who obviously has no insight into the prol
lems which confront her and Foster. However, he agreed i
see the probationer as often as he could, possibly invite him i
his home and pursue the plan along the lines of the discussion.

On the 12th P. O. conferred with Miss Jameson, investigate
of the *Home Relief Bureau,* District Office No. 66 and an ap
pointment was made for the 18th for a conference at which th

investigator and the supervisor were present. The case was discussed in all its aspects and the Home Relief Bureau decided to make provision for supplementary relief to this family and if necessary place them on a regular relief budget.

On the 18th probationer telephoned that he began working as a millinery salesman for the *Chic Hat Shop at 62 English Street, Newark, N. J.* at a wage of $25. a week.

At the employment visit made on the morning of the 21st, P. O. observed the probationer about his duties in the millinery shop, which is located on the main business street of Newark. Since he appeared to be quite busy waiting on customers, P. O. returned later in the day. The probationer explained that he had worked for these employers some years ago and they agreed to re-employ him after considerable pleading on his part. He explained that the hours of his employment are from nine in the morning until about seven in the evening, and for that reason it is extremely difficult for him to report in person. The matter of family support payments was discussed with him. He stated that he had given his wife $5.00 last Sunday, and that he will pay as much as he can. P. O. carefully went over with him his budget, and he finally agreed to make payments of $9.00 a week. He was directed to forward his contribution to this Department, which will make application to the Court for a *family support order.*

On the 25th probationer's wife was seen at the home. Probationer's wife related that on Sunday night, the 23rd, at about 10 o'clock, the probationer, quite drunk and noisy, forced his way into her flat, awakened the children, and nearly terrified her "out of her wits." It appears that the purpose of this visit was to see his "beloved children" and to become conciliated with his wife. She stated that the probationer used vile language, created a disturbance, but she finally got him out of the flat. Mrs. Foster, after some discussion, agreed to permit the probationer to visit the children on Sundays. She also informed the P. O. that Miss Jameson had visited the home on the 24th and had promised immediate assistance.

Family Support

On March 27th, 1937 Judge Blank upon our recommendation directed Foster to pay $9.00 a week for the support of his family through this Department.

The probationer was again seen in his place of employment on the 28th, when he denied that at the time of his visit to his wife's flat he had been drunk or noisy. P. O. pointed out to him the futility of antagonizing his wife and advised him that arrangements had been made to have him visit the children on Sunday at about noon. Probationer readily acquiesced to this.

Foster introduced P. O. to the manager of the store who verified the probationer's statement that he earns no more than $25.00 a week. The manager also assured the P. O. that the probationer could have his job as long as he was orderly and did his work satisfactorily. The manager, Mr. Jones, also stated that he expected the month of April to be a busy one, and that it would be difficult to give the probationer time off for reporting.

As Mr. Jones was somewhat familiar with the case, the home situation was explained in part to him and he promised to see that the provisions for the support of the children would be carried out.

Dr. Blank was advised that employment conditions prevented Foster from keeping his appointments at the Clinic. The doctor agreed that for the present treatment could be held in abeyance. If the probationer continues to work regularly, efforts will be made to secure evening appointments for him.

AJS:AM

E. FORM AND STATISTICS

1. A very important aspect of recording in the Probation Department of the Court of General Sessions is the form and substance of the various reports to the court and the other relatively standardized forms which must be used in specific situations. These reports, although standardized provide the the probation officer with wide latitude so that the interested authorities are given a comprehensive and individualized pic-

ture of the probationer and his situation. Each probation officer is provided with a Book of Forms which cover the following reports:

A. Application to Establish Terms of Restitution.

B. Application to Suspend Payments.

C. Application for Permission to Leave the Jurisdiction of the Court.

D. Application for Permission to Hold the Issuance of Bench Warrant in Abeyance.

E. Request for Non-Issuance of Bench Warrant.

F. Letter to District Attorney for Return of Violator.

G. Request for Date of Hearing (Violation of Probation).

H. Violation of Probation Report.

I. Supplementary letter (Violation of Probation).

J. Application for Extension of Probationary Period.

K. Permission to Close Case (and revoke Bench Warrant).

L. Summary to Psychiatric Clinic (for Re-examination).

M. Discharge from Probation Report.

2. The probation officer is responsible for securing and keeping up to date the information which is asked for upon:

A. The Field Sheet

    (a) Identifying Data.

    (b) Personal Data.

    (c) Legal Data.

    (d) Contacts with probationer.

    (e) Collateral visits.

    (f) Payments in Restitution or Family Support.

    (g) Record of Earnings.

    (h) Interested agencies.

B. The Face Card

    (a) Identifying data.

    (b) Personal data.

(c) Legal data.

(d) Contacts with probationer.

(e) Collateral Visits.

(f) Payments in Restitution and Family Support.

(g) Employment History.

(h) Details re Immediate Family.

(i) Details re Other Relatives.

(j) Interested persons and agencies.

C. Termination Slip

(a) Identifying Data.

(b) Response

1. Reports.
2. Conduct.
3. General Attitude.

(c) Changes in Home and Environment.

(d) Employment

1. Steady or irregular.
2. Position.
3. Wages.
4. Reasons for leaving.
5. Attitude toward work.

(e) Schooling during probation.

(f) Restitution or Family Support.

(g) Rearrests.

(h) Health Treatment.

(i) Agencies contacted for probationer.

(j) Agencies contacted for probationer's family.

D. The Daily Supervision Sheet

    (a) Contacts with Probationers

        1. Personal, Mail, Telephone Reports.

        2. Verification of Employment, Earnings, Savings.

        3. Home and Employment Visits.

    (b) Contacts with Social Agencies

        1. By visits, mail, telephone or at office.

    (c) Other Contacts

        1. By visits, mail, telephone or at office.

E. Monthly Time Report

    (a) Distribution of Time.

    (b) Case load.

    (c) Number of visits.

    (d) Expenses.

F. Monthly Statistical Sheet

    (a) Data re Active, Mail and Bench Warrant Cases.

    (b) Data re employment of probationers classified into regular, irregular, part time, unemployed and unemployable.

    (c) Data re Earnings of probationer.

    (d) Data re Savings of probationers.

Chapter IX

THE COMMUNITY'S CONTRIBUTION TO CRIME

The New York City Housing Authority, desirous of obtaining adequate information concerning the relationship of slum areas to crime, requested the Probation Department of the Court of General Sessions to institute a statistical survey of crime and juvenile delinquency in relation to the slums in the City of New York.

To facilitate the study, a Committee was formed under the title of "Committee on Crime and Delinquency of the New York City Housing Authority." This Committee included the Chief Probation Officer as Chairman, John N. Stanislaus, Probation Officer of the Court of General Sessions, and Bernard Botein, Assistant District Attorney of New York County.

The Probation Department welcomed this opportunity to make a contribution to the eradication of the slums, and Mr. Stanislaus was assigned to train and direct the staff in gathering the source material, and to correlate the findings. His intense interest and energy, attention to detail, and evaluation of findings are worthy of the highest commendation.

The findings of the survey were presened in the book "The Slum and Crime." One thousand copies of this book were published by the New York Housing Authority through a grant of Federal funds. The books were distributed to housing commissions and other interested agencies, and to university and public libraries both here and abroad. Although the issue has long since been exhausted, we are constantly receiving requests from interested agencies and persons for copies of the book.

In acknowledging receipt of the completed survey, Langdon Post, Chairman of the New York City Housing Authority, and Tenement House Commissioner of the City of New York, stated:

"I requested the Probation Department of the Court of General Sessions to conduct this survey because of its outstanding national reputation and the constructive contributions to the study of crime causation which it has made in the past. My expectations were amply met by the most comprehensive crime survey that has ever been made in the City of New York."[1]

Commenting on the contents of the published book, Senator Robert F. Wagner stated at the Conference of Mayors of the United States at Washington, D. C.:

"I wish that every man and woman in America would read a book published for the New York Housing Authority in 1934, entitled: 'The Slum and Crime.' It proves irrefutably that every slum area, every ramshackle rural hovel is a corroding influence that saps the strength and character of the younger generation."[2]

The following outline of the survey and the data which it revealed are excerpts from "The Slum and Crime":

Limitations upon Study:

The staff for the survey was provided by the Civil Works Administration in sufficient numbers to carry through the program which was developed. Working quarters were provided by the Tenement House Department in its Brooklyn office. The personnel consisted of 170 workers, untrained and inexperienced in the field of criminology. Trained research workers were lacking. Remuneration of the staff was on a relief basis.

Because limitations were placed on the time of the study, the survey could not be extended beyond a study of offenses for one year. The year 1930 was selected for two reasons. The statistical findings could be correlated directly with census figures for population, and we believed that the full impact of the depression had not been felt until about the latter part of the year selected. Uncertainty as to how much of the crime statistically shown was attributable to depression conditions thereby would be somewhat minimized.

Even for the study of a one year period, the data had to be gathered from many sources. A study in distribution obviously is based on the

---

[1]Post, Langdon. Letter to the Chief Probation Officer, November 15, 1934.
[2]*New York Evening Post,* November 20, 1935.

residence of offenders. The addresses of those arrested were procurable only from the police precinct blotters and visits also had to be made to the various courts for data on those convicted. The more extensive the data sought, the longer would be the time required for their transcription.

The practical choice, then, lay in limitation of the type of data to be secured.

Character of Study:

The survey makes no pretense to furnish more than an index of crime and juvenile delinquency in substandard areas. Statistics, after all, only measure volume. They do not and cannot explain crime causation.

Any study of crime must begin with the individual. Otherwise how explain certain obvious facts. The facts, for instance, that of two given individuals within the same family, one is an honest citizen and the other a criminal. Another fact equally to be explained is that while a considerable number of slum dwellers may commit crimes, the majority do not. The neighborhood environment of all is the same. The answer, of course, is the individual.

The realistic necessity for individual case studies does not preclude the use of statistics. The value of these as indicia is immeasurable. Only as we have these indices in every increasing numbers, can we form a correct estimate of the crime problem. The innumerable factors it involves, even in the case of a single delinquent, is best illustrated by case study.

A number of case studies taken from the files of the Probation Department of the Court of General Sessions, which were selected both on the basis of the offender's residence in the areas studied and because of the social situations which they graphically illustrated, were included in the study.

The Slum and Crime:

As social reflexes, the same conditions which made slums are often present in delinquent careers. Bad housing, low income levels or poverty itself, the weakened grip of regulatory institutions like the family, objectionable groupings, unwholesome or inadequate recreational outlets are but some. The full meaning of the slum and crime will only reach the mind in a confused form unless all these situations are understood, separately and clearly. Even then the delinquent still remains to be studied as a person.

Thinking on the slum frequently freezes into the conviction that crime is its only output. The conviction and its implication that environment alone makes a delinquent are scientifically untenable. Were such the case, then Park Avenue would be a paradise, and a penthouse there insurance against misbehavior.

The belief that when slums are abolished, all crime will cease automatically is likewise a fallacy. Demolishing the slum unquestionably will reduce delinquency. The prediction that it will do away with it entirely, utterly ignores the personal element in crime. The same outcome has been predicted for the abolition of capital. Much room for doubt as to so utopian a prediction remains after we consider the result of the Soviet experiment in this respect.[3]

The slum is alike the by-product of changes in the economic structure and of social hindsight. An instance of these changes, one that is traditionally cited, is the industrial revolution. Along with great prosperity it produced great poverty and the slum. This historical fact, combined with current experience, should indicate forcefully that most slum conditions are at root the resultant of larger social and economic forces.

The Slum—An Area of Minimum Choice:

The slum, as conceived by sociologists, is a natural, an interstitial or an area of minimum choice. All three designations ultimately repose on the idea of social disorganization, as opposed to plan and solidarity. The disorganization is seen readily in bad housing, poverty and dependency, overcrowding, within and congestion outside the home, and higher incidence rates for disease, crime and juvenile delinquency.

---

[3]cf. Boris Brasol, *The Elements of Crime*, Oxford University Press, New York, 1932, p. IX, for a discussion of these points.

It is often forgotten that the slum is the home of a large law abiding population. The same economic pressures that compel people to live in it, act also to keep them there. At no time is this more apparent than during economic upheavals. The world depression has thrust aside the Darwinian theory of the weak falling by the wayside as the only explanation for economic incompetence and poverty. The disabilities occasioned by depression have reduced thousands to a slum level of existence;—thereby proving that poverty is not an exclusive product of the slum but that the slum is usually its end result.

Cultural groups best exemplify social selection, the second force operative in natural areas. Groups of this kind are built up from such elements as a common racial origin, language, traditions and folkways. A large number, those with immigrant backgrounds especially, prefer to remain within the orbit of their own cultural group. Change would necessitate new adaptations for which they may have neither the desire nor the initiative, nor even yet the means.

Social selection works similarly to make the slum a habitat for antisocial groupings. Cultural levels and living standards, as Shulman has noted, are lower. There is neither neighborhood solidarity in the community sense, nor that strongly organized group opinion which frequenly acts like a brake upon individual misbehavior. Attitudes either of apathy or indifference, toward acceptable modes of behavior and individual delinquencies are common. The criminally inclined, in consequence, find a greater leeway and a safer hideout in the slum than elsewhere.

It is this presence of the law abiding and the criminally minded that gives the slum a distinctively heterogeneous character. In view of this, any broad statement about the criminality of all slum dwellers would be as inaccurate as it is manifestly unjust to the law abiding populace. The fact that the slum is a delinquency area is attributable in part to its being an area of minimum choice and also to the social distintegration which occurs in such an area.

The Slum—A Delinquency Area:

Studies in this, other cities and abroad indicate forcefully that the slum is a locus of adult crime and juvenile delinquency. Where the

260

studies are incomplete, it is in understanding the facts. Obviously only apprehended delinquents can be enumerated. No estimate can be given of unapprehended offenders whose number unquestionably would swell the totals.

The substandard areas, notably those in Manhattan, were found to contain a greater percentage of delinquents per one thousand of population than the non-slum sections. Here to cite but a few are the supporting statistics. Forty-three out of every thousand residents of the slums were arrested during 1930. Twice as many juveniles adjudged delinquents came from the slum as compared with the non-slum sections. One-third of all the felons convicted in General Sessions and Kings County courts resided in the Manhattan slums. More than half the number of Manhattan residents convicted of robberies, assaults and murders came from substandard areas. Most striking of all, is the findings about murder convictions. Twelve out of every thirteen persons convicted of murder were residents of slum areas. The trend, as indicated in the foregoing figures, is neither unique nor insignificant. It is wholly in keeping with findings in other cities.

Noteworthy is the reference to physical deterioration. Wherever it characterizes an area, delinquency rates are high. Elmer noticed this in his Minneapolis-St. Paul Survey.[4] The other cities studied by Shaw and McKay—Philadelphia, Seattle, Cleveland, Birmingham, Denver and Richmond, showed a like situation.[5] New York is no exception. During a survey here in 1930 by the New York State Crime Commission, Shulman ascertained what Shaw had discovered in Chicago, and what delinquency studies in any large city reveal with striking uniformity—the fact that a deteriorated is also a delinquency area.

Environment and Delinquency:

Social environment is not a matter that can be reduced to the simplicity and precision of a multiplication table. It is composed of many forces, mostly intangible and hence immeasurable. On no two persons

---

[4]Manuel C. Elmer, *Maladjustment of Youth in Relation of Density of Population,* Publication of the American Sociological Society, Chicago, 1925, vol. 20, pp. 138-140.
[5]Clifford R. Shaw and Henry D. McKay, *Social Factors in Juvenile Delinquency,* National Commissions on Law Observance and Enforcement. Reports on the Causes of Crime, Washington, D. C. 1931, vol. II, pp. 140-188.

does it act alike. This assures a different outcome for environment upon individuals even within the same family, and explains the difficulty of treating the outcome mathematically.

Delinquency, for example, can be measured on a distributional scale. One area will be found to have more delinquents than another. While the greater prevalence suggests that the behavior problems these delinquents represent are allied in some degree to their social environment, it does not explain their underlying causation. Only that approach, which a blend of the psychological and the sociological and which the case method best embodies, can supply the real answer.

Some of the links in this connection have been ascertained through social exploration, group and individual case studies. An example is Thrasher's competent study of gangs in Chicago.[6] Sociologists, on the basis of such accumulated data have drawn tentative conclusions about environment as a positive factor in delinquent behavior.

Group relationships outside the family are among the environmental forces with a more direct implication for delinquency. At the root of these is the association habit, one that lies deep in all normal humans. Combined with the emulative it is frequently a habit that leads into unwholesome and sometimes criminal associations. The choice of associates by adolescents at any time requires discrimination. A much greater selectivity is necessary amid so heterogeneous a population as that of slum areas. Adult delinquents, though not in every instance professionally criminal, abound in such areas. This condition gives emphasis to the danger unsupervised youths, and especially those in deteriorated regions, incur in forming companionships promiscuously.

The case histories in the Probation Department of the Court of General Sessions are rich in examples of what ill-advised associations produce. Approximately three thousand of these cases were inspected during the present study. The inspection disclosed that a large number of the offenses were perpetrated by two or more youths acting in concert. The groupings occurred with greater frequency in slum areas. Points of association usually included residence in the same vicinity and the intimacy of the same age groups. Relatively few of the groupings possessed stigmata characteristic of professional criminal gangs.

---

[6] Frederick M. Thrasher, *The Gang*, University of Chicago Press, Chicago, 1929.

One member at least of such groups had been delinquent previously. As often there was a non-delinquent, at once impressionable and possessed of the emulative habit.

Initiation in crime demands no long apprenticeship. Nowhere is it more easily facilitated than in the slum. It is this facilitation, even acceleration of delinquent growth, that is a direct environmental influence in slum areas.

Housing and Delinquency:

No picture where only situations outside the home are sketched can completely illustrate the relation of environment to delinquency. The home is the primary or immediate environment of a person. As such, its influences are the first and longest to play upon him.

Antagonisms arise where there is overcrowding. Little or no space is afforded for the free expression of personality. Irritations as well as harmful repressions ensue; jealousies also and those deep-seated resentments which always produce emotional combustion. The most damaging effects of this are upon personality, though instances are far from scarce of physical assaults, incited by long smouldering grudges, no less than impulsive reactions to irritations.

Inaedquate play space is a major characteristic of the overcrowded home. Children are handicapped the most. More than any, it is the one factor that compels them to seek outdoors what they are denied inside the home. Together with inadequate playgrounds, it best explains street life and recreation in congested areas. Both are acknowledged paths to delinquency in many case.

Housing must be accepted as an influence in behavior. The fact that areas of bad housing are notable for high delinquency rates suggests a relationship. The fact, however, that the physical cannot be separated from the social, economic and personal elements that constitute a home, shows the inherent difficulty in isolating housing as a separate element for study in relation to malbehavior.

It must be acknowledged that the value of statistical studies relating housing to delinquency is limited. The reasons for this are best set forth by James Ford, who states:

263

"No adequate studies of the causes of crime which properly isolate housing factors are available at this time. Nor does it seem probable that housing factors can be sufficiently isolated from other environmental factors, or from conditions of family life, moral training and the mental and emotional make-up of the individual, to make such a study convincing."[7]

As an outstanding fact in a slum environment, bad housing is a direct challenge to social action. The knowledge that we still have such housing is startling enough. The added revelation that antiquated slum dwellings are tenanted, over-tenanted at that, raises doubt both as to our social conscience and our boast of world leadership in social progress. Certainly that progress cannot be reflected in crime reduction until the areas where crime and delinquency flourish most are eradicated.

The experience of large European cities furnishes ample evidence of the desirable benefits to be gained from improved housing. Assuredly the most desirable is a reduction in behavior disorders. A concrete illustration in Liverpool, a city notorious for its bad housing, is given by J. H. Clarke.[8]

One area before its demolition, had 202 arrests per annum. After it was reconstructed, the number decreased to 84 and eight years later to 4 per annum. The same progressive change occurred in all areas that had been rehabilitated.

Slum Clearance as Crime Control:

Results like the foregoing have obtained wherever there has been slum clearance.

The delinquent may be removed from a bad environment, but the environment remains for others. He may be confined behind prison walls, reformed and then returned to the world outside. Economic pressure forces him back into the setting whence he came. The revolution in his case has been solely that of a wheel. With the difference that only a vicious circle has been traversed.

---

[7]James Ford, *Improved Housing as a Means of Crime Prevention,* Annals of the American Academy of Social and Political Sciences, May 1926, p. 177.
[8]John Joseph Clarke, *The Housing Problem,* Isaac Pitman's Sons, London, 1920, pp. 218-219.

Facts like these compel the recognition of environment as an objective for social reform along with the individual. No person, least of all a delinquent residing in the slums, lives in a vacuum. The net of crime prevention accordingly must be flung far and wide. The slum must be abolished, for crime prevention as well as for humanitarian reasons.

No better substitutes have yet been designed to replace a decent home, a suitable neighborhood, adequate and supervised recreation, as constructive pressures upon the individual. Where all are operative, delinquency rates are lowest. The neighborhood should be the unit of reconstruction; socially as well as physically. Anything short of this would be neither slum clearance nor crime prevention.

The slum, as already suggested, is not one but a set of problems. Some are deep-seated in the economic, others in the social structure. Others still are the accompaniments of the city's growth upwards and outwards. Poverty is in the slum, along with disease and crime. The law abiding rub elbows with the criminally minded. The delinquent plays with the non-delinquent child. For all, there is the same wretched housing, the same overcrowding, the same street life and the same restricted play space.

These are the community's contribution to crime and as it improves the social setting, slum clearance will help to disentangle the skein which is crime, wherein environmental influences and personal traits are confusingly enmeshed.

Abstract of Findings:

The most offender concentrations occur in Manhattan. They coincide with population congestion, vary in degree of severity and are mainly in Harlem and the lower East Side. Although largely within, they are not confined exclusively to substandard areas.

The slum areas collectively have higher offender ratios to population and to the square block than the non-slum sections of Manhattan. The incidence rates of juvenile delinquency in the slum are high and suggest the possibility that adult patterns of misconduct are emulated freely.

The higher incidence rates of crime and juvenile delinquency indicate that the substandard are major delinquency areas. Conclusions about the causes of this situation cannot be arrived at scientifically unless the case method is the approach used.

More than half the Manhattan felons who were convicted of robberies, assaults and murders came from substandard sections. Those residing elsewhere were convicted more frequently of larcenies and burglaries. The margin of difference, however, is small, numbering sixteen convictions for larceny and two for burglary.

During 1930, offenders living in Manhattan who were sentenced to State Prison totalled 499. Of this number 284 dwelt in the substandard areas of that borough. Measured by institutional commitments, the deteriorated areas contributed more than their share to the crime costs of the community.

Central place in any criminal census no longer belongs to the middle-aged offender. It has been usurped by youth, along with the monopoly in robberies and burglaries. The average delinquent today has yet to reach his thirtieth year. Whether he comes from the slums or the suburbs, he is usually a native born white, still in the twenties.

The age shift in criminality is neither sudden nor yet is it a signal for pessimism. The youthful may indeed be the most serious offender. He likewise is the most curable, provided that he is treated immediately and intelligently. When his social implementation is in the slum, the cure must depend also for its permanency upon new surroundings. The delay in supplying these, if for no other reason than as social insurance against tomorrow's crime and juvenile delinquency, makes society and not youth the real culprit.

The maximum for juvenile offenders is reached between the thirteenth and sixteenth years. Out of 3,660 adjudged delinquent in Manhattan and Brooklyn, 2,738, or 75 percent, came within these age brackets. They embrace the period of puberty and also represent the upper limits of Children's Court jurisdiction.

During 1930, 6,110 male and female adolescents living in Manhattan were arrested. In other words, 64 out of every thousand males between

16 and 20 years of age allegedly violated the law. The Brooklyn rate is lower. There, 40 in every thousand adolescent males were arrested. A marked increase is observable in the rate for the slum areas of both boroughs. In Manhattan it is 74 per thousand; in Brooklyn, 59 per thousand.

The form crime assumes among adolescents is shown by the character of their felonies. Robbery, followed by larceny and assault, led among Manhattan adolescents. There is no deviation from this sequence when slum and non-slum sections are compared.

As a criminal, the young adult is more conspicuous than the adolescent. With the latter he divides responsibility for approximately fifty percent of the more serious offenses. Frequently he is found in ranks of gangsters and racketeers with whom spectacular crimes are a forte. Whatever new direction criminal activities have taken during recent years, the young adult usually is the one who has shared it.

Outstanding . . . is the percentage of felony convictions chargeable to young adults. There were 272 such convictions involving Manhattan residents, of whom 144 belonged in slum areas. The figures for Brooklyn are striking. The second largest number of felony convictions is in this age group. Although the young adult is less frequently convicted of misdemeanors and petty offenses than are older age groups, he is responsible for an undue proportion.

Statistical support is given . . . to the belief that an increase in age is accompanied by a decrease in criminality. The viewpoint is further borne out by figures for the 36 and the upwards age group.

Two facts stand out sharply when the sex composition of offenders is considered statistically. First and most obvious is the fact that an overwhelming majority of offenders are males. As much does this apply to juvenile delinquents as to felons.

Among the more salient findings as to the composition of the offender population are the youthfulness of the serious offender, the relative infrequency with which females appear in delinquent situations and the preponderance of native-born offenders. The adolescent and the youthful adult male unquestionably are the most conspicuous factors in crime today. Youths between the ages of 16 and 20 were convicted of' felonies more frequently than any other age group of Brooklyn residents. With an advance in age, seemingly there is a decrease in criminality. The upper age levels are composed mostly of alcoholics, vagrants and persons convicted of Disorderly Conduct. Among females, delinquency was found to reach a peak in the 26 to 35 age group, which contains a majority of the women convicted of felonies, misdemeanors and prostitution.

One-fourth of the felony convictions involving Manhattan residents were attributable to the foriegn born. The majority of foreign-born offenders residing both in Manhattan and Brooklyn were charged with petty offenses. In the face of these statistical findings the belief that the foreign born are responsible for most of our crime is utterly untenable. Crime is a native product.

Recreation in the Slums:

Between the misuse of leisure time and delinquency there is often a straight line relationship. Nowhere does this so frequently hold true as in the slums. There the street is the principal playground. Opportunities for wholesome recreation are notoriously limited. More often than otherwise, the play life of a child is unsupervised.

In the fourteen areas under consideration, 61,720 children were tabulated. The majority appeared to overage from 9 to 15 years of age. Of the 61,720 counted, 55,191 were on the streets and 5,801 in playgrounds. Many were observed to be loitering and to be taking no active interest in the street games. Others were engaged in such mischievous activities as throwing sticks under passing automobiles and starting bonfires, often dangerously near to buildings. Shooting craps and playing "cops and robbers" were conspicuous among the various play habits observed. Most of the children, however, were engrossed in playing handball, tag, and other innocuous games.

Apart from their insufficient number, playgrounds in the substandard areas are poorly situated and, on the whole, inadequately equipped. Few measure up to accepted standards of size, equipment and relative remoteness from dangerous traffic arteries and crossings. From the standpoint of delinquency prevention, they are also deficient, notably in their failure to attract children who stand in greatest need of wholesome play life.

Poolrooms are almost three times as numerous as playgrounds in the substandard areas. With pool playing and with many poolrooms, there is no quarrel. It is against the small and obscure poolroom, frequently encountered in the slums, that sociologists and welfare workers have levelled their criticisms. Mostly, these center around the acknowledged fact that such poolrooms are "hang-outs" for loafers, petty gamblers and criminals.

From the limited aspects briefly touched upon, it is apparent that nowhere are recreational facilities more urgently needed than in the slums. Repeatedly it has been said that playgrounds are cheaper to build than reformatories. To say this, is not to assume that delinquency is attributable, in the last analysis, to the absence of adequate play space. Wholesome and properly supervised recreation, however, is a powerful ally in checking delinquent behavior.

The longer we tolerate social conditions that help to foster delinquent behavior, the more problems we heap up for ourselves and for the coming generation. Actually we beget the criminal of tomorrow. Common sense, along with a sense of economy, dictates that if we are to reduce our criminal population, bigger and more vigorous steps than any we are now taking are vitally necessary.

The slum clearance project gives promise of being one such step. As it replaces outmoded dwellings with modern housing and provides large sized, suitably equipped and properly supervised playgrounds, it also becomes an effective social weapon in the warfare against crime.

Chapter X

SUMMER CAMP WORK

Summer Camp Work, more popularly known as "Fresh Air Work," originated with the Children's Aid Society about fifty years ago. Al though originally inaugurated to provide summer vacation for sick and under-nourished children, the service has gradually been extended so as to apply also to healthy children from under-privileged homes Although its value as an opportunity for the recuperation of sickly children is apparent, just as important is the service that summer camp render in developing desirable behavior patterns and building character

In addition to providing a form of supervised recreation which i not available to children in the slum areas, present-day summer camp are utilizing the services of psychologists, psychiatrists and trained social workers so as to meet and attempt to resolve behavior problem and to carry into effect educational programs.

Experience and studies have patently revealed the far-reaching effec which Summer Camp Work has had not only in assisting the children themselves, but also in improving the relationship between social agency and family. As a result the progress of other aspects of the treatmen plan was facilitated.

Probation Camp Work

The Probation Department of the Court of General Sessions ha accepted, as have other social agencies, summer camp work as an in tegral part of its treatment program.

The importance of this phase of our work is obvious when it i recognized that a large proportion of probationers reside in slum areas The physical aspects of their home life are characterized by wretched living conditions, congestion, poor sanitation, etc. The children of many of these families live in circumstances which tend to produce emotional imbalance, a warped social outlook and physical pathology. The parents poor concepts of child rearing and control become especially evident during the summer months when the children are away from school, and hese children, during this period, are in a greater measure exposed o the unwholesome street influences of slum areas. Recognition of this situation provided this Department with an opportunity to extend its crime prevention program.

For the most part, the children sent to the summer camps are drawn from under-privileged families, and suffer from malnutrition, poor habits of hygiene, lack of cleanliness, etc. The normal, healthy routine and wholesome food at camp benefits them immeasurably.

Another direct result of the integration of summer camp work into our treatment program has been the improved relationship which develops between this Department and the probationers and their families. Providing of summer vacations for children is to the probationers a tangible and concrete manifestation of our sincere interest in them and their families.

Method of Procedure

As it was found inefficient for individual probation officers to attend to the numerous preliminary steps preparatory to sending the children to summer camps, one probation officer was selected to direct and supervise the details incident to this program. Mr. Theodore Concevitch, the Probation Officer in charge of these activities for the past ten years, has administered this service in a manner which has reflected credit on the Department.

The probation officers select the children who would most benefit by camp vacations. They then submit the names and addresses to the officer in charge of summer camp work, who makes all the subsequent necessary arrangements which include complying with the requirements of the Department of Health of the City of New York.

A study was made of approximately one hundred and twenty-eight camps. The officer, who was fully acquainted with the case histories of the children, was in a position to select that camp which was most suitable to the particular needs of the individual children. Careful selection was essential since in addition to the behavior problems which some of the children manifested, a large number of them were suffering from definite physical disabilities. Every effort was made to place

271

children in particular camps which were best equipped to handle pathological conditions such as cardiac, tubercular, and malnutrition cases It was also found that certain camps by virtue of the type of counsellors employed, were best able to cope with behavior disorders.

This process of classification begins during the latter part of February or the early part of March of the year in which the children are to be sent to camp. The first step is to have the children examined physically so that where possible, existing defects could be corrected or ameliorated. Treatment and advice revolves about such organic conditions as heart dysfunctions, tuberculosis, poor teeth, tonsils, adenoids, skin infections, ear, nose and throat conditions. In some instances, regular weekly follow-up work is conducted until the actual departure for camp.

All children are examined four or five months prior to leaving for camp. This entails securing the cooperation of physicians and clinics and arranging for the children's appearance at specified times. These examinations reveal that the hair of a large number of children are infected with nits and vermin; many are suffering from malnutrition Visual oral and nasal pathologies are quite frequent and two cases of scarlet fever were discovered as well as a number of cardiac and tubercular conditions. Less than 25% of the children sent to summer camps were found to be in perfect physical condition.

At the inception of our summer camp program a surprising number of families were totally indifferent to our efforts. It was only through vigorous and personal attention both by the supervising probation officer and the probation officer in charge of camp work that we seecured the necessary cooperation from the parents.

Twenty-four hours before being sent to camp, every child is re-examined. This is done so as to determine what has been done to correct physical disabilities and to ascertain whether or not any child has acquired any new pathology. The child's address is also checked against the index of contagious diseases kept by the Board of Health, so as to determine whether the child is residing at an address where contagious diseases exist. If this is true, the child is not permitted to leave for camp, lest it might prove a source of infection to other children.

Cooperating Agencies

This Department has been fortunate in securing excellent cooperation from the agencies which operate the summer camps to which our children are sent. Workers with these agencies who were unfamiliar with problems of delinquency were readily convinced that the children of our probationers were no different than those of other families in similarly impoverished circumstances.

We were also successful in having a number of children sent to private homes throughout the eastern states. These children met qualifications made by the families desiring them. Such specifications included age, religion, special abilities, etc. In many cases the same child was requested year after year by the same family. During the past five years a limited number of mothers and their children, who were under five years of age, were provided with twelve-day vacations.

In the ten years during which this work has been carried on, the following agencies and camps have cooperated with this Department in the successful development of our camp program:

1. The Herald Tribune Fresh Air Fund
2. Christian Herald Summer Home
3. Catholic Charities
4. Salvation Army
5. Jewish Vacation Association
6. Protestant Welfare League
7. Children's Aid Society
8. Association for Improving Conditions of Poor
9. Boys' Club
10. East Side Vacation Camps Association
11. Life's Summer Camps
12. Jay Gee Camp
13. Little Wanderers Home
14. Newark Female Charitable Society
15. Institute for Family Service
16. Brace Memorial Newsboys' Home
17. Brooklyn Bureau of Charities

18. University Settlement
19. Hudson Guild
20. Greenwich House
21. Harlem House
22. Bellevue-Yorkville Health Centre
23. Mulberry Health Centre
24. Harlem Health Centre (Health Department Station)
25. Church of All Nations
26. Il Progresso Italo-Americano Daily
27. Ella Fohs Camp
28. Seventh Masonic Camp
29. Gad Lodge Vacation Foundation
30. Young Men's Christian Association
31. Young Men's Hebrew Association
32. Vanderbilt Clinic

During the ten years of summer camp service, this Department was instrumental in providing fifteen hundred and twenty-nine children, relatives of our probationers, with summer vacations. The number of children sent to camp each year since 1927 follows:

Year		Number
1927		8
1928		139
1929		179
1930		189
1931		193
1932		201
1933		233
1934		114
1935		130
1936		143
Total		1,529

It is to be noted that in the year 1927, the first year of our work, only eight children were sent to camp. This is attributable to the fact that the difficulties of organizing this new project plus the preliminary work necessary in securing contact with camp agencies, hospitals, clinics, etc. restricted attention to all but a few especially needy families.

Avoiding Identification

The need of protecting children from any unfavorable comment because of the delinquency of some member of their family, was immediately recognized and met. Despite the fact that frequent contacts were necessary in having the children examined at the Clinics, meeting them at their homes, taking them to the railroad stations, meeting them there in order to return them to their homes, etc., at no time were any of these children's fellow campers apprised of their situation.

The probation officer and his assistants were addressed as "counsellor" and in all letters addressed to the worker the words "Welfare Department of General Sessions" were used. This precaution was also observed in the allotment sheets which accompanied the children to the various camps. The executives of the various camps who were, of course, aware of the children's status, took especial care to avoid identifying the children to others as coming from a delinquent family. During the ten years of our work in this field, not a single complaint has come to our attention that children from the homes of probationers were discriminated against because of their family situation.

Length of Vacations

At the inception of the summer camp work movement there developed the custom that the vacation period at welfare vacation camps should be of two weeks duration. It is rather apparent that this period of two weeks is too brief a time in which to attain all of the objectives sought in regard to the improvement of conditions existing in these children; especially in consideration that their disabilities, physical, emotional, or social have developed over a number of years. During the first two years that this Department engaged in this work the average vacation period was of two weeks duration. However, during succeeding years, a large number of children were able to pass more than two weeks in camp. Of late, approximately twenty per cent of the children received vacations ranging from three to six weeks. In order to provide continuity for the work, an effort was made to send the same children to the same camps during successive summers. According to the camp records, children returning to camps at which they had previously had vacations, were found to adjust more readily to camp activities. Especially manifest was their desire to renew acquaintanceship with the other children with whom they had had contact during the previous summer. Of course, it is apparent that in some instances it was not possible to follow up, in this manner, the summer camp work of the previous year. If a family's economic condition improved to the extent that they would not be eligible for this aid or when probationers were discharged from probation, the children thereafter, except in isolated instances, were not eligible for reenrollment.

However, it was incumbent upon the supervising probation officer to follow out the recommendations made by the camp authorities with a view towards correcting physical disabilities or psychic maladjustments.

Evaluation

Persons on probation represent a group which has had conflict with society in a criminal sense. In addition, the children sent to camp constitute an underprivileged group. It follows logically, then, that these children were exposed to a greater degree than the average child to the unwholesome conditions which motivated the anti-social conduct which resulted in contact with this Department. A study of these children revealed that the indicated combination of circumstances resulted in their having irregular habits of personal hygiene, eating, sleeping, etc. The intelligent routine of camp life resulted in the correction of these and similar undesirable behavior patterns.

The process of training was evolved so as to create self-confidence where it had heretofore been lacking. Association with other children has led to the development of a social consciousness where previously there had been timidity, isolation and a feeling of rejection. Mutual participation in cooperative tasks and supervised play activities, engendered in the children a new found willingness to submit to authority. There was a marked carry-over of this attitude to the home life of the children.

Children who were handicapped by serious ailments such as cardiac disorders and tuberculosis, as well as those suffering from malnutrition were sent to health camps where they were the recipients of specialized treatment developed to meet their individual needs. A number of camps maintain social service departments which develop long range treatment programs for the children and has had contact with them during subsequent years. Camp psychiatrists were of inestimable value in treating behavior problems.

Camp programs, play or study, as the general rule include the following subjects:

1. Astronomy	16. Flowers and Trees
2. Athletics	17. Fungi
3. Birds	18. Handicraft
4. Boating	19. Hiking
5. Boxing	20. Indian Life
6. Campcraft	21. Knot Tying
7. Camp Paper	22. Life Saving
8. Canoeing	23. Music
9. Cooking	24. Public Speaking
10. Dramatics	25. Photography
11. Domestic Sciences	26. Religious Services
12. Citizenship	27. Riding
13. Diving	28. Sailing
14. Entertaining	29. Sewing
15. First Aid	30. Swimming

In addition to the physical improvement which was easily discernible in these children, their social and character development was manifested by marked improvement in their family and social relationships subsequent to their return from camp. Although it is difficult to tabulate this type of development, a survey reveals definitely favorable results in the following phases of community activity:

1. Mixing with others.
2. Cooperating with other members of the family.
3. Courtesy.
4. Religious practices.

277

5. Assuming responsibilities.
6. Displaying courage.
7. Respect for property.
8. Self-confidence.
9. Responsiveness to parents.
10. Volunteering to help others.
11. Personal tidiness.
12. Industriousness.
13. Good manners and etiquette.
14. Assuming leadership.
15. Improved health.

Another interesting survey was conducted, the results of which, however, cannot be definitely correlated with summer camp activity because of the absence of a control group and of necessary identifying social data. The names of the fifteen hundred and twenty-nine children who had been sent to summer camps through this Department were checked with the social service exchange. It was found that only three of these children subsequently came into contact with law enforcement agencies. The remainder were unknown to any court or correctional institution. It is not too much to assume that the new, wholesome experiences of camp life were, at least to some extent, positive crime prevention influences.

A statistical analysis of the results obtained through this Department's activities in connection with summer camp work is not possible. However, our experience as well as the experience of other social service agencies has unequivocally revealed that lessons of self-reliance and mutual cooperation have resulted in the development of children who grow into better and healthier citizens.

Chapter XI

DIVISION OF INVESTIGATION

CHART 1

CASES INVESTIGATED

Year	Male	Female	Total*
1927	2,287	106	2,393
1928	2,139	79	2,218
1929	2,214	75	2,289
1930	2,842	85	2,927
1931	2,819	98	2,917
1932	2,761	102	2,863
1933	2,427	86	2,513
1934	2,799	99	2,898
1935	2,382	110	2,492
1936	2,242	120	2,362
Total	24,912	960	25,872*
		3.71% of total	

*After "Cases Investigated" and "Dispositions," all totals will be 25,858 as 13 Male and 1 Female will be dropped. These 14 were discovered to be under 16 years of age by our Investigator, as follows:

1927	1 Male	
1928	1 "	
1930	5 "	
1931	4 "	and 1 Female
1933	1 "	
1934	1 "	

DIVISION OF INVESTIGATION

CHART 2

Dispositions of Cases Investigated

	Penal and Correctional Institutions		Placed Under Supervision		Institution for Mental Defectives or Insane		Other Dispositions	
	Male	Female	Male	Female	Male	Female	Male	Femal
1927	1,631	54	579	46	34	—	43	6
1928	1,541	51	532	24	50	—	16	4
1929	1,585	50	564	21	52	1	13	3
1930	2,012	47	733	31	50	1	47	6
1931	2,167	65	559	31	32	—	61	2
1932	2,132	66	532	35	9	—	88	1
1933	1,871	54	432	28	24	1	100	3
1934	2,157	68	520	29	25	1	97	1
1935	1,813	64	468	35	30	2	71	9
1936	1,686	69	455	39	30	2	71	10
Totals	18,595	588	5,374	319	336	8	607	45
	74.64% of Total Male Invest.	61.25% of Total Female Invest.	21.57% of Total Male Invest.	33.23% of Total Female Invest.	1.35% of Total Male Invest.	.83% of Total Female Invest.	2.44% of Total Male Invest.	4.69% of Tota Female Invest
Grand Total	19,183 74.15% of Total Investigations		5,693 22% of Total Investigations		344 1.33% of Total Investigations		652 2.52% of Tota Investigations	

280

CHART 3

Color of Offenders

	White				Colored				Yellow		Red	
				% of Total Invest.				% of Total Invest.		% of Total Invest.		% of Total Invest.
	Male	Fe-male	Total	Same Yr.	Male	Fe-male	Total	Same Yr.	Male	Same Yr.	Male	Same Yr.
1927	1,748	76	1,824	76.25	530	30	560	23.41	8	.33	—	—
1928	1,600	56	1,656	74.70	523	23	546	24.63	14	.63	1	.04
1929	1,675	45	1,720	75.14	532	30	562	24.55	4	.17	3	.13
1930	2,121	62	2,183	74.71	703	23	726	24.84	11	.38	2	.07
1931	2,067	53	2,120	72.80	737	44	781	26.82	10	.34	1	.03
1932	1,966	57	2,023	70.66	786	45	831	29.03	6	.21	3	.10
1933	1,661	49	1,710	68.07	755	37	792	31.53	10	.40	—	—
1934	1,993	55	2,048	70.69	793	44	837	28.89	10	.35	2	.07
1935	1,588	61	1,649	66.17	781	49	830	33.31	13	.52	—	—
1936	1,382	61	1,443	61.09	840	59	899	38.06	18	.76	2	.09
	17,801	575	18,376	71.07	6,980	384	7,364	28.48	104	.40	14	.05

DIVISION OF INVESTIGATION

CHART 4

AGES AND SEX

	Male	Female	Total	% of Total Investigated
16	852	12	864	3.34
17	1,313	22	1,335	5.16
18	1,489	31	1,520	5.88
19	1,498	34	1,532	5.93
20	1,377	38	1,415	5.47
21	1,326	33	1,359	5.26
22	1,283	68	1,351	5.23
23	1,286	61	1,347	5.21
24	1,175	46	1,221	4.72
25	1,034	40	1,074	4.15
26	999	45	1,044	4.04
27	993	43	1,036	4.01
28	944	37	981	3.79
29	889	30	919	3.55
30	732	26	758	2.93
31-35 inclusive	3,014	157	3,171	12.26
36-40 inclusive	2,013	120	2,133	8.25
41-45 inclusive	1,183	49	1,232	4.76
46-50 inclusive	685	29	714	2.76
over 50	814	38	852	3.29
	24,899	959	25,858	

DIVISION OF INVESTIGATION

CHART 5

Age Groups and Sex

	Male	% of Total Male Invest.	Female	% of Total Female Invest.	Total	% of Total Investigations
6-20	6,529	26.22	137	14.29	6,666	25.78
21-25	6,104	24.52	248	25.86	6,352	24.57
26-30	4,557	18.30	181	18.87	4,738	18.32
31-35	3,014	12.11	157	16.37	3,171	12.26
36-40	2,013	8.08	120	12.51	2,133	8.25
41-45	1,183	4.75	49	5.11	1,232	4.76
46-50	685	2.75	29	3.02	714	2.76
over 50	814	3.27	38	3.96	852	3.29
	24,899		959		25,858	
6-21 inclusive	7,855	31.55	170	17.73	8,025	31.04

283

DEPARTMENT OF INVESTIGATION

CHART 6

COMPARISON OF AGE GROUPS

PERCENTAGE OF TOTAL INVESTIGATIONS—BY YEARS

	10-Year Periods	1927	1928	1929	1930	1931	1932	1933	1934	1935	1936
16-30		25.78	25.13	28.06	28.35	29.77	29.02	24.76	22.53	22.75	24.24	22.90
21-25		24.57	24.58	25.94	25.29	24.88	27.06	25.46	24.00	22.40	22.39	23.62
26-30		18.32	19.11	17.37	17.39	18.45	16.28	17.74	18.79	20.06	18.82	19.22
31-35		12.26	12.33	11.73	10.75	10.54	11.85	12.12	14.37	12.94	13.40	12.70
36-40		8.25	8.99	7.53	7.78	7.84	7.14	9.47	8.60	8.80	8.19	8.04
41-45		4.76	3.80	4.01	4.54	4.14	3.67	5.06	4.98	5.83	5.66	5.93
46-50		2.76	2.34	2.25	2.84	1.98	2.40	2.62	3.07	3.28	3.49	3.39
over 50		3.29	3.72	3.11	3.06	3.40	2.58	2.76	3.66	3.94	3.81	4.19
16-21 inclusive		31.04	30.06	33.11	33.64	35.49	35.85	29.55	27.39	27.79	29.01	27.90

CHART 7

NATIVITY OF OFFENDERS

BY YEARS
% OF TOTAL INVESTIGATED

	Native Born	Foreign Born	Dependency Born	Unknown
1927	68.77	28.01	3.09	.13
1928	69.28	27.56	3.02	.14
1929	72.65	23.85	3.45	.04
1930	75.91	21.63	2.46	—
1931	74.59	21.05	4.22	.14
1932	73.32	22.21	4.47	—
1933	74.20	21.14	4.66	—
1934	76.08	19.64	4.25	.03
1935	77.53	18.22	4.25	—
1936	79.55	15.16	5.25	—

285

DIVISION OF INVESTIGATION

CHART 8

NATIVITY OF OFFENDERS

BY COLOR

	White	% Total White	Colored	% Total Colored	Yellow	Red	Total	% Total Invest.
Native Born	12,818	69.75	6,366	86.45	19	10	19,213	74.30
Foreign Born	4,936	26.86	618	8.39	62	4	5,620	21.73
Dependency Born..	614	3.34	376	5.11	23	—	1,013	3.92
Nativity Unknown	8	—	4	—	—	—	12	.05
	18,376		7,364		104	14	25,858	

NATIVITY OF PARENTS OF NATIVE BORN OFFENDERS

BY COLOR

		% Native Born White		% Native Born Colored				% Total Native Born	% Total Invest.
Native Born Parents	4,250	33.16	5,903	92.73	6	7	10,166	52.91	39.31
Foreign Born Parents	7,132	55.64	189	2.97	13	1	7,335	38.18	28.37
Mixed Parentage..	1,077	8.40	131	2.06	—	1	1,209	6.29	4.68
Dependency Born Parents	7	.05	10	.16	—	—	17	.09	.07
Parentage Unknown	352	2.75	131	2.09	—	1	486	2.53	1.88
	12,818		6,366		19	10	19,213		

DIVISION OF INVESTIGATION

CHART 9

NATIVITY OF FOREIGN BORN OFFENDERS

Abyssinia	2	Dutch Guiana	1	Newfoundland	10
Africa (Country		Dutch West Indies	4	New Zealand	2
Unknown)	8	Ecuador	6	Nicaragua	7
Albania	6	Egypt	11	Nigeria	1
Algeria	12	England	174	Norway	24
Arabia	2	Esthonia	3	Nova Scotia	10
Argentine	16	Finland	25	Palestine	5
Armenia	9	France	50	Panama	42
Australia	4	French Guiana	2	Paraguay	1
Austria	343	French West Africa	4	Persia	1
Azore Islands	2	French West Indies	4	Peru	9
Bahama Islands	3	Germany	363	Poland	355
Belgium	15	Greece	157	Portugal	27
Bermuda	16	Guatemala	6	Rumania	86
Bolivia	1	Haiti	10	Russia	829
Brazil	11	Holland	31	San Domingo	17
British Guiana	16	Hungary	102	San Marino	1
British Honduras	3	Iceland	1	San Salvador	1
British West Africa	1	India	18	Scotland	68
British West Indies	367	Ireland	281	Serbia	5
Bulgaria	5	Isle of Cyprus	4	Siam	1
Canada	143	Isle of Gihalei	1	South America	81*
Canary Islands	1	Isle of Mauretania	1	Spain	117
Cape Verde Islands	4	Italy	1037	Sweden	40
Chile	29	Japan	14	Switzerland	30
China	46	Jugoslavia	12	Syria	21
Colombia	7	Korea	2	Tunisia	2
Costa Rica	10	Liberia	6	Turkey	62
Cuba	130	Lithuania	22	Ukrania	1
Czechoslovakia	35	Macedonia	1	Uraguay	1
Danish West Indies	7	Malta	8	Venezuela	9
Danzig Free State	1	Mexico	79	Wales	6
Denmark	41	Montenegro	3	West Coast—Africa	2
Dominican Republic	3	Morocco	4		

---

*Not separated into countries in 1927-1931.

CHART 10

RELIGIONS

	Number	% of Total Investigations
Catholic	13,103	50.67
Protestant	8,911	34.46
Jewish	3,261	12.61
Greek Catholic	298	1.15
Greek Orthodox	88	.34
Christian Science	55	.21
Mohammedan	31	.12
Confucian	40	.15
Buddhist	8	
Shintoist	1	
7th Day Adventist	3	
Other	16	.06
Mormon	1	
Spiritualist	1	
Freethinker	2	
None	39	.15
Unknown	16	.06

DIVISION OF INVESTIGATION

CHART 11

EDUCATION OF OFFENDERS

Last Schooling	Number	% of Total Investigated
Public School	19,955	77.17
Graduated	3,286	12.71
High School	3,688	14.26
Graduated	558	2.16
College	530	2.05
Graduated	193	.75
Continuation, Vocational or Business Schools	543	2.10
No Schooling	1,018	3.94
Unknown	124	.48

SCHOOL CHARACTERISTICS—FOR 1932-1936 INCLUSIVE

TOTAL OF 13,126 CASES

	Number	% of Total
Truancy	676	5.15
Excessive Truancy	1,158	8.82
Backward Pupil	1,142	8.70
Disciplinary Problem	885	6.74

DIVISION OF INVESTIGATION

CHART 12

MARITAL STATUS

	Male	% of Total Male	Female	% of Total Female	Total	% of Total
Single	15,437	62.00	304	31.69	15,741	60.87
Married	6,308	25.33	329	34.31	6,637	25.67
Separated	2,143	8.61	200	20.86	2,343	9.06
Widowed	505	2.03	77	8.03	582	2.25
Divorced	258	1.04	32	3.34	290	1.12
Common Law	234	.94	17	1.77	251	.97
Unknown	14	.06	—	—	14	.05
	24,899		959		25,858	

DIVISION OF INVESTIGATION

CHART 13

LIVING CONDITIONS

	Number	% of Total
Parents	6,226	24.08
Family or Relatives	7,508	29.04
Furnished Rooms	7,956	30.77
Lodging Houses	936	3.62
Hotels	437	1.69
Vagrants	1,354	5.24
Others	1,353	5.23
Unknown	88	.34
	25,858	

ECONOMIC STATUS

1932-1936 INCLUSIVE

TOTAL CASES, 13,126

	Number	% of Total 1932-1936
Poverty	2,139	16.30
Poor	7,737	58.94
Fair	2,367	18.03
Good	727	5.54
Prosperous	78	.59
None	30	.23
Unknown	48	.37

DIVISION OF INVESTIGATION

CHART 14

Broken Homes

Homes Broken When Defendant 16 Years or Under 12,245   47.35% of Total

Parents Living or Dead
of Offenders 16-21 Years Inclusive

(Total Investigated in this age group, 8,025)

Both Parents Living	4,319	53.82% of Total
Father Dead	1,646	20.51% of Total
Mother Dead	1,045	13.02% of Total
Both Parents Dead	761	9.48% of Total
One or Both Unknown	254	
One or Both Parents Dead	3,452	43.01% of Total

DIVISION OF INVESTIGATION

CHART 15

Unemployment at Time of Offense

Year	Unem-ployed	% of Total	Em-ployed	% of Total	School-Boys	House-wives	Re-tired	In Insti-tutions	Un known
1927	1,000	41.79	1,348	56.35	—	—	—	2	42
1928	1,145	51.65	1,028	46.37	—	—	—	—	44
1929	1,164	50.58	1,074	46.92	4	—	1	—	46
1930	1,769	60.54	1,138	38.95	6	—	—	1	8
1931	1,944	66.76	937	32.18	16	2	—	4	9
1932	1,836	64.13	996	34.79	8	4	—	—	19
1933	1,534	61.07	932	37.10	22	6	—	13	5
1934	1,642	56.68	1,197	41.32	29	14	—	10	5
1935	1,417	56.86	1,012	40.61	33	29	—	1	—
1936	1,225	51.86	1,056	44.71	53	21	—	7	—
Total	14,676	56.76	10,718	41.45	171	76	1	38	178

CHART 16

1932-1936 INCLUSIVE

Year	Total Exam.	Nor-mal	% of Total Exam.	In-ferior	% of Total Exam.	Vener-eal Dis-ease	% of Total Exam.	Chronic Alco-holic	% of Total Exam.	Drug Ad-dicts	% of Total Exam.
1932	2,088	1,510	72.32	221	10.58	184	8.81	129	6.18	44	2.11
a1933	2,327	1,655	71.12	259	11.13	215	9.24	162	6.96	55	2.36
b1934	2,745	2,031	73.99	217	7.91	238	8.67	241	8.78	46	1.68
c1935	2,410	1,929	80.04	173	7.18	146	6.06	111	4.61	57	2.37
d1936	2,168	1,738	80.17	104	4.75	161	7.43	97	4.47	71	3.27
Total	11,738	8,863	75.51	976	8.31	944	8.04	740	6.30	273	2.33

a1933—10 Alcohol-Venereal; 4 Drug-Venereal; 3 Drug-Alcohol; 1 Alcohol-Drug-Venereal.
b1934—22 Alcoholic-Venereal; 3 Alcoholic-Drug Addict; 3 Venereal-Drug Addict.
c1935— 4 Alcoholic-Venereal; 2 Alcoholic-Drug Addict.
d1936— 2 Drug Addict-Venereal; 1 Alcoholic-Drug Addict.

DIVISION OF INVESTIGATION

CHART 17

CONTRIBUTORY FACTORS

	Number	% of Total
Economic Factors		
Poverty	1,499	5.80
Unemployment	6,238	24.12
Occupational Influences and Temptations	1,666	6.44
Economic Incompetency	3,510	13.58
Physical and Mental Factors		
Mental Disease (Insanity)	104	.40
Mental Defect (Retarded)	1,290	4.99
Mental Peculiarity	367	1.42
Physically Defective or Diseased	417	1.61
Emotional Immaturity and Instability	3,833	14.82
Lack of Normal Emotional Outlets	663	2.56
Environmental Factors		
Bad Associates	15,136	58.54
*Bad Home Conditions	8,940	34.57
Lack of Religious or Moral Training	6,177	23.89
*Broken Home	2,432	9.41
Domestic Disharmony and Incompatability	235	.91
Institutionalization	616	2.38
Sex Factors		
Immorality (Sex Excesses)	1,647	6.37
Sex Perversion	261	1.01

*From 1927-1931—Broken Homes were incorporated under Bad Home Conditions.

CHART 17-A

CONTRIBUTORY FACTORS
Continued

	Number	% of Total
Alcohol and Drugs		
Alcoholism	5,755	22.26
Drug Addiction	525	2.03
Excessive Desires and Ambitions		
Love of Pleasure and Luxury	3,334	12.89
Love of Adventure	486	1.88
Greed	792	3.06
Excessive Ambition	444	1.72
Gambling	1,360	5.26
Personal Deficiencies		
Easily Influenced or Weak-Willed	7,174	27.74
Irresponsibility and Carelessness	4,654	17.80
Jealousy	389	1.50
Laziness	2,795	10.81
Inferiority Complex	1,064	7.98
Fixed Ideas	193	.75
Lack of Wholesome Interests	2,878	11.13
Anti-Social Attitude	2,330	9.01

CHART 18

Offenses

	Male	Female	Total	% of Total Investigations
Abandonment	69	11	80	.31
Abduction	28	1	29	.11
Abortion	4	5	9	—
Accessory to Felony	2	—	2	—
Arson	73	10	83	.32
Assault 1st and 2nd Deg.—Pugnacity	1,364	65	1,429	5.52
Assault 2nd Deg.—Pugnacity and Unlawful Entry	1	—	1	—
Assault 1st and 2nd Deg.—Sex	188	—	188	.73
Assault 3rd Deg.—Pugnacity	1,797	124	1,921	7.43
Assault 3rd Deg.—Sex	720	4	724	2.80
Bank Laws Vio. Sect. 340 and 453	3	—	3	—
Bigamy	215	31	246	.95
Blackmail	2	1	3	—
Bribery	4	1	5	—
Bringing Stolen Property into State	1	—	1	—
Bucket Shop Vio. Sec. 390 P. L.	4	—	4	—
Burglary	1,095	4	1,099	4.25
Burglary and Assault 3rd Deg.	4	—	4	—
Burglary and Grand Larceny	4	—	4	—
Burglary and Petit Larceny	14	—	14	.05
Carnal Abuse of Children, 483a and 483b P. L.	18	—	18	.07
Coercion	40	—	40	.15
Compounding a Misdemeanor	1	—	1	—
Compulsory Prostitution, 2460 P. L.	40	5	45	.17
Compulsory Prostitution of Wife, 1090 P. L.	1	—	1	—
Compulsory Prostitution and Living Proceeds of Prostitution, 1148 P. L.	1	—	1	—
Concealing Escaped Prisoner	—	1	1	—

CHART 18-A

OFFENSES
Continued

	Male	Female	Total	% of Total Investigations
Conspiracy	47	5	52	.20
Conspiracy to Commit Forgery	4	—	4	—
Contempt	1	—	1	—
Corrupt Bargain for Appointment—1832 P. L.	11	—	11	.04
Corrupt Use of Position or Authority, 775 P. L. Sub. 3	2	—	2	—
Criminally Receiving Stolen Property	168	5	173	.67
Damaging Building or Vessel by Explosion, 1420 P. L.	1	—	1	—
Defacing or Removing Identification Marks, 436a P. L.	1	—	1	—
Deserting Children	1	—	1	—
Discharging a Firearm, 1906 P. L.	5	—	5	—
Disorderly Conduct	2	2	4	—
Driving While Intoxicated	2	—	2	—
Drugs, Possessing or Selling	182	8	190	.73
Education Law Vio.	2	—	2	—
Election Law Vio. Sec. 262 or 783 or 765	7	—	7	—
Endangering Life or Health of Child	7	1	8	—
Escaping Lawful Custody	25	1	26	.10
Extortion	151	10	161	.62
Failure to Appear on Bail Bond	4	1	5	—
Failure to Provide for Child, 482 P. L.	5	3	8	—
Failure to Secure Compensation	9	—	9	—
False Affidavit, 43 P. L.	2	1	3	—
False Canvass of Ballots, 753 or 766 P. L.	7	—	7	—
False Entry in Books of Corporation, 665 P. L.	1	—	1	—
False Financial Statement	15	1	16	.06
False Impersonation, 928 P. L.	2	1	3	—
False Registration	7	—	7	—
False Statement in Bail Bond	—	1	1	—

CHART 18-B

OFFENSES
Continued

	Male	Female	Total	% of Total Investigations
Feloniously Concealing Stolen Property Knowingly	1	—	1	—
Filing Forged Document, 2051 P. L.	4	—	4	—
Forgery	693	50	743	2.87
Forgery and Grand Larceny 2nd Deg.	2	—	2	—
Fraud in Obtaining Employment, 939 P. L.	2	—	2	—
Fraud in Obtaining Property for Charitable Purposes, 934 P. L.	1	—	1	—
Fraud in Securing Organization of Corporation, 661 P. L.	3	—	3	—
Homicide	538	48	586	2.27
Hypothecation of Customer's Securities, 956 P. L.	1	—	1	—
Impairing Morals of Minor	136	1	137	.53
Impersonating Officer, 931 P. L.	3	—	3	—
Incest	1	—	1	—
Insurance Law Vio., Sec. 341a	2	—	2	—
Issuing Fraudulent Check or Draft, 1293a P. L.	5	—	5	—
Keeping Disorderly House, 1146 P. L.	8	14	22	.08
Keeping Gambling or Betting Establishment, 973 P. L.	1	—	1	—
Keeping Place for Game of Policy, 974 P. L.	15	—	15	.06
Kidnapping	12	2	14	.05
Larceny, Grand	3,467	175	3,642	14.08
Larceny, Grand, 2nd Deg. and Petit Larceny	1	—	1	—
Larceny, Petit	5,906	281	6,187	23.93
Libel	2	—	2	—
Living on Proceeds of Prostitution, 1148 P. L.	30	—	30	.12
Living on Proceeds of Prostitution and Petit Larceny	1	—	1	—
Maintaining a Nuisance	7	—	7	—
Maintaining Woman for Prostitution, 887CC, Sub. E	2	—	2	—
Malicious Injury to Property	47	3	50	.19
Malicious Mischief	8	—	8	—

CHART 18-C

OFFENSES

Continued

	Male	Female	Total	% of Total Investigations
Misappropriation of Funds by Officers of Bank, 305 P. L.	6	—	6	—
Misconduct of Officers of Corporation, 665 P. L.	1	—	1	—
Misleading Advertising, 421 P. L.	3	—	3	—
Obscene Pictures and Art, 1141 P. L.	1	—	1	—
Obtaining Property by False Pretenses, 932 P. L.	2	1	3	—
Obtaining Property by False Statement, 1293b P. L.	4	—	4	—
Obtaining Signatures to Written Instrument by False Pretenses	1	—	1	—
Oppression, 854 P. L.	13	—	13	.05
Pawning Borrowed Property, 941 P. L.	3	—	3	—
Perjury	32	11	43	.17
Pointing a Firearm, 1901 P. L.	1	—	1	—
Possessing a Blackjack	5	—	5	—
Possessing Burglars' Tools	265	1	266	1.03
Possessing Explosives, 1895 P. L.	7	—	7	—
Possessing Knife	3	—	3	—
Possessing Machine Gun	8	3	11	.04
Possessing Policy Slips	2	—	2	—
Possessing Weapons, 1897 P. L.	880	10	890	3.44
Preventing or Dissuading Witness from Attending, 2441 P. L.	1	—	1	—
Presenting False Proof in Support of Claim in Insurance, 1202 P. L.	2	—	2	—
Procuring Marriage License Unlawfully, 1451 P. L.	1	—	1	—
Public Officer Taking Illegal Fees, 885 P. L.	1	—	1	—
Rape	98	—	98	.38
Rape and Abduction	1	—	1	—
Rape and Burglary	1	—	1	—

CHART 18-D

OFFENSES

Continued

	Male	Female	Total	% of Total Investi- gations
Receiving Deposits in Insolvent Bank, 295 P. L.	2	—	2	—
Resisting Officer in Discharge of His Duty, 1851 P. L.	1	—	1	—
Robbery	3,064	41	3,105	12.01
Robbery, Assault and Grand Larceny	2	1	3	—
Robbery and Assault	1	—	1	—
Robbery and Bigamy	1	—	1	—
Robbery and Possessing Burglars' Tools	1	—	1	—
Robbery and Possessing Weapon, 1897 P. L.	1	—	1	—
Seduction	3	—	3	—
Seduction under Promise of Marriage	1	—	1	—
Seizing and Taking State Military Stores	1	—	1	—
Sending Annoying or Threatening Letters	17	—	17	.07
Sodomy	34	—	34	.13
Subornation of Perjury	1	—	1	—
Suppression of Evidence, 814 P. L.	1	—	1	—
Taking Unlawful Fees, 1826 P. L.	2	—	2	—
Trade Mark, Vio. Sect. 436 P. L. or 2354 P. L.	7	—	7	—
Unauthorized Use of Motor Vehicle, 1293a P. L.	2	—	2	—
Unlawful Assembly	1	—	1	—
Unlawful Entry	3,142	14	3,156	12.21
Unlawful Entry and Petit Larceny	1	—	1	—
Using Forged or Altered Evidence	1	—	1	—
Vio. Motor Vehicle Laws	5	—	5	—
Vio. Workman's Compensation Law, Sec. 24 (Unlawfully Accepting Fees)	1	—	1	—
	24,899	959	25,858	—

DIVISION OF INVESTIGATION

CHART 19

Comparison of Offenses by Age Groups with Total Investigations by Age Group

1932-1936

Age Group	Total in Age Group Inv. 1932-1936 No.	% of Total	Petit Larceny No.	% of Total	Assault 3rd Deg. No.	% of Total	Unlawful Entry No.	% of Total	Assault 1st and 2nd No.	% of Total	Grand Larceny No.	% of Total	Forgery No.	% of Total	Burglary No.	% of Total	Robbery No.	% of Total	Homicide No.	% of Total
16-20	3,079	23.46	842	29.40	256	18.74	651	41.62	130	15.10	230	13.94	11	3.87	107	19.14	631	37.21	55	14.75
21-25	3,095	23.58	628	21.93	319	23.35	361	23.08	203	23.58	322	19.52	32	11.27	161	28.80	585	34.49	84	22.52
26-30	2,485	18.93	503	17.56	259	18.96	224	14.32	198	23.00	312	18.91	59	20.77	135	24.15	319	18.81	66	17.70
31-35	1,717	13.08	347	12.12	198	14.49	164	10.49	132	15.33	259	15.70	55	19.37	59	10.55	97	5.72	64	17.16
36-40	1,136	8.65	223	7.79	128	9.37	83	5.31	69	8.01	231	14.00	55	19.37	57	10.20	38	2.24	30	8.04
41-45	720	5.49	153	5.34	88	6.44	41	2.62	65	7.55	118	7.15	40	14.08	21	3.76	16	.94	27	7.24
46-50	415	3.16	77	2.69	50	3.66	19	1.22	26	3.02	95	5.76	19	6.69	14	2.50	5	.29	20	5.36
over 50	479	3.65	91	3.18	68	4.98	21	1.34	38	4.41	83	5.03	13	4.58	5	.89	5	.29	27	7.24
	13,126		2,864		1,366		1,564		861		1,650		284		559		1,696		373	

Note—Offenders convicted of two or more offenses in one vase, such as Burglary and Petit Larceny, etc., are included under the more serious offense.

DIVISION OF INVESTIGATION

CHART 20

First Offenders

Year	Number	% of Total Invest.
1927	1,044	43.65
1928	885	39.92
1929	853	37.27
1930	1,233	42.20
1931	1,142	39.22
1932	815	28.47
1933	825	32.84
1934	943	32.55
1935	768	30.82
1936	685	29.00

CHART 21

SUMMARY OF PREVIOUS COURT RECORDS OF OFFENDERS
1932-1936 INCLUSIVE

Year	1st Offenders			% of Total Inv.	Previous Juven. Record 1st Adult Ct. Appearance			% of Total Inv.	Previous Ct. Appearances 1st Conviction			% of Total Inv.
	Male	Female	Total		Male	Fe-male	Total		Male	Female	Total	
1932	761	54	815	28.47	130	1	131	4.58	422	11	433	15.12
1933	775	50	825	32.84	122	1	123	4.90	218	3	221	8.80
1934	884	59	943	32.55	167	—	167	5.76	227	7	234	8.08
1935	712	56	768	30.82	126	4	130	5.22	211	10	221	8.87
1936	618	67	685	29.00	124	4	128	5.42	205	6	211	8.93
Totals	3,750	286	4,036	30.75	669	10	679	5.17	1,283	37	1,320	10.06

29.74% of Total Male Inv. 55.32% of Total Female Inv.

5.31% of Total Male Inv. 1.93% of Total Female Inv.

10.17% of Total Male Inv. 7.16% of Total Female Inv.

	Number	% of Total Inv. 1932-1936
No. with Juvenile Court Records	2,611	19.81
No. with Juvenile Court Convictions	2,310	17.59
No. with Adult Court Records	8,403	64.02
No. with Adult Court Convictions	6,944	52.52
No. with Juvenile and Adult Court Convictions	1,480	11.28
No. with Juvenile Institutional Commitments	1,661	12.65
No. with Adult Institutional Commitments	5,444	41.47
No. with Juvenile and Adult Institutional Commitments	971	7.40
No. with Juvenile Probation Record	1,397	10.64
No. with Adult Probation Record	1,707	13.00
No. with Juvenile and Adult Probation Records	258	1.97

DIVISION OF INVESTIGATION

CHART 22

PREVIOUS JUVENILE RECORDS

1932-1936

Juvenile Court Appearances .... 2,611—19.81% of Total Investigations
     Total Appearances—5,080
Juvenile Court Convictions .... 2,310—17.59% of Total Investigations
     Total Convictions—4,025
Juvenile Institutional Commitments .... 1,661—12.65% of Total Investigations
     Total Commitments—2,375
Juvenile Probation Records .... 1,397—10.64% of Total Investigations
     Total Number of Probations—1,878
Violations of Juvenile Probation .... 298—21.33% of Probationers
     Total Number of Violations—355
No. Committed for Violation of Probation 189—13.53% of Probationers
     Total Number of Commitments—196
Juvenile Parole Records .... 1,020— 7.77% of Total Investigations
     Total Number of Paroles—1,484
Violations of Juvenile Parole .... 354—34.71% of Parolees
     Total Violations—458
No. Committed for Violation of Parole........ 292—28.63% of Parolees
     Total No. of Commitments—371

DIVISION OF INVESTIGATION

CHART 23

Previous Adult Court Records of Offenders

1932-1936

No. with Court Appearances .... 8,403—64.02% of Total Investigations
    Total No. of Appearances—30,524

No. with Court Convictions .... 6,944—52.52% of Total Investigations
    Total No. of Convictions—19,562

No. with Lower Court Convictions .... 5,088—38.76% of Total Investigations
    Total No. of Convictions in Lower Courts—12,305

No. with Higher Court Convictions .... 3,915—29.83% of Total Investigations
    Total No. of Convictions in Higher Courts—6,750

No. with Federal Court Convictions .... 442— 3.37% of Total Investigations
    (Includes Court Martials)
    Total No. of Federal Court Convictions—507

No. with both Lower and Higher Court
    Convictions .... 2,277—17.35% of Total Investigations

No. with both Juvenile and Adult Court
    Convictions .... 1,480—11.28% of Total Investigations

No. with previous appearances in General
    Sessions .... 2,912—22.18% of Total Investigations
    Total No. of appearances—4,465

No. with previous conviction in General
    Sessions .... 2,464—18.77% of Total Investigations
    Total No. of convictions—3,805

Number previously Investigated by this
    Department .... 1,954—14.89% of Total Investigations
    Total No. of Previous Investigations—2,329

DIVISION OF INVESTIGATION

CHART 24

1932-1936

No. with Institutional Commitments............. 5,444—41.47% of Total

    Total No. of Commitments—13,429

        No. previously in State Prisons........ 1,132— 8.62% of Total Investigations

        No. previously in Napanoch .... 90— .69% of Total Investigations

        No. previously in Mattewan 20

        No. previously in Central Islip........ 6 .32% of Total Investigations

        No. previously in Other Institutions
           for mental ills 16

No. with both Juvenile and Adult Institu-
    tional Commitments .... 971— 7.40% of Total

DIVISION OF INVESTIGATION

CHART 25

PREVIOUS ADULT PROBATION RECORDS

1932-1936

No. with Probation Record .... 1,707—13.00% of Total
      Total No. of Probations—1,968
No. with Lower Court Probation .... 815— 6.21% of Total
      Total Lower Court Probations—965
No. with Higher Court Probation .... 929— 7.08% of Total
      Total Higher Court Probations—978
No. with Federal Court Probations .... 25— .19% of Total
      Total Federal Court Probations—25
No. with Juvenile and Adult Probation Records............... 258— 1.97% of Total
No. with Previous General Sessions Probation Record...... 532— 4.05% of Total
No. who Violated Previous Probations .... 708— 5.39% of Total
      (includes present offense)
      Total Violations—803

DISPOSITION OF PREVIOUS VIOLATIONS

No. Committed	338	No. of Times	343
No. Continued	124	No. of Times	143
No. Warrants Filed	215	No. of Times	216
No. Other Dispositions	67	No. of Times	67
No. Dispositions Pending	34	No. of Times	34

DIVISION OF INVESTIGATION

CHART 26

Previous Adult Parole Records

No. with previous Parole Record .... 2,896—22.07% of Total
　　　Total No. of Paroles—4,900

No. with violated Paroles (includes present offense) .... 1,993—15.18% of Total
　　　Total No. of Violations—2,724

Dispositions of Violations

No. Committed	742	Total Times	930
No. Continued	57	Total Times	59
No. Warrants Filed	1,563	Total Times	1,673
No. Other Dispositions	57	Total Times	58
No. Dispositions Pending	4	Total Times	4

DIVISION OF SUPERVISION

CHART 1

CASES RECEIVED FOR SUPERVISION

	Probation		Deferred Sentence		Transfer		Total		% Placed on Probation of	Grand
	M	F	M	F	M	F	M	F	Total Invest.	Total
1927	569	45	24	—	3	—	596	45	26.66%	641
1928	482	24	66	3	1	1	549	28	25.92%	577
1929	490	16	96	6	6	—	592	22	26.56%	614
1930	653	31	93	3	12	—	758	34	26.65%	792
1931	494	27	96	5	14	—	604	32	21.32%	636
1932	479	27	33	5	12	—	524	32	19.00%	556
1933	448	28	22	1	7	2	477	31	19.87%	508
1934	516	29	14	2	4	1	534	32	19.36%	566
1935	484	35	7	1	4	—	495	36	21.15%	531
1936	447	40	11	2	7	—	465	42	21.17%	507
Total	5,062	302	462	28	70	4	5,594	334		5,928

Taken over January 1, 1927 from consolidated agencies............ 677

Total Cases Supervised 6,605

DIVISION OF SUPERVISION

CHART 2

PLACED UNDER SUPERVISION

BY OFFENSES COMMITTED

	Male	Female	Total	% Total Recd. for Supervision	% Total Invest. for Same Offense
Abandonment	47	8	55	.94	68.75
Abduction	2	—	2	.034	——
Abortion	1	4	5	.09	——
Accessory to Felony	1	—	1	.017	——
Arson	10	4	14	.24	16.87
Assault 1st and 2nd	119	7	126	2.15	7.79
Assault 2nd and Unlawful Entry	1	—	1	.017	——
Assault 3rd	688	33	721	12.32	27.26
Bank Law Vio., Sec. 340	1	—	1	.017	——
Bigamy	74	19	93	1.59	37.80
Bribery	3	—	3	.05	——
Bringing Stolen Prop. into State	1	—	1	.017	——
Bucket Shop Vio.	1	—	1	.017	——
Burglary	70	—	70	1.20	6.37
Burglary 3rd and Petit Larceny	4	—	4	.07	——
Carnal Abuse of Child, 483B P. L.	1	—	1	.017	——
Coercion	12	—	12	.20	30.00
Common Gambler	1	—	1	.017	——
Concealing Escaped Prisoner	—	1	1	.017	——
Conspiracy	18	5	23	.39	44.23
Corrupt Bargain for Apptment., 1832 P. L.	4	—	4	.07	——
Corrupt Use Position or Authority, 775 Sec. 3, P. L.	1	—	1	.017	——
Criminally Receiving Stolen Prop.	44	1	45	.77	26.01
Deserting Child	1	2	3	.05	——
Disorderly Conduct	—	1	1	.017	——
Drugs, Poss. and Selling	10	—	10	.17	5.26
Education Law Vio.	2	—	2	.034	——
Election Law Vio., 783 P. L.	1	—	1	.017	——
Endangering Life or Health of Child, 483 P. L.	1	1	2	.034	——
Escaping Lawful Custody	6	—	6	.10	——
Excess Interest—453, Bank Law	2	—	2	.034	——
Extortion	23	6	29	.50	18.01
Failure Provide for Child, 482 P. L.	—	2	2	.034	——
Failure Ssecure Compensation	10	—	10	.17	——
False Affidavit, 43 P. L.	—	1	1	.017	——
False Financial Statement	9	—	1	.017	——
False Proof of Loss	1	—	1	.017	——
False Rumor on Stock or Bond, 926 P. L.	1	—	1	.017	——

311

CHART 2-A
Placed Under Supervision
By Offenses Committed
Continued

	Male	Female	Total	% Total Recd. for Supervision	% Total Invest. for Same Offense
Filing Forged Document	1	—	1	.017	——
Forgery	199	31	230	3.93	30.96
Fraud in Obtaining Empl., 939 P. L.	1	—	1	.017	——
Fraud in Securing Organization of Comp., 661 P. L.	1	—	1	.017	——
Homicide	4	1*	5	.09	——
Hypothecation Customer's Securities, 956 P. L.	1	—	1	.017	——
Impairing Morals of Minor	9	—	9	.15	6.57
Impersonating Officer, 931 P. L.	1	—	1	.017	——
Issuing Fraudulent Check or Draft, 1292 P. L.	2	—	2	.034	——
Keeping Disorderly House, 1146 P. L.	—	2	2	.034	——
Keeping Place for Game of Policy, 974 P. L.	6	—	6	.10	——
Kidnapping	—	1	1	.017	——
Larceny, Grand	829	52	881	15.05	24.19
Larceny, Petit	2,208	124	2,332	39.84	37.69
Libel	3	—	3	.05	——
Malicious Injury to Property	27	—	27	.46	54.00
Malicious Mischief	2	—	2	.034	——
Obtain Prop. by False Prtenses, 932 P. L.	—	1	1	.017	——
Omit to Provide for Child, 482a P. L.	6	1	7	.12	——
Oppression, 854 P. L.	2	—	2	.034	——
Pawning Borrowed Prop., 941 P. L.	3	—	3	.05	——
Perjury	11	8	19	.32	44.19
Pointing a Gun, 1906 P. L.	1	—	1	.017	——
Possessing Burg. Tools	11	—	11	.19	4.14
Possessing Explosives, 1895 P. L.	2	—	2	.034	——
Possessing Knife	1	—	1	.017	——
Possessing Policy Slips	1	—	1	.017	——
Possessing Shotgun	1	—	1	.017	——
Possessing Weapon, 1897 P. L.	54	3	57	.97	6.40
Prevent Witness from Attending, 2441 P. L.	1	—	1	.017	——
Public Health Law Vio., Sec. 174	1	—	1	.017	——
Rape	15	—	15	.26	15.31
Receiving Deposits in Insolvent Bank, 295 P. L.	1	—	1	.017	——
Robbery	78	4	82	1.30	2.64
Seduction Under Promise of Marriage	1	—	1	.017	——
Sending Annoying Letter	5	—	5	.09	——
Sending Threatening Letter, 551 P. L.	3	—	3	.05	——
Sodomy	1	—	1	.017	——
Trade Mark Vio.	6	—	6	.10	——
Transaction by Broker after Insolvency, 955 P. L.	1	—	1	.017	——
Unauthorized Use Motor Vehicle, 1293a P. L.	1	—	1	.017	——
Unlawful Entry	850	6	856	14.62	27.12
Unlawful Registration	1	—	1	.017	——
	5,524	330	5,854	—	——

*Witness in Murder Case—No conviction but supervised by order of Judge.

DIVISION OF SUPERVISION

CHART 3

PREVIOUS PROBATION EXPERIENCE

(Includes Deferred Sentences and Transfers)

	First Probation		Second Probation		Third Probation		Fourth Probation		Fifth Probation		Sixth Or Over		Total
	M	F	M	F	M	F	M	F	M	F	M	F	
1927	567	42	20	3	4	—	4	—	—	—	1	—	641
1928	504	26	39	2	5	—	—	—	1	—	—	—	577
1929	532	21	47	1	9	—	3	—	—	—	1	—	614
1930	693	32	47	2	15	—	2	—	1	—	—	—	792
1931	541	32	47	—	11	—	—	—	3	—	2	—	636
1932	478	31	35	—	8	1	3	—	—	—	—	—	556
1933	424	27	40	4	8	—	3	—	1	—	1	—	508
1934	493	32	27	—	10	—	3	—	1	—	—	—	566
1935	445	35	42	1	6	—	1	—	—	—	1	—	531
1936	421	41	36	1	7	—	—	—	—	—	1	—	507
	5,098	319	380	14	83	1	19	—	7	—	7	—	
Total	5,417		394		84		19		7		7		

% of Total
Received for
Supervision 91.38%   6.65   1.42   .32   .12   .12

DIVISION OF SUPERVISION

CHART 4

RECEIVED UNDER SUPERVISION

BY AGE GROUPS

	Male	Female	Total	% Total Recd. for Supervision	% Total Same Age Groups Investigated
16-20 years	2,065	53	2,118	36.18	31.77
21-25 "	1,173	84	1,257	21.47	19.79
26-30 "	753	70	823	14.06	17.37
31-35 "	536	39	575	9.82	18.13
36-40 "	413	39	452	7.72	21.19
41-45 "	245	14	259	4.42	21.02
46-50 "	151	10	161	2.75	22.55
Over 50 "	188	21	209	3.57	24.53
	5,524	330	5,854		
16-21 yrs. incl.	2,351	67	2,418		30.13

CHART 4-A

RECEIVED THROUGH TRANSFERS

By Age Groups

	Male	Female	Total
16-20 years	35	1	36
21-25 "	14	—	14
26-30 "	8	1	9
31-35 "	4	2	6
36-40 "	3	—	3
41-45 "	3	—	3
46-50 "	1	—	1
Over 50 "	1	—	1
Unknown	1	—	1
	70	4	74

315

DIVISION OF SUPERVISION

CHART 5

	Male	Female	Total
Abandonment	5	—	5
Arson	1	—	1
Assault to Rob	5	—	5
Bigamy	1	—	1
Breaking and Entering	1	—	1
Bringing Stolen Property into State	3	—	3
Burglary	4	—	4
Burglary 3rd and Grand Larceny	1	—	1
Burglary 3rd and Petit Larceny	1	—	1
Compulsory Prostitution	1	—	1
Desertion	2	—	2
Disorderly Person	1	—	1
Embezzlement	2	—	2
False Pretenses	2	—	2
Forgery	3	—	3
Homicide	1	—	1
Larceny, Grand	12	2	14
Larceny, Petit	14	1	15
Perjury	1	—	1
Possessing Hypnotic Needle	—	1	1
Rape	1	—	1
Tampering with Automobile	2	—	2
Unauthorized Use of Motor Vehicle	4	—	4
Worthless Checks	1	—	1
Unknown*	1	—	1
	70	4	74

*Accepted Conditionally—Further information never received and case returned to original jurisdiction.

DIVISION OF SUPERVISION

CHART 6

MAXIMUM DURATION OF PROBATION PERIOD

(Includes Transfers Total 5,438)

Year	1 Mo.	4 Mo.	6 Mo.	1 Yr.	1½ Yr.	1 Yr. 9 Mo.	2 Yr.	2½ Yr.	3 Yr.	4 Yr.	4½ Yr.	5 Yr.	6 Yr.	7 Yr.	7½ Yr.	8 Yr.	10 Yr.	15 Yr.	20 Yr.	Unoff. Prob. Prd.
1927	—	—	1	194	—	—	185	—	148	3	—	86	—	—	—	—	—	—	—	—
1928	—	—	4	134	—	—	130	—	164	7	—	69	—	—	—	—	—	—	—	—
1929	—	—	—	109	—	—	180	—	157	2	—	64	—	—	—	—	—	—	—	—
1930	4	—	1	102	—	—	184	—	308	3	—	94	—	—	—	—	—	—	—	—
1931	—	—	1	23	—	—	103	—	306	2	—	100	—	—	—	—	—	—	—	—
1932	—	—	—	13	—	—	72	—	318	—	—	115	—	—	—	—	—	—	—	—
1933	—	2(1)	—	17	1	—	91	1	324	2	—	47	1(2)	—	—	—	—	—	—	—
1934*	—	—	1	17	1	—	80	2	390	1	—	46	—	1	1	—	9	—	—	—
1935	—	—	2	17	2	—	128	14	304	2	—	44	—	2	4	—	4	2	—	1
1936	4	2	—	16	1	1	126	17	220	—	1	86	1	3	2	1	17	2	1	1
Totals				642	4	1	1,279	34	2,639	22	1	751		6	7		30			
% of Total Placed on Prob. and Transfers	.07	.04	.18	11.81	.07	.02	23.52	.62	48.53	.40	.02	13.81	.02	.11	.13	.02	.55	.04	.02	.02

(1) Transfers to us.
(2) Transfers to us.

*Change in law in 1934 Relative to Maximum Probation Period.

317

DIVISION OF SUPERVISION

CHART 7

Disposition of Closed Cases

			% of 6,605 Cases Supervised During Ten Years
Discharged		3,862	58.47%
Favorable—3,073—46.52% of Total Supervised			
Guarded — 789—11.95% of Total Supervised			
Committed on Violation of Probation		831	12.58
Committed on new charges—our cases closed		89	1.35
Died		81	1.35
Deported or left country		52	.79
Transferred		11	.17
Bench warrants filed in Clerk's office		70	1.06
Bench warrants filed in District Attorney's office		3	.05
Permission of Court to close cases		96	1.45
Moved to other states	4		
In institutions for mental ills	16		
In institutions for Feebleminded	3		
On parole	29		
On probation in other courts	2		
D. A. refused to extradite	13		
In Children's Village	2		
Gypsies—supervision impossible	2		
In sanitarium for Tuberculosis	1		
In City Home	1		
Under care of Veterans Bureau	1		
Absconded	22		
Indictments dismissed		3	.05
Suspended Sentence—no probation		8	.12
(of this number 1—on parole			
1—to be deported)			
Suspended Sentence—No probation on deferred sentence		1	.015
Discharged on Violation of Probation		7	.11
On probation to Special Sessions	1		
Suspended sentence continued	2		
On parole	1		
Good Behavior while absconded	3		
Bench warrants withdrawn		10	.15
To be on parole	2		
In Central Islip State Hospital	1		
In Puerto Rico	1		
In other states	2		
Maximum probation period expired	2		
Permission to close cases	2		
Other dispositions		8	.12
Total Cases Closed		5,132	

DIVISION OF SUPERVISION

CHART 8

Success and Failure

Years	Success	Success Prognosis Guarded	Failure
1927-1931 incl.	73.89%	8.05%	18.06%
1932	84.02	5.43	10.55
1933	84.80	6.22	8.98
1934	83.42	7.09	9.49
1935	83.81	6.32	9.87
1936	84.37	5.69	9.94

CHART 8-A

Percent of Total Failures Due to Rearrests for New Offenses

Years	%
1927-1931	38.82
1932	39.05
1933	36.30
1934	29.82
1935	36.07
1936	24.75

DIVISION OF SUPERVISION

CHART 9

BENCH WARRANTS ISSUED

Year	For Rearrests			For Absconding			For Misconduct			Total		
	Male	Fe-male	Total	Male	Fe-male	Total	Male	Fe-male	Total	Male	Fe-male	Total
1927	38	1	39	53	7	60	9	1	10	100	9	109
1928	49	3	52	92	3	95	21	1	22	162	7	169
1929	54	1	55	71	—	71	25	3	28	150	4	154
1930	86	1	87	103	6	109	50	—	50	239	7	246
1931	130	3	133	97	3	100	44	—	44	271	6	277
1932	116	4	120	87	6	93	15	—	15	218	10	228
1933	93	1	94	54	—	54	16	4	20	163	5	168
1934	88	3	91	62	5	67	26	2	28	176	10	186
1935	99	4	103	62	1	63	16	1	17	177	6	183
1936	80	—	80	61	2	63	21	3	24	162	5	167
Totals	833	21	854	742	33	775	243	15	258	1,818	69	1,887

SUMMARY

Rearrests .... 854—45.26% of Total B.W.
Absconders .... 775—41.07% of Total B.W.
Misconduct .... 258—13.67% of Total B.W.
Females .... 3.66% of Total B.W.

320

CHART 10

BENCH WARRANTS

LENGTH OF TIME UNDER SUPERVISION WHEN WARRANTS WERE ISSUED—
ACCORDING TO MAXIMUM SUPERVISION PERIOD
IN MONTHS

Max. Length of Supervision Period	Under 3	3-5	6-8	9-11	12-17	18-23	24-35	36-47	48-59	60 & Over	Total	% of Total B.W. Issued
4 Months	1	—	—	—	—	—	—	—	—	—	1	.05
6 "	1	—	—	—	—	—	—	—	—	—	1	.05
1 Year	37	35	33	30	8	—	—	—	—	—	143	7.58
1½ "	—	—	—	—	2	—	—	—	—	—	2	.11
2 "	54	86	71	63	91	70	6	—	—	—	441	23.37
2½ "	2	—	—	—	2	1	—	—	—	—	5	.27
3 "	125	159c	117	101	160	119	185	11	—	2	979	51.88
4 "	1	—	5	1	1	3	5	5	—	—	21	1.11
5 "	28	31	21a	18	44	26	41	25	25	4b	263	13.94
10 "	—	—	—	—	1	—	—	—	—	—	1	.05
Deferred Sentence	15	10	3	1	1	—	—	—	—	—	30	1.59
Totals	264	321	250	214	310	219	237	41	25	6	1,887	
% of Total B. W.	13.99	17.11	13.25	11.34	16.34	11.61	12.56	2.17	1.32	.32		

a—1933—1 Duplicate B. W. Issued—Original Warrant—Dec. 3, 1919—Duplicate June 10, 1933.

b—1934—1 Duplicate B. W. Issued—Original Warrant—Aug. 21, 1925—Duplicate Sept. 26, 1934.

c—1934—1 Duplicate B. W. Issued—Original Warrant—Dec. 20, 1921—Duplicate Jan. 4, 1934.

DIVISION OF SUPERVISION

CHART 11

Disposition of Bench Warrants

Total

	Male	Female	Total	% of Total B.W.
Committed	818	28	846	44.83
Probation Continued	498	21	519	27.50
(71 Male, 3 Female Committed on New Charges)				
Cases Closed or Discharged	200	4	204	10.81
(112 Male, 3 Female Committed on New Charges)				
(13 D. A. Refused to Extradite)				
(11 B. W. Filed in Clerk's Office)				
B. W. Filed at Penal Institutions	42	—	42	2.23
Died	15	—	15	.79
Deported	7	—	7	.37
Bail Forfeited and Absconded	1	—	1	.05
In Institutions for Insane	2	—	2	.11
Unapprehended	232	15	247	13.09
(59 Male, 1 Female Filed in Clerk's Office)				
(3 Filed in D. A. Office)				
Dispositions Pending	3	1	4	.21
	1,818	69	1,887	

1927 - 1936

SUCCESS AND FAILURE

Lined ■ = Failure

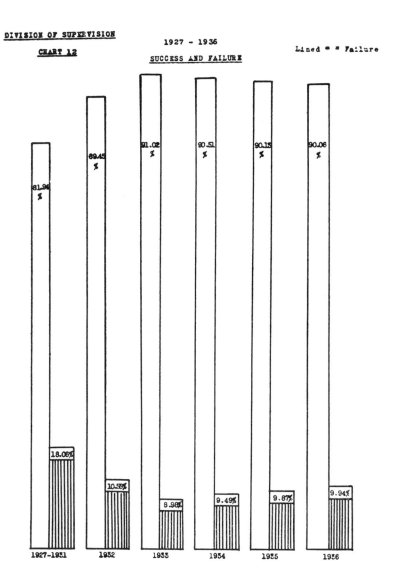

81.94%

89.45%

91.02%

90.51%

90.15%

90.06%

18.06%

10.55%

8.98%

9.49%

9.87%

9.94%

1927-1931   1932   1933   1934   1935   1936

ROSTER OF STAFF

Chief Probation Officer
IRVING W. HALPERN

Deputy Chief Probation Officers
EDWARD S. PORTER · JEROME A. WALSH

Assistant to Chief Probation Officer
WILLIAM V. CHIECO

Assistants to Deputy Chief Probation Officers

HARRY M. GOLDMAN
HENRIETTA HENIUS

ELMER W. REEVES
FREDERIC J. LEVY (Acting)

Probation Officers

THOMAS F. BURKE
PHILIP COHEN
THOMAS C. COLLINS
THEODORE CONCEVITCH
EDWARD A. DERMODY
WILLIAM S. DILLON
RAYMOND DISCO
BYRON G. DODGE
ARDSLEY J. DONNELLY
JOSEPH R. DORSEY
PATRICK J. DUFFY
EDWARD D. DUNNE
MAXWELL FALK
JOSEPH R. FLOOD
IRVING FORTGANG
PETER GAMBARO
ALEXANDER GITTES
FRED N. GRANICH
CHARLES P. HENRY
JAMES L. HUSSEY

HARRY KATZMAN
MARTIN C. KELLY
JOHN J. F. LARKIN
WILLIAM G. LEONHARDT
JOHN J. MORGAN
ALICE C. MORIARTY
DANIEL J. MULHOLLAND
JOHN J. MURPHY
FRANCIS O'BRIEN
RAYMOND C. O'CONOR
HELMER O. OLESON
RINALDO J. PISARRA
GEORGE H. ROYAL
HERMAN D. SCHEFF
ABRAHAM SIMON
JOHN N. STANISLAUS
ABRAHAM J. STOCKHEIM
JANE D. WYLIE
MARCUS M. ZETKIN
(Vacancy)

325

Chief Clerk

Terese Jason

Bookkeeper

Helen L. Schneider

Assistant Bookkeeper

Arthur Crown

Statistician

David A. Krosnick

Secretary-Stenographers

Clara M. Leiser   Ella Reeves

Stenographers

Jean Blaustein
Anna L. Corrigan
Agnes V. Daley
Rosalie Gilbert
Florence B. Gray
Jeanne E. A. Grosz
Lottie Hirsch
Sally McDermott
Rose A. Mullaly
Anna G. Munno

Rebecca Neidich
Sybil B. Poston
Ida Rabinowitz
Lily C. K. Rogers
Hannah A. Ruff
Geraldine Schlossberg
Gussie Schlossberg
Ann M. Schofield
Mildred Senner
Gwendolyn Sturges
(2 Vacancies)

Record Clerks

FANNIE FRIEDWALD

GERTRUDE PILGRIM
(Vacancy)

Typists

MARGARET M. ALFERO

FRANCES BROWN

JESSIE COTMAN

EVA FOX

PAULINE K. GREENBLUM

MOLLIE KALINA

ANNE T. ROSENBAUM

RUTH M. VAN DEUSEN

Switchboard Operator

MAE M. CURRAN

Information Clerk

ANNA C. RYAN

327

PATTERSON SMITH REPRINT SERIES IN
CRIMINOLOGY, LAW ENFORCEMENT, AND SOCIAL PROBLEMS

1. Lewis: *The Development of American Prisons and Prison Customs, 1776-1845*
2. Carpenter: *Reformatory Prison Discipline*
3. Brace: *The Dangerous Classes of New York*
4. Dix: *Remarks on Prisons and Prison Discipline in the United States*
5. Bruce *et al: The Workings of the Indeterminate-Sentence Law and the Parole System in Illinois*
6. Wickersham Commission: *Complete Reports, Including the Mooney-Billings Report.* 14 Vols.
7. Livingston: *Complete Works on Criminal Jurisprudence.* 2 Vols.
8. Cleveland Foundation: *Criminal Justice in Cleveland*
9. Illinois Association for Criminal Justice: *The Illinois Crime Survey*
10. Missouri Association for Criminal Justice: *The Missouri Crime Survey*
11. Aschaffenburg: *Crime and Its Repression*
12. Garofalo: *Criminology*
13. Gross: *Criminal Psychology*
14. Lombroso: *Crime, Its Causes and Remedies*
15. Saleilles: *The Individualization of Punishment*
16. Tarde: *Penal Philosophy*
17. McKelvey: *American Prisons*
18. Sanders: *Negro Child Welfare in North Carolina*
19. Pike: *A History of Crime in England.* 2 Vols.
20. Herring: *Welfare Work in Mill Villages*
21. Barnes: *The Evolution of Penology in Pennsylvania*
22. Puckett: *Folk Beliefs of the Southern Negro*
23. Fernald *et al: A Study of Women Delinquents in New York State*
24. Wines: *The State of the Prisons and of Child-Saving Institutions*
25. Raper: *The Tragedy of Lynching*
26. Thomas: *The Unadjusted Girl*
27. Jorns: *The Quakers as Pioneers in Social Work*
28. Owings: *Women Police*
29. Woolston: *Prostitution in the United States*
30. Flexner: *Prostitution in Europe*
31. Kelso: *The History of Public Poor Relief in Massachusetts: 1820-1920*
32. Spivak: *Georgia Nigger*
33. Earle: *Curious Punishments of Bygone Days*
34. Bonger: *Race and Crime*
35. Fishman: *Crucibles of Crime*
36. Brearley: *Homicide in the United States*
37. Graper: *American Police Administration*
38. Hichborn: *"The System"*
39. Steiner & Brown: *The North Carolina Chain Gang*
40. Cherrington: *The Evolution of Prohibition in the United States of America*
41. Colquhoun: *A Treatise on the Commerce and Police of the River Thames*
42. Colquhoun: *A Treatise on the Police of the Metropolis*
43. Abrahamsen: *Crime and the Human Mind*
44. Schneider: *The History of Public Welfare in New York State: 1609-1866*
45. Schneider & Deutsch: *The History of Public Welfare in New York State: 1867-1940*
46. Crapsey: *The Nether Side of New York*
47. Young: *Social Treatment in Probation and Delinquency*
48. Quinn: *Gambling and Gambling Devices*
49. McCord & McCord: *Origins of Crime*
50. Worthington & Topping: *Specialized Courts Dealing with Sex Delinquency*

51. Asbury: *Sucker's Progress*
52. Kneeland: *Commercialized Prostitution in New York City*
53. Fosdick: *American Police Systems*
54. Fosdick: *European Police Systems*
55. Shay: *Judge Lynch: His First Hundred Years*
56. Barnes: *The Repression of Crime*
57. Cable: *The Silent South*
58. Kammerer: *The Unmarried Mother*
59. Doshay: *The Boy Sex Offender and His Later Career*
60. Spaulding: *An Experimental Study of Psychopathic Delinquent Women*
61. Brockway: *Fifty Years of Prison Service*
62. Lawes: *Man's Judgment of Death*
63. Healy & Healy: *Pathological Lying, Accusation, and Swindling*
64. Smith: *The State Police*
65. Adams: *Interracial Marriage in Hawaii*
66. Halpern: *A Decade of Probation*
67. Tappan: *Delinquent Girls in Court*
68. Alexander & Healy: *Roots of Crime*
69. Healy & Bronner: *Delinquents and Criminals*
70. Cutler: *Lynch-Law*
71. Gillin: *Taming the Criminal*
72. Osborne: *Within Prison Walls*
73. Ashton: *The History of Gambling in England*
74. Whitlock: *On the Enforcement of Law in Cities*
75. Goldberg: *Child Offenders*
76. Cressey: *The Taxi-Dance Hall*
77. Riis: *The Battle with the Slum*
78. Larson *et al: Lying and Its Detection*
79. Comstock: *Frauds Exposed*
80. Carpenter: *Our Convicts.* 2 Vols. in 1
81. Horn: *Invisible Empire: The Story of the Ku Klux Klan, 1866-1871*
82. Faris *et al: Intelligent Philanthropy*
83. Robinson: *History and Organization of Criminal Statistics in the United States*
84. Reckless: *Vice in Chicago*
85. Healy: *The Individual Delinquent*
86. Bogen: *Jewish Philanthropy*
87. Clinard: *The Black Market: A Study of White Collar Crime*
88. Healy: *Mental Conflicts and Misconduct*
89. Citizens' Police Committee: *Chicago Police Problems*
90. Clay: *The Prison Chaplain*
91. Peirce: *A Half Century with Juvenile Delinquents*
92. Richmond: *Friendly Visiting Among the Poor*
93. Brasol: *Elements of Crime*
94. Strong: *Public Welfare Administration in Canada*
95. Beard: *Juvenile Probation*
96. Steinmetz: *The Gaming Table.* 2 Vols.
97. Crawford: *Report on the Penitentiaries of the United States*
98. Kuhlman: *A Guide to Material on Crime and Criminal Justice*
99. Culver: *Bibliography of Crime and Criminal Justice: 1927-1931*
100. Culver: *Bibliography of Crime and Criminal Justice: 1932-1937*